WORKS ISSUED BY

THE HAKLUYT SOCIETY

RUSSIAN EMBASSIES TO THE
GEORGIAN KINGS

VOLUME II

SECOND SERIES
No. CXXXIX

ISSUED FOR 1970

'The men of Erzurum attacked by Simūn.' This is the only known
likeness of Mad Simon of Kartli.

From the *Sheja'atname* of Asafi, MS. TY 6043, fol. 109r. of Istanbul University Library.

RUSSIAN EMBASSIES TO THE GEORGIAN KINGS

(1589 - 1605)

VOLUME II

Edited with Introduction, Additional Notes, Commentaries and
Bibliography by

W. E. D. ALLEN

Texts translated by

ANTHONY MANGO

CAMBRIDGE
Published for the Hakluyt Society
AT THE UNIVERSITY PRESS
1970

PUBLISHED BY

THE SYNDICS OF THE CAMBRIDGE UNIVERSITY PRESS

Bentley House, P.O. Box 92, 200 Euston Road, London, N.W.1

American Branch: 32 East 57th Street, New York, N.Y. 10022

© THE HAKLUYT SOCIETY 1970

Library of Congress Catalogue Card Number: 70–85707

Standard Book Numbers:

521 01030 6   Vol. I

521 01031 4   Vol. II

521 01029 2   set of two vols.

Printed in Great Britain
by Robert MacLehose & Company Limited
at the University Press Glasgow

CONTENTS

VOLUME II

v

CONTENTS

CONTENTS

vii

LIST OF MAPS AND ILLUSTRATIONS

LIST OF MAPS

VOLUME II

LIST OF ILLUSTRATIONS

VOLUME II

NOTES ON RUSSIAN RELATIONS
WITH KAKHETI AND KARTLI
BETWEEN 1590 and 1604

(refs. Belokurov, *Snosheniya*, pp. 223–65, 314 ff.; Brosset, *EC/BHP* Nos. 16–18, cols. 239–72, Nos. 19–21, cols. 288–302; also see Introduction, pp. 79–83.)

THE Georgian ambassadors Prince Suliman[1] and Khurshit who travelled to Russia with Zvenigorodski reached Moscow on 30 November 7099 (1590). On 13 December they were received in audience by Tsar Fedor. In his speech Suliman called King Alexander the Tsar's tributary and asked for protection against Shevkal.

King Alexander's letter, which the Georgian ambassadors brought with them, complained of raids by mountaineers who were secure in their fastnesses. The King asked for more falcons, three icon-painters and a gunner.

On 7 March 1591, the Georgian ambassadors were informed at the Posolski Prikaz that Alexander was being granted everything he had requested, with the exception of the gunner because all the gunners were at Pskov. The Russians were told by the Georgian ambassadors that Alexander could muster an army of 40,000 men and that it would need one month to reach Shevkal's land.

On 19 April the Georgian ambassadors were received by Patriarch Job and later the same day by Boris Godunov whom they asked to intercede with Tsar Fedor on Alexander's behalf and ensure that a Russian army would be sent against Shevkal. Boris promised that this would be done. The promise to help Alexander against Shevkal was repeated at the farewell audience.

[1] For Prince Suliman (Suleyman), see Commentary 36.

The Georgian ambassadors were given leave to return to King Alexander in April 1591 (7099). They were accompanied by the Tsar's new ambassadors Vasili Timofeyevich Pleshcheyev (who was given for the occasion the rank of *dvoryanin* and Lord Lieutenant of Kozel) and under-dyak Timofey Kudrin with instructions to tell Alexander that the Tsar, in reply to his entreaty, was sending an army under Prince Grigori Zasekin to wage war on Shevkal. They took with them three icon-painters (to replace the men who had stayed in Georgia after Zvenigorodski's embassy) and falconers with falcons. Pleshcheyev was instructed to tell the Georgian ambassadors, when they reached the Terek, that the expedition against Shevkal would be undertaken by 5,000 of the Tsar's men with firearms and a muster of 10,000 Cherkesses; the Georgians were to be prevented from witnessing the build-up of Russian forces. The ambassadors were given a message for King Alexander to hold off his own attack on Shevkal until he heard from Zasekin. They were also instructed to try and persuade Simon of Kartli to come under the Tsar's 'hand'. Patriarch Job's letter to Alexander made no reference to spiritual matters, nor were any clerics sent with the embassy. (Pleshcheyev's *stateyny spisok* is not published by Belokurov.)

Pleshcheyev and Kudrin returned from Georgia in December 1592 (7101). They were accompanied by King Alexander's ambassadors Prince Aram[1] and Archimandrite Kiril. They were received by Godunov on 3 January 1593, to whom they conveyed Alexander's thanks for Zasekin's expedition against Shevkal. (The result of this minor expedition appears to have been the capture and burning of Andreyevo in 1592; Shevkal was wounded in the fighting; the Russians then withdrew.) Aram and Kiril petitioned that the Russians should occupy Tarku and use it as a base for further operations against Shevkal; they wanted the Russians to open up the road to Georgia

[1] For Prince Aram, see Commentary 61 (c).

across Shevkal's domains. The Georgian ambassadors were told in July 1593 that the Tsar was giving instructions for a force of 15,000 men under Prince Andrey Khvorostinin to march against Shevkal; Tarku was to be occupied and Russian men and Alexander's ally the Krym-Shevkal were to be installed there.

Prince Ivan Nikitich Vsevolodski was sent to Georgia in July 1593 (7101), when Aram and Kiril returned home. He carried Godunov's letter informing Alexander of Khvorostinin's expedition and asking him to order his own army to Tarku and to send his son Yuri to Moscow to do homage to the Tsar. King Alexander was told in the letter not to send any of his children as hostages to Turkey or Persia without referring the matter to the Tsar. (Belokurov published no documents relating to Vsevolodski's embassy other than Boris's letter.)

Vsevolodski returned in December 7103 (1594). He was accompanied by Alexander's ambassadors Khurshit and Aram who carried a letter to Godunov in which the King wrote that Khvorostinin had ravaged and burnt many of Shevkal's places by the sea but never got close to Kakheti, with the result that the road through the Kumukh land remained closed. Alexander promised to send his son Yuri and his army to the Terek as soon as it was cleared. Alexander asked Godunov to petition the Tsar to send an expedition against Shevkal which would build a fort in the land of the Ghazi-Kumukhs. Khurshit and Aram remained in Russia until 1596 when they were sent home in the company of the Russian ambassadors Kuzma Petrovich Sovin and Andrey Polukhanov.

Sovin left Moscow on 6 June and, after a delay in Astrakhan, reached Terki on 11 October. The winter was already advancing when the ambassadorial party arrived at Soni on 28 November. To spare the exhausted and underfed horses, they had to march on foot day and night through the snow. On 7 December Alexander's aznauri Farsadan met them and escorted them to

Buyutan (Boetan) where the King was wintering in southern Kakheti on the banks of the Belakanis-tsqali, famed for its abundance of game.

Discussions dragged on for the following two months until the end of February 1597. The Georgians were at pains to explain their difficulties in mounting an attack against Shevkal across the high ridges of Daghestan. (There was some justice in their hesitations, since it took a nineteenth-century Russian army sixty years to impose their authority over the warlike tribes of these formidable ranges).

In April the Russians moved to Gremi and were assigned a camp at the village of Shilda. Here Georgians and Russians engaged in acrimonious disputes on their respective relations with the Kabardan princes. At last Sovin asked for leave to depart but King Alexander was in no hurry to let the Russians go, since it is evident that their continued presence gave him some prestige and potential bargaining power in the diplomatic game he had to continue to play between the changing Ottoman sultans and the Safavid Shah Abbas. Sovin was informed that snow still blocked the passes and, further, that the King was awaiting the return of a messenger despatched by him to King Simon of Kartli.

Between May and September the King persisted in his delaying tactic, and it was not until 3 October 1597 that Sovin finally left Gremi on the three weeks' ride to Soni. But he found no escort from the Terek waiting for him at Lars; instead, he received instructions to pass the winter in Kakheti and thus returned to Tog a week before Christmas. The unfortunate Polukhanov was ill and the ambassador's dragoman died. In April of the following year (1598), Sovin dined with the King at Aloni and at last took his leave.

On 5 June Sovin reached Soni, accompanied by a return Georgian mission to Moscow. The Kakhian representatives were Suliman Bayindirli and the dyak Levan Yankov (a

Russian rendering of 'son of Ianko'= G. Iankoshvili).[1] At Soni the party had to wait three months, for again no escort had been sent from the Terek to meet them – a fact which Brosset attributes to the uncertain conditions following the accession of Boris Godunov as Tsar in Moscow.

Sovin and the Georgian ambassadors Prince Suliman and dyak Levan at last reached Astrakhan in October 1598 (7107); they wintered there and arrived in Moscow on 9 July 1599. Tsar Boris received them on 23 August. They brought a letter in which Alexander complained that, although twelve years had elapsed since he first petitioned the Tsar and came under his hand, he had received no aid from the Tsar's army. He wrote: 'You are a great Sovereign and it will be improper for us to go on pestering you all the time. You sent us your bountiful royal word saying "I have taken King Alexander and his entire land into protection under my royal hand, and I shall not allow anybody to ravage your land." We had faith in this royal word and placed our hopes in you; but our land was laid waste in subsequent raids . . . There is nothing more to say . . .' In a letter to Boris he complained that Tsar Fedor had not sent him any falcons that year and that the Tsar's gifts were so poor as to be unfit even for a commoner. On 8 September 7108, the Georgian ambassadors were received by Patriarch Job and in July 1601 (7109) they were given leave to return home (they apparently complained that they had not been issued with sufficient food in Moscow).

Ivan Nashchokin and Ivan Levontyev were ordered on

[1] Brosset (EC/BHP, Nos. 16–18, col. 371, n. 134) states that in the rescript of King Alexander, which the ambassadors brought with them, the name of Revaz Mugalbegov appears instead of that of dyak Levan. Brosset professes to be unable to identify the family name Mugalbegov, but if we take the Russian termination – begov to be a translation of Georgian aznaurishvili, we can identify the stem Mugal-; this may correspond to the well-known Georgian princely name Maghala-shvili (cf. Chap. 2, p. 105, n. 3, for 'Mokholey's son Keleya' = Kolya Maghalashvili).

25 August 7109 (1601), to accompany Suliman and Levan to Georgia. They were instructed to take all necessary precautions while travelling between Kazan and Astrakhan so as not to suffer at the hands of 'outlaw Cossacks, Zaporozhians, Cherkesses and Tartars' (Belokurov, p. 330). In his message to Alexander Tsar Boris made no reference to the King's complaints; he expressed readiness to keep Alexander under his royal hand just as Fedor had done, and promised to send an army under Ivan P. Romodanovski against Shevkal; Alexander was asked to send his army to combine with the Russians for these operations. Boris also asked Alexander to renew his oath of allegiance saying that the failure of Khvorostinin's expedition (in 1594) was due to Alexander's failure to send his army against Shevkal at the same time. In case Alexander complained of delays in the dispatch of the Russian army against Shevkal, Nashchokin and Levontyev were asked to draw his attention to the great fire at Astrakhan, witnessed by the Georgian ambassadors, when the suburb (*posad*) and the blockhouse (*ostrog*) were destroyed with heavy loss of the food and various stores needed for an expedition; among the property destroyed were the houses of Russian, Bukharan and Ghilan merchants. Stocks sufficient for five, six or even ten years were normally stored at Astrakhan; now everything was lost (Belokurov, p. 337).

Nashchokin and Levontyev were accompanied by two iconpainters (to replace the men sent earlier) and four carpenters skilled in building churches. They also carried five falcons (one died at Murom).

They were held up by bad weather on the Volga and only reached Astrakhan on 7 November. The journey was marked by continuous bickering with Suliman who complained of inadequacy of provisions. There were further delays at Astrakhan and further arguments with Suliman about the onward journey.

In a letter from Gremi dated 27 September (? 7111–1602) the ambassadors reported that they had reached Georgia on 1 July 1602. They were received by Kings Alexander and David who took the oath to the Tsar. King David then set off against Aristov of Soni 'and he sent us off to an empty spot, in the woods. And we suffered dishonour and great hunger there. We sent the interpreter Dmitri and the under-dyak Timokha to King David to say that we were dying of hunger. The King got angry and he sent us, your servants, far from him to Zagem in the month of August. And at Zagem, Sire, we suffered even greater hunger and great dishonour; at that time of the year even local inhabitants leave Zagem for the mountains because of the heat. And your Majesty's falconers, and the under-dyak and *streltsy* and many of our men, died and we, your servants, are ill.' King David returned to Gremi from his expedition against Aristov in October and sent messengers to fetch the ambassadors. But he fell ill and died on the fifth day. Alexander, who then returned to the throne, told the ambassadors: 'Sixteen years have passed since I grasped the tail of the Muscovite Sovereign's coat, but I have seen no help. And you, ambassadors, have misled me . . .' 'And King Alexander said improper words and he imprisoned us, your servants.'

Nashchokin and Levontyev wintered in Georgia. They left Astrakhan on their way back to Moscow on 13 September 1603. Nashchokin died at Kazan. The remainder of the party – which included Kiril, Alexander's ambassador – were at Nizhni Novgorod on 7 December.

PART II

THE EMBASSY OF TATISHCHEV AND IVANOV
(1604–5)

CHAPTER 8

GEORGIANS AT THE COURT OF BORIS GODUNOV

[The Georgian ambassador Kiril and his men, who travelled to Russia in the company of Nashchokin and Levontyev on their way back from the court of King Alexander, left Astrakhan on 13 September 1603. Nashchokin died in Kazan. [Levontyev and the Georgians left Kazan on 30 November and reached Nizhni Novgorod on 7 December.] Nashchokin and Levontyev having complained to the Tsar of their ill-treatment when they were in Georgia, retaliatory action was taken against the monk Kiril: he and his men were issued with 'scanty provisions', just enough not to be hungry. The Georgians were detained in Nizhni Novgorod and the Tsar's letter of 31 December contained instructions that 'no foreigners or Russians' were to be admitted to the Georgian ambassadors and that 'nobody should converse with them about anything and none of their men should wander about the market-place or the streets needlessly'. The attendant Russian squire was instructed to accompany the Georgian ambassadors every time they left their quarters. On 30 January 1604 the Tsar gave orders to have the Georgian ambassadors brought to Moscow. On 18 February they were received by Tatishchev and dyak Grigori Klobukov at the Posolski Prikaz[1].]

The Georgian King Alexander's ambassadors, the monk Kiril (377) and the under-dyak Savva were received on the 18th of February by the gentleman of the Privy Council and Master of the Horse [*yaselnichi*] Mikhail Ignatyevich Tatishchev[2] and dyak Grigori Klobukov[3] at the Posolski Prikaz, at the command

---

[1] For the history of the Posolski Prikaz, see Commentary 45.

[2] For the rank of *yaselnichi* and the background of Mikhail Tatishchev, see Commentary 46.

[3] Dyak Grigori Klobukov, nicknamed *zloba*, the spiteful, was himself

of the Sovereign Tsar and great Prince Boris Fedorovich of all Russia. The attendant officers Grigori Elizarov and Misyur Solovtsev had been sent to fetch the Georgian ambassadors. Horses from the royal stables and a sledge from the Chudov monastery were sent for the Archimandrite, and a sledge-horse and a sledge from the royal stables for the underdyak. There were forty town gentry in clean mourning attire in the ante-chamber of the Posolskaya Palata, while *streltsy* in ordinary uniforms were placed in the square in front of the (378) Posolskaya Palata. When King Alexander's ambassadors drove into the walled town, they were taken past the Razryadny Seni,[1] and they alighted from the sledges in front of the Posolskaya Palata. When they entered the chamber the gentleman of the Privy Council and Master of the Horse Mikhail Ignatyevich and dyak Grigori Klobukov got up and asked the monk whether he was a priest; he replied that he was an Archimandrite. So they asked for his blessing and went back to their seats, and they bade the Archimandrite and under-dyak Savva sit down, too.

After they had remained seated for a short while, Tatishchev said to the monk Kiril: 'Kiril! By what custom did King Alexander say many unseemly things about the great Sovereign Tsar and great Prince Boris Fedorovich, Autocrat of all Russia, things which the mind refuses even to contemplate?...'

(380)   The monk Kiril replied: 'Far from such things having been done or uttered, I am seized with fright even when I hear such unseemly things from you. I am a Greek by birth and a

the son of a *dyak* whose duties had included participation in diplomatic missions. In 1598 he was a member of the council which brought Godunov to the throne. In 1601 he was sent to Tsarev-Borisov for talks with Crimean ambassadors, and in 1603–4 he was the head of the Novgorod department (*RBS*, under name).

[1] The antechamber to the Razryadny Prikaz, the Department concerned with military affairs and fortifications; the service records which determined the seniority of the nobility were kept in this Prikaz (ref. Brockhaus and Efron).

Christian. A fast for the salvation of our souls has begun for all Orthodox Christians. I swear on my Christian faith and my monastic vows and my priesthood that at the court of my lord King Alexander I heard no unseemly speeches about the great Sovereign Tsar...'

Tatishchev and dyak Grigori then said: 'When King David (382) left Shemta[1] on an expedition against Prince Aristov who holds a fief from him, he sent Ivan Nashchokin and Ivan Levontyev to an uninhabited spot in the forest of Morkanch.[2] They experienced hardships when they were encamped there;

---

[1] *Shemta* = Shua-mta, a monastery five or six versts to the south of Telavi, to the left of the route from central Kakheti to Tbilisi, leading up the valley of the Turdis-tsqali across the pass over the Gombori mountains. The name means literally 'amidst the mountains'; for the monastery is surrounded on three sides by woods and high peaks (cf. Bakradze, *Akty*, Vol. 5, p. 1100). An ancient cult centre, with shrines dating back to the seventh century A.D., Shua-mta rose to fame as the favourite residence of Tinatin, the first queen of King Levan. About 1527–8 she endowed a church and monastery which Chubinashvili (*AK*, Vol. 1, pp. 440–5 and Vol. 2, pls. 353–9) describes as an outstanding monument of the renaissance of Kakhian architecture during the first half of the sixteenth century. In September 1850 Brosset (*VA, Ier Rapport*, pp. 57 ff.) crossed the Gombori mountains to Shua-mta and noted the wild beauty of the countryside and the lack of security from Lesghian bandits. Chubinashvili (Vol. II, pl. 359b) reproduces a faded fresco portrait of Tinatin and Levan. For a description in English of Shua-mta, see Taqaishvili, 'Antiquities of Georgia' in *Georgica*, Vols. 4–5 (1937), pp. 109–11 and pls. xv–xviii.

[2] *Morkanch*: Although Alexander describes Morkanch as 'a large place' frequented by his father 'King Levont', the meticulous Wakhusht, writing only a century and a quarter later, makes no mention of Morkanch. It is possible that the Russian form 'Morkanch' may be a distortion of the name of the village of Mukhrawan which lay between Martqopi and Ujarma. In 1850, Brosset was told by peasants that in the forest about three versts from Ujarma were the ruins of an ancient citadel and the remains of a residence of King Gurgaslan who flourished in the fifth century A.D. (cf. *VA, Ier Rapport*, p. 56). Attributions to King Gurgaslan were as common as those to Queen Tamar or to Tamerlane, and there is a possibility that here was 'the large place' frequented by 'King Levont'. It may well have been destroyed during the repeated devastations of Kakheti by Shah Abbas I.

wattle huts[1] were made expressly for them, and they received scanty provisions, and even these were issued every other day and sometimes once in three days; nor could they buy provisions anywhere. The ambassadors' men wandered through the woods and fed on apples, but the attendant officer gave orders not to let them into the woods, and to beat and tie up their men. Their horses were let out on waste land, and the Georgian peasant watchmen cut off the horses' tails,[2] insulted them and threw stones at the horses; many horses died because of it. The ambassadors sent the falconer Afanasi and the interpreter Dmitri to King Alexander in the monastery of Alaverdi, but King Alexander replied that he had given his realm to his son David and that the matter was no concern of his. He said that he knew everything which David did to the ambassadors; while he had been king, the Sovereign's men had not been subjected to such dishonour and ignominy.'

The monk Kiril said: 'His royal Majesty's ambassadors were quartered in houses at Morkanch. Morkanch is a large place; in previous years King Alexander's father King Levont went there every year, and always lived there in the summer in order to feel cooler. It is an old custom in the Iberian land to make wattle huts. The ambassadors were lodged in whatever quarters there happened to be. His royal Majesty's ambassadors did not suffer any dishonour, and they were issued with sufficient provisions. I do not know anything about thieving by attendant officers.'

Tatishchev and the dyak said: 'And Ivan Nashchokin and

[1] Wattle huts: temporary summer dwellings thrown up by the peasants – in contrast to the often luxurious tents under which the nobility and court officials would spend the hunting and campaigning seasons. For a wattle hut of the period, see Castelli's drawing reproduced in Allen, *HGP*, tail-piece to p. 256.

[2] 'Cut off the horses' tails': probably for the very saleable horse-hair – the motive being profit rather than malice. This lamentable practice still persists among the 'tinkers' of Ireland and is one of the reasons for their unpopularity among farmers.

Ivan Levontyev also wrote to King David that they were suffering great hardship on account of their quarters and through lack of provisions and the behaviour of the attendant officers, and King David commanded that they be moved far away from him, to Zagem. And at Zagem the attendant officer lodged them in the stables behind the King's court, where the King's donkeys had been stabled and which were full of droppings. They were issued with scanty provisions every other day or once in three days. They sold their clothes and belongings there and bought provisions in that way. The falconers and the under-dyak and *streltsy* and many of their men died there.'

And the monk Kiril said: 'His Royal Majesty's ambassadors Ivan Nashchokin and Ivan Levontyev sent to King David the under-dyak Timofey and the interpreter Dmitri asking for the king's permission to go and trade at Zagem. King David repeatedly sent messengers to them and told them himself (383) that it was very hot at Zagem, and that people felt very bad because of the heat, but they replied that they were not afraid of the heat. So the King gave them freedom of action. And they went on their own. The ambassadors lodged at Zagem in houses near the King's court and not in stables; the houses were ordinary ones – there is but one house at Zagem that is better: the royal court where the king lives . . . The ambassadors were given sufficient provisions and were subjected to no dishonour.'

Tatishchev and the dyak then said: 'When King David came to Krym he bade Ivan Nashchokin and Ivan Levontyev come to him there. They came on the 16th of October. And the attendant officer had their camp pitched in the forest, in an empty garden belonging to a doctor, and gave orders for their tent to be erected. And within the hour Prince Aram and ambassador Suliman and the same attendant officer Petr and you, monk Kiril, came to them from King David and asked angrily on behalf of the King why they encamped in a doctor's garden close to Krym. Yet it was the attendant officer himself who had had their camp pitched there. The attendant officer beat the men who were putting up the tent and gave orders for the tent to be brought down on top of Ivan Nashchokin and Ivan Levontyev, and they narrowly missed being crushed by the tent. They were ejected from that spot at about four o'clock at night, and were taken back some five *versts* to an uninhabited spot in the forest, where they were abandoned on their own. They remained encamped there for a long time.'

The monk Kiril said: 'King David had sent messengers to fetch the ambassadors and he bade them come to him at Krym. And when they came to Krym they encamped near the king's court in a garden, and they had the king's tents erected. They encamped there without the king's knowledge. King David became angry with them because of it, and he commanded that they be moved to another spot. God and his Majesty the Tsar are free to do what they please: the deed was done by King David and not by King Alexander, and King David did not listen to his father in anything. His royal Majesty should extend his mercy to King Alexander, and should not subject him to his wrath because of King David's misdeeds. I do not know and did not hear of any dishonour which the attendant officer might have caused the ambassadors...'

(387)   Tatishchev and dyak Grigori also said: 'On the 12th day of January the Turkish Pasha of Genzha, Kaikhosr,[1] came to Zagem with King Alexander; Prince Yuri had asked the Pasha for his daughter in marriage. And the Pasha was lodged in the king's forecourt and he supped with the king every day, and Prince Yuri sat at table below him. And some three days later the Turkish *chaush* Illi-aga arrived, and the king

[1] For the Turkish Pasha of Genzha, Kaikhosr, see Commentary 47.

had him quartered in some Armenians' houses near his court; yet he had his royal Majesty's men quartered far away from him.'

And the monk Kiril said that the Pasha of Genzha was a Georgian by birth. He came to Zagem with King Alexander in order to effect a reconciliation between the king's sons King David and Prince Yuri; that the Pasha's wife and daughters are of the Christian faith, but he himself is a Moslem. 'Prince Yuri asked for his daughter in marriage because she is a Christian and the daughter of a great man, and I believe that Prince Yuri married her in the summer. His royal Majesty's ambassadors were not lodged near the Turkish *chaush* on purpose.'

Tatishchev and dyak Grigori said: 'And it is also written in Ivan Nashchokin and Ivan Levontyev's report: King Alexander told them – "The Sovereign wished to defend me but he will not defend me; there is no need even to ask for protection. None will be forthcoming".'

And the monk Kiril said that he did not ever hear at King Alexander's court such unseemly speeches about his royal Majesty; at King Alexander's court they always hear the king boast of the Tsar's mercy and protection.

Tatishchev and dyak Grigori went on: 'It is also written in the report: When the ambassadors left Zagem and were proceeding to Krym, the attendant officer brought them to a farmstead at about four o'clock in the night; the officer himself settled in the house, while they were quartered under the eaves near the house. From there as far as Krym they travelled without the attendant officer, who abandoned them. And as for the men who died at Krym of hardships, the king ordered that they should not be buried near a church, and they were buried in a waste piece of ground.'

And the monk Kiril said: 'If attendant officers behaved in that way, they did it lawlessly without the king's knowledge;

King Alexander did not command them to behave in that way.' He, Kiril, had not heard of it.

(388)   Tatishchev and dyak Grigori said: 'And it is also written in the report: "*Streltsy* went to a fair in the village of Elon. Turks and Georgians beat them and wounded three men. Ivan Nashchokin and Ivan Levontyev sent messages to King Alexander about this, and the king told the interpreters: 'Why do you quarrel with the Turks? They have come to me on business and they are my friends. They are inept not to have done you to death.' " '

And the monk Kiril said that he did not know about this and had not heard anything.

The gentleman of the Privy Council and Master of the Horse Mikhail Ignatyevich Tatishchev and dyak Grigori Klobukov asked the monk Kiril: 'It is written in the letter of Ivan Nashchokin and Ivan Levontyev that King David had marched against Prince Aristov who holds a fief from him. What are the present relations of Prince Aristov and King Alexander, and for what reason did King David take the field against him?'

And the monk Kiril said: 'When King Alexander's son David became king in the Iberian realm, Prince Aristov seceded from him. He did not want to let through his land our sovereign's ambassador Prince Suliman[1] together with your Sovereign's ambassadors who were travelling from your great Sovereign Tsar and great Prince Boris Fedorovich of all

[1] For Prince Suliman, see Chap. 6, p. 203, n. 1, above and Commentary 36. Since the days of the Zvenigorodski mission, fifteen years earlier, Suliman Bayindirli had become rather a controversial figure. On his return from a mission to Moscow in 1601 he got himself into a dispute about his allowances with the Russian envoy Nashchokin; while waiting in Kazan, his tumultuous orgies with a Georgian merchant called Mamuka had attracted the attention of the *voyvode*; and in Astrakhan he had run out of funds and become involved in some dingy transaction with a Russian merchant, Pervusha Izborenin, which had provoked an official investigation (see Brosset, *EC/BHP*, Vol. II, Nos. 19–21, cols. 290, 296, 301).

Russia. On his arrival Suliman reported to Alexander and to King David that Aristov was seceding from them. It was for this reason that King David led his army against him and intended to wage war on him. And Aristov exchanged messages with King David and made peace with him, and he recognised the authority of the Iberian kings as of old.'

Tatishchev and Klobukov questioned the monk: 'Why had King Alexander relinquished the throne to his son Prince David, and how long did King David reign and how did he pass away?'

And the monk Kiril said: 'King Alexander had for his sins been sick of the fever for a long time, and for three days he lay so weak as if he were dead, and there was but slight breathing. And, despairing of his life, his sons Prince David and Prince Yuri at that time began discussing together who would ascend the throne; and disputes began. Traitors were causing trouble between them: they told Prince David that his brother Yuri was plotting to murder him; and they told Prince Yuri that David wanted to kill him. And because of this Prince Yuri fled. And those same traitors who had been causing the trouble told Prince David that his brother Yuri had fled to the Turk. And David with his close counsellors pursued him; and when he had caught up with Yuri, they placed between them the *abreks*[1] and exchanged messages about peace. And they made peace there and confirmed it by kissing the cross and signing charters. Prince David gave a (389) fief to his brother Yuri and himself ascended the throne. And members of his entourage plotted among themselves to kill King David. They came to Prince Yuri suggesting that he should ascend the throne and that they would kill King

---

[1] *Stali mezh sebya abreku: abrek* can mean 'mountaineer', 'outlaw', 'mercenary'. The idea was apparently to reduce the chance of fighting by introducing a buffer group. I am indebted to Dr N. Andreyev for this suggestion.

David, and should Prince Yuri not want to ascend the throne they would kill him also. Prince Yuri replied that he did not want to violate his oath. King David came to King Alexander, his father, and held on to his leg saying that he was guilty because he had ascended the throne while he, his father, was still alive. And the same traitors who had been stirring up quarrels between David and his father and his brother, began telling him: "The bird flies in the air. If you catch it, it is in your hands, but if you let it go you will not see it again. God has given the realm into your hands and you do not know how to hold it." And King David sent messengers to his father Alexander, asking for the royal banner and hat and the sword and belt. That is their custom instead of coronation.[1] And David thought that should his father not send him the regalia and not give up the throne, he would have his father strangled. And it became known to King Alexander that his son was plotting to kill him; he yielded the throne to him and he placed his trust in God and said: "Should I remain alive, God will again give me my realm." And Prince Yuri fled at that time to the Iberian Metropolitan. Simon's son Yuri[2] learnt that Prince Yuri was with the Metropolitan and wrote to King David about it. And King David wrote to Simon's son Yuri to guard Prince Yuri and not let him leave that place. Simon's son Yuri had him surrounded and guarded by his men; King David then came and captured him and, having put him in irons, sent him into confinement. King David remained on the throne for about a year; and he began behaving in an un-Christian way: he did not respect his father, and he caused him

[1] For Georgian coronation customs, see Commentary 48.

[2] 'Simon's son Yuri' – Giorgi X of Kartli who assumed the administration of Kartli after his father had been captured by the Turks in 1600. He appears to have been a man of moderation and good will who made genuine but abortive efforts to ransom his father; and he had been responsible for the reconciliation of his father with Alexander of Kakheti (see Brosset, EC/BHP, Vol. II, Nos. 16–18, col. 266). Further on this king, see text below, Chaps. 13–15, and particularly 13, p. 469, n. 1.

much hardship through hunger and nakedness and thirst, and he beat many of his father's entourage, and intended to kill others. King David killed seventeen members of the entourage: he cut off the heads of some and he had others cast from high walls.[1] And he then thought of killing a member of the entourage by the name of Storozan. Having learnt about it, Storozan fled to the church of the Immaculate Mother of God and stood in the church doors so that the king should not kill him.[2] But King David sent his men and commanded them to cut off Storozan's head on the spot, and he spilled blood in the church. And on learning about this King Alexander was greatly distressed; he ran to the church of the Immaculate Mother of God in his *boshmanki* [? house shoes], threw his hat on the ground and cursed his son King David. And from that moment King David sickened: first he suffered from toothache, and then a swelling came upon him; his belly split on the seventh day, and his entrails fell out and he died; and such evil stench emanated from him that a man could not stand close.[3] (390)

And when King David was no more King Alexander sent people to fetch his son Prince Yuri; he commanded that he

[1] For the feud between the Kakhian princes, see Commentary 49.

[2] Storozan: Brosset, *EC/BHP*, Vol. II, Nos. 16–18, col. 269, = 'Sorozon, Srozan ou plutôt Saridan', an *aznauri* in the confidence of King Alexander who, in February 1597 had negotiated with the Russian envoys, Sovin and Polukhanov. The church would seem to have been that of the Assumption of the Mother of God in Gremi, see Chubinashvili, *AK*, pp. 494–5, and n. 6, who attributes the building of the bell tower to Queen Tinatin in 1535. A daughter of Mamia I Gurieli, she had been repudiated by King Levan in favour of a daughter of the Shevkal Kara Musal. She died only in 1591 (*Chronique Géorgienne*, p. 25).

[3] The meaning of the Russian word *boshmanki* is not quite clear, and the reading *bashmaki* is suggested. About King David's death Professor Hermann Lehmann writes (21 Nov. 1963), 'The disease you describe sounds very much like a *Welchii* infection, or a gas gangrene arising from a lesion in the mouth – more one really cannot say. Our mouths are full of these organisms and this is the reason why bites from monkeys and men are so dangerous. It is conceivable that the father's curse lowered the resistance of his son.'

should be removed from prison, and he blessed him for kingship; and he rules himself, too . . .'

And the monk Kiril returned to his quarters . . .

On Sunday 4 March the Sovereign Tsar bade the ambassador of the Iberian King Alexander the monk Kiril and under-dyak Savva attend on him. . . . They alighted from their sledges outside the Posolskaya Palata . . . from where they walked across the square and along the parvis of the church of the Annunciation. At that time the Sovereign Tsar was seated in his royal seat in the central Gold Painted Hall;[1] he wore a cherry-coloured velvet coat and a black hat; and Prince Fedor Borisovich of all Russia, clad in a brocade coat and a black hat sat near the royal place, on the Sovereign's left. Boyars and equerries and great gentlemen clad in plain dress . . . sat with the Sovereign. Gentlemen and officials sat in the ante-chamber, and other gentlemen and boyars' sons and under-dyaks in clean plain attire stood on the porch; the *streltsy* near the church of the Annunciation and in the square wore clean uniforms and carried no arms.

When the Iberian ambassadors came into the Sovereign's presence, the equerry Mikhail Mikhaylovich Saltykov[2] pre-(391) sented the ambassadors to the Sovereign and to the Prince . . . And the monk Kiril delivered to the Sovereign Tsar King Alexander's speech. . . . And having done so he presented King Alexander's letter. The Sovereign Tsar and Prince Fedor Borisovich were gracious to the monk Kiril and gave him their hands to kiss and enquired after his health . . . The Tsar then bade the ambassadors return to their quarters . . .

[1] For 'the central Gold Painted Hall', see Commentary 50.
[2] Perhaps a son of Mikhail Glebovich Saltykov, nicknamed Krivoy (the One-Eyed), a boyar to whom Tsars Fedor and Boris entrusted diplomatic assignments in negotiations with Poland and Sweden. Krivoy later went over to the False Dmitri and became a supporter of the Polish party; a son Ivan, who was also pro-Polish, was executed in Novgorod in 1611 (cf. Brockhaus and Efron).

The following petition was sent by the monk Kiril to the (395)
gentleman of the Privy Council and Master of the Horse
Mikhail Ignatyevich Tatishchev and to dyak Grigori Klobukov
by the attendant officers:

To the Sovereign Tsar and great Prince Boris Fedorovich
of all Russia: your royal Majesty's servant, the monk in holy
orders Kirilo Ksanfopul, who prays to God for King Alexander
Levontyevich of the Georgian land, makes obeisance. My
lord King Alexander has sent me, Sire, to your royal Majesty
with instructions to petition and complain to you, Sire, of the
behaviour of your royal ambassadors Ivan Afanasyevich
Nashchokin and Ivan Levontyev . . . Your royal Majesty's
ambassadors behaved not in accordance with your royal command, but in an unseemly and improper way. Our sovereign
King Alexander and his son Prince David repeatedly sent
his gentlemen to your royal ambassadors bidding them come (396)
and carry out their embassy . . . but your royal ambassadors
paid no heed . . . And it was with great difficulty that they were
prevailed upon to attend on our sovereign King Alexander and
deliver their embassy . . . And the falcons, Sire, which they
brought with them, were dead . . . After the audience our
sovereign King Alexander commanded that your Majesty's
ambassadors be escorted to the camp where they were
quartered. And, Sire, your Majesty's ambassadors began
trading with the Turkish ambassador, the *chaush*, selling
sables and martens in exchange for pieces of velvet and gold
silk; and they did not attend to your royal affairs. And, Sire,
our sovereign daily issued as provisions to your Majesty's
ambassadors one barren cow and four sheep and five cockerels,
200 ordinary loaves and eight white loaves, and ten buckets of
grape wine, and as much minor stuff as they wanted; and the
ambassadors were also paid each two hundred silver pieces[1]

---

[1] *R. efimki*, the name given to silver coins of West European origin,
used as currency in Russia. It is a corruption of Joachimsthaler, a silver

for their expenses. And, Sovereign, the ambassadors' camp was pitched in a cool spot, at Morkanch, near the king's court; and a church was built for them so that they should not be short of anything. But Ivan Levontyev's men began behaving lawlessly: they beat two women and a peasant to death; and, Sire, your Majesty's interpreters Dmitri Ivanov and Ivan Sergeyev witnessed the murder. And, Sire, it was again there, at Morkanch, that Ivan Levontyev's men broke at night into a peasant's hut, took a cauldron by force and beat the peasant and his wife till they were half dead; the same interpreters know about this. And Ivan Levontyev bade his men sell the cauldron in Kabarda. And these same men of Ivan Levontyev forced their way into the village of Satilani[1] and wanted to violate a woman, but she screamed; the men then snatched from the hut a *batman*[2] of silk and a pair of striped silk drawers, and went off into the woods. Many tearful complaints against them were made, Sire, to King Alexander because of their acts of violence. And, Sire, our sovereign sent one of his gentlemen to your Majesty's ambassadors with instructions to tell them to respect and fear your royal Majesty, give orders to their men not to behave lawlessly, rob, oppress or beat people to death in the future, not to allow their men to go drinking in taverns and to protect the Georgians from them. But your Majesty's ambassadors gave no protection against these men; (397) they abused us, your servants, and our sovereign King Alexander suffered shame and great distress through it. And, Sire, these same men of Ivan's, in company with Terek Cossacks – so that there were nine of them – seized a man's wife at Shuvamtez[3] and carried her into the woods and violated

coin first minted in the Bohemian town of Joachimsthal in 1518. It bore the effigy of St Joachim. (See *EB*, 14th ed., Vol. 7, 507a.)

[1] 'The village of Satilani': not identifiable in Wakhusht.

[2] An oriental measure of weight: a Persian *batman* could be equal to 11 lb. 8 oz. or 5 lb. 12 oz. (cf. *EI* and longer article in *IA*).

[3] Shuvamtez/Shuvaytez = Shuamta, see p. 381, n. 1 above.

her; and this woman died in the forest as a result of their violence. Her husband and her father-in-law came and brought her dead out of the forest, and they petitioned our sovereign, King Alexander. And for the sake of your Majesty, our sovereign did not cause any dishonour to your Majesty's ambassadors for it, but he was distressed and sad over it. Your Majesty's ambassadors asked our sovereign's permission to go and trade at Zagem, four days' march from the town; not wanting to anger them – for the sake of your Majesty – our sovereign let them go to Zagem for trading after the Feast of the Dormition. And there, at Zagem, they robbed merchants from many lands, they removed by force their turbans and hats and clothes and money, they dishonoured the women, snatched the hats off their heads and sold them for drink in taverns. When our sovereign heard of their acts of violence from Jews and from Armenians and from Moslems and from Christians, from all kinds of people, he sent me, your servant, to your Majesty's ambassadors with instructions to say that they behaved badly, that they had spread ill-fame and shame into many lands, that they robbed many people, brought shame upon women and beat people to death. And I, your royal Majesty's servant, came to these men of theirs who were drinking in a tavern, and began telling them, without scolding, that they did not fear your royal Majesty, but were behaving lawlessly, beating people, robbing and drinking in taverns. And, Sire, the ambassadors' men and the same outlaw Terek Cossacks wanted to beat me with cudgels, and they cursed and insulted the honour of the mother of our sovereign King Alexander.[1] And I, your servant, escaped from them on horseback...'

[1] Doubtless a reference to the common Russian term of abuse *sukin syn*, 'son of a bitch', applied here to King Alexander. More than forty years ago the present writer was involved in quite a nasty brawl in a tavern in Zakopane in the Polish Carpathians arising out of the use of this expression by someone drinking there.

(398)   On 9 March the monk Kiril and under-dyak Savva were received by the Sovereign's boyars in the parvis of the church of the Annunciation near the Kazenny Dvor;[1] the boyars and the equerries and the gentlemen of the Privy Council and the Privy Council dyaks were all present . . . When the Georgian ambassadors came to the walled city they were first taken to the Posolskaya Palata where they waited until the boyars who were with the Sovereign came to the Kazenny Dvor . . . When they joined the boyars the great boyars enquired after their health and bade them be seated on a bench opposite them. And after a little while dyak Grigori Klobukov delivered the speech in accordance with the written message:

'Our great Sovereign Tsar and great Prince Boris Fedorovich, autocrat of all Russia and his royal Majesty's son, the (399) great sovereign Prince Fedor Borisovich of all Russia have commanded us to say: We sent Ivan Nashchokin and Ivan Levontyev as envoys to King Alexander. They wrote to us from Astarakhan – and Ivan Levontyev confirmed it orally – that King Alexander had said improper words and dishonoured them, that they suffered great restrictions and were subjected to great duress and hardships. And on the basis of their report the great Sovereign Tsar extended his wrath to King Alexander and his disfavour to you, and he was about to command that you be sent from Nizhni back to King Alexander. But Prince Fedor Borisovich petitioned his father . . . to extend his grace to King Alexander and overlook his misbehaviour, if he was guilty of any; so he graciously commanded you, Kiril, to come to Moscow . . . The great Sovereign Tsar and his royal Majesty's son listened to your petition in which you accused

[1] The *Kazenny Dvor*, the Tsar's Treasure, stood next to the Cathedral of the Annunciation. First mentioned in 1578; in the first half of the seventeenth century it was incorporated in the Patriarch's Palace. The Treasury's cellars extended below the Cathedral of the Annunciation (Brockhaus and Efron, and *Kreml Moskvy*).

our Sovereign's ambassadors of dishonouring King Alexander and of perpetrating many actions which were not in accordance with the Sovereign's command. And the great Sovereign Tsar and his royal Majesty's son graciously commanded you to see their most luminous royal eyes. And you submitted King Alexander's letter to our great Sovereign ...

With regard to the forts which King Alexander wrote (400) about . . . our great Sovereign Tsar and his royal Majesty's son Prince Fedor Borisovich have extended their grace to King Alexander and will command that the forts be built. And they have commanded us, the boyars, to question you, Kiril, as to where these forts ought to be built, and what the distance is between these emplacements, and what the local resources are. And as for King Alexander's complaints about our Sovereign's envoys . . . the great Sovereign Tsar and his royal Majesty's son have commanded that dyak Ivan Levontyev be executed ...'

And the monk Kiril said: '. . . King Alexander with his sons and grandsons and the whole of their Iberian land kissed the cross on their promise to remain for ever without seceding under his royal Majesty the great Sovereign's exalted hand ... We now petition the Sovereign to show mercy and not have dyak Ivan Levontyev executed, because our sovereign King Alexander is of the Christian faith and he does not need Christian blood; furthermore we are now in Lent ...

'With regard to the forts . . . the first should be built in the Kumyk land at Tarku; Tarku is some fifteen versts distant from the Sovereign's blockhouse on the Koysu, and some six days' march from Terek-town; it is a suitable spot with a natural stone wall, and Shevkal has his court there; there is (401) much timber and much arable land by this town; stone for the building of fortifications and lime are plentiful there; the town has many springs of water and there is a mill standing on the watercourse. The Sovereign should be merciful and have a fort erected also in another spot, near the Salting of Tuzluk;[1] it is a suitable spot with a great salt lake similar to the one near Astarakhan, and it is some five versts from Tarku; sulphur and saltpetre are extracted there. And should only the Sovereign be merciful, let him command that a fort be erected in a third spot, too – on the Boynak river; there had been a fort of King Alexander's[2] at that spot and at the site there are towers attached to the houses. The site is populous, and in the neighbourhood there are many villages and hamlets; grapes and arable land and timber are plentiful; the river is great at this spot, bigger than the Terek, and it is possible to come up the river from the sea in ships. The distance from the sea to this site is some fifteen versts, and it is a day's march from Tarku. Two roads lead from there. One is towards Derbent – and it is about a day's march from the site to Derbent; and the other road is towards the Iberian land, to the Kazy-Kumyks, and it is two days' march to the Kazy-Kumyks . . .'

(402)   On 12 March 7112 [1604], Mikhail Ignatyevich Tatishchev and dyak Grigori Klobukov called on the monk Kiril at his

(403) lodgings at the command of the Sovereign Tsar . . . And having remained seated for a short while, Mikhail and Grigori went out on to the porch; the monk Kiril and under-dyak Savva and King Alexander's men went out with them. And Mikhail and Grigori gave orders that Ivan Levontyev be led from Nicholas's Cross[3] past the quarters of the Iberian ambassadors, so that the monk Kiril should see. And as Ivan Levontyev was being led past the ambassadors' lodgings he

---

[1] For the approaches to Tarku and further details on the Kumukhs, see Commentary 51.

[2] For 'Alexander's fort', see Commentary 52.

[3] The crossroads near the St Nicholas Gate, in the north-east corner of the Kremlin walls. The gate, built in 1491 by a Milanese architect, Petrus Antonius Solarius, was farthest from the Cathedral square and the Tsar's Palace (cf. Brockhaus and Efron). For a contemporary miniature of a public knouting, see *OI/PF/xv–xvii vv.*, p. 342.

was knouted. On seeing this the monk Kiril prostrated himself and supplicated with tears his royal Majesty to extend his grace to King Alexander and not have Ivan Levontyev executed...

Mikhail and Grigori then said to the monk Kiril: 'In his letter King Alexander has asked his royal Majesty our great Sovereign to command the building of three forts in the Kumyk lands – at Tarku, Tuzluk and on the Boynak. But when his royal Majesty ... sent Prince Andrey Khvorostinin and his assistants with a large army against Shevkal, they said that those places were unsuitable for fort-building: that they (404) lacked water, that timber was far away, and that great mountains rose above them from where Kumyks would begin pressing and killing the men in the forts.' Kiril should therefore tell them the whole truth about those places.

And the monk Kiril said: 'The site of Tarku in the Kumyk land is some two versts from the sea-shore. In old days a stone castle stood there on high ground; and this mountain forms a ridge towards the sea away from the big mountains. It is thickly wooded and is some thirty *sazhen* high; a stone tower now stands on the very summit of the mountain and from this tower gun-fire can carry to the sea and in every direction. On one side of the mountain away from the sea there is a stone quarry; and at the foot of the quarry, some twenty *sazhen* or more from the summit, Shevkal's court, consisting of stone buildings and of huts, stands on the mountain side. And to one side, behind Shevkal's palace, there is a second stone tower and the site of an old castle. There had been a stone wall on two sides of the mountain. In order to fortify the place it is necessary again to build a stone or a timber wall from two sides towards the old towers across the old castle site. Stone for fortifications is most plentiful here and there is limestone too; big trees, oak and other suitable timber, are to be found one verst from Tarku and even less. And at the

very bottom, below Shevkal's palace, there is a stone mosque. At the time I, Kiril, was there, there were some three hundred peasant homesteads; and now there are some twenty or thirty homesteads, and perhaps more, where people live permanently; Tarku is never deserted. Shevkal's fighting men come there from time to time, when the crops ripen, and they bury the grain in pits and in the mountains, taking care lest the Sovereign's men come from the Koysu. And when they have stored the grain they again ride off to Shevkal in the mountains. There is no river here, but many springs of water both on the mountain and at the foot of the quarry; the spot and the water are very healthy for men and beasts. They build mills along the watercourses which flow from the springs. It is fifteen versts from the Koysu blockhouse to Tarku, and from Koysu to the Terek it is three days' march. And from Tarku there is a direct road to the Georgian land, to Zagem, across the mountains, along which people travel with pack-horses; it is impossible to travel with carts, because there are great mountains and gorges. And it is half a day's march along that road from Tarku to Tarkali; and from Tarkali it is half a day's march to the Kafyr-Kumyks; and from the Kafyr-Kumyks there is a day's march to the Kazy-Kumyks; and from the Kazy-Kumyks it is two days' travelling to the Georgian land and to Zagem.[1] Shevkal and his sons mostly
(405) live in the mountains of the Kazy-Kumyks, because this spot is farthest away from the Russian forts and is easy to defend: there are no forts but one has to cross great mountains and gorges. Should the Sovereign's men find him in those parts, he would have but one way out - to flee to the Turk's towns of Shemakha and Baku; he will not go to Derbent, because this fort is not strong and is deserted. The Turk's fort of Derbent is a day's march from Tarku, and can be seen from the upper tower of Tarku. The journey from Derbent to Baku takes

[1] For the route from Tarku to Zagem, see Commentary 53.

three days, and from Baku to Shemakha – three days. From Tarku direct to Shemakha, without going through Baku, it takes five days. Shevkal cannot expect assistance from these towns, because they themselves fear the coming of the Sovereign's men.

And the second fort should be erected near the salt lake that is called Buzlyk, some twenty versts near the lake;[1] and this lake is some five versts from Tarku. There is much good salt in this lake. Timber and arable land and grass-land are plentiful at this spot and there are many springs of water; the spot is healthy for men and beasts. And near this lake the land is flat. And apart from this spot there is no salt anywhere in the mountains. Should only a fort be built here, Shevkal would be greatly pressed and suffer hardship; and all the mountaineers would have nowhere to get their salt from.

And the third spot is the site of an old town on a mountain overlooking the river Boynak a day's march from Tarku. The Boynak river has left the mountains there and flows towards the sea. There are still walls and towers at this site, but in a ruinous state; and the size of this site in length and across is three hundred *sazhen* each way. The town had been built by King Alexander of Macedon. There are numerous villages and hamlets near this old site, and there is plenty of grapes and arable land and timber, and it is a very healthy place for men and beasts. That river Boynak is the size of the river Koysu. The distance from the sea up the river is some fifteen versts to the old site, and one can sail up from the sea in ships. Two roads lead from the site: one goes towards Derbent and the other to Shemakha and to Baku; it is approximately a day's march from Boynak to Derbent, and it takes four days to Shemakha, and from Shemakha to Baku it takes two days.

[1] Buzlyk presumably an error for Tuzluk. The sentence, as given by Belokurov, would appear to be incomplete. For Tuzluk, see further Commentary 51.

When a fort is built at that spot all these roads will be controlled.[1]

[On 18 March the Georgian ambassadors were received with great ceremony by Patriarch Job. During the following weeks they were frequently supplied with provisions from the royal kitchens. On 21 April the Georgians were received by Tsar Boris in farewell audience, immediately after he had received the Persian ambassadors Lachin-bek and his assistants. The Georgian ambassadors were given gifts and allowed to kiss the hand of the Tsar and of Prince Fedor.[2] On 26 April they were received in farewell audience by the Patriarch. Meantime, on the 21, the Russian attendant officers were given instructions to see to it that nobody should sell any falcons or gerfalcons to the Georgian ambassadors, or bring them cuirasses, bows and arrows or swords for sale. The Georgian ambassadors were sent back home in the company of the Russian ambassadors Tatishchev and dyak Ivanov.]

[1] For the site and history of Boynak, see Commentary 51.

[2] For ceremonial leave-taking of the Tsar, cf. Herberstein (Hakluyt Society ed.) Vol. II, pp. 132–3. I have been unable to trace references to the embassy of Lachin-bek in the documents on Russo-Persian affairs published by Veselovski. Brosset (*EC/BHP*, Vol. II, Nos. 19–21, col. 308, n. 50) observes that this ambassador left before the new Russian mission (of Tatishchev and Ivanov) and was met near Kasimov in the month of June by Ivanov, who himself only joined Tatishchev at Kazan. Müller (*Sammlung*, Vol. v/i, pp. 168–9) states that the Persian ambassador 'Latschin Buk' arrived in Moscow on 28 August 1603, and was received by the *pristav*, Prince Fedor Andreyevich Zvenigorodski. He brought with him very costly gifts, including a gold chair or camp-stool (*Sessel*) set with precious stones. On 4 September he had an audience of Tsar Boris.

CHAPTER 9

MINUTIAE

FROM the Tsar and great Prince Boris Fedorovich of all (420) Russia, to our ambassadors the gentleman of the Privy Council and Lord Lieutenant of Mozhaysk Mikhail Ignatyevich Tatishchev and our dyak Andrey Ivanov: We have sent to you by Fedor Suleshev[1] our instructions and letters, and all documents which you will need and which relate to the embassy to Iberia, as well as the bounty which has been sent by us to the Iberian King Alexander and to his son Prince Yuri, and to King David's queen[2] and to other royalty and princes, and also some in reserve. An inventory over the signature of our dyak Afanasi Vlasyev[3] has been sent to you

[1] Suleshev, Fedor: The Suleshevs or Suleshovs were of Crimean Tartar origin. Fedor may have been brother or cousin of Prince Yuri Yansheyevich Suleshov who married, c. 1610, Marfa Mikhaylovna Saltykova, niece of Marfa Ivanovna Romanova, and had a distinguished and adventurous career under the first Romanov Tsars (cf. *RBS* under name).

[2] 'King David's Queen'; Ketevan, daughter of Ashotan, Prince of Mukhrani of the collateral line of the Kartlian Bagratids. She married David of Kakheti about 1581 and was the mother of Taymuraz I, King of Kakheti, 1605–63. She was tortured to death by order of Shah Abbas I, 12 Sept. 1624 and was canonized as a saint and martyr of the Georgian Church (cf. Brosset, *HG*, Vol. ii/i, p. 634; Genealogical Trees; also pp. 166 and 190 – recounting the loss of her relics owing to the fall of a horse while crossing the Aragvi in 1723). For details, including the Queen's interest in Catholic missionaries in Shiraz, see Tamarati, *EG*, pp. 482 ff., with reproduction of idealized portrait after Sabinini. Also learned article by Z. Avalishvili, 'T'eimuraz I and his poem "The Martyrdom of Queen K'et'evan'" in *Georgica*, Nos. 4 and 5 (1937), citing many original sources, a penetrating study of Georgian–Persian relations; and Commentary 8.

[3] Vlasyev, Afanasi, head of the Posolski Prikaz, 1601–5 (see Chap. 8, p. 379, n. 1). He had been sent on embassies to Emperor Rudolf II in 1595 and 1599. In 1600 he was one of the Russian plenipotentiaries who

by Fedor, listing our instructions, letters and all documents and the bounty which we have sent . . . and the items sent in reserve, and the presents sent to King Alexander by Patriarch Job who prays to God for us. The box with the documents has Afanasi's seal, and the chests with gifts are sealed with the Treasury dyaks' seal . . .

(421)   The[1] ambassadorial documents and the presents should not be allowed to get wet. And Suleshev must have the boxes accompanied and carried by men when crossing very muddy and unpaved parts, so that on no account should anything in these boxes get wet. He must camp in inhabited places. For the protection of the gifts he must take ten watchmen from among officials in towns, and from among the inhabitants of town-ships and villages and post-stations where he happens to camp; and he must take all precautions on the road and while camping. If he considers it [necessary] . . . he must take an escort from the towns so as to deliver the consignment safely. He must travel in haste after the ambassadors Mikhail Ignatyevich and Andrey, without delaying anywhere . . . by day and by night. On getting to the ambassadors, he must give them the Sovereign Tsar's letter and inventory of all docu-ments and the gifts. After taking from them a report for the Sovereign Tsar, he should travel to Moscow and on arrival there he should come and hand in the report to dyak Afanasi Vlasyev at the Posolski Prikaz.

negotiated the twenty-year armistice with Poland. After the death of Tsar Boris, Vlasyev made his submission to the False Dmitri and became Grand Secretary and Court Treasurer. Dmitri sent him to Cracow to fetch his bride, Marina Mniszech (cf. Purchas, Vol. xiv, p. 163). (Vlasyev had had experience of a similar mission before–since, in 1602, he had been sent to welcome the Danish Prince John, the suitor of Tsar Boris's daughter, Xenia.) After the accession of Vasili Shuyski, Vlasyev was appointed commander at Ufa – an honourable exile (cf. Brockhaus and Efron).

[1] Belokurov notes that of the instructions given to Suleshev only this fragment has survived.

Inventory of documents from the Posolski Prikaz sent to the ambassadors ...:

Instructions on how they are to conduct the Sovereign Tsar's affairs while they are with King Alexander in the Georgian land.

Another and secret instruction which Mikhail Ignatyevich must keep; and a specimen letter on a scroll addressed to King Alexander about the secret affair – which must be kept together with the instructions.[1]

A specimen letter on a scroll, addressed to King Simon's son Prince Yuri. And letters to Simon's brothers, to King Roston[2] the son of Constantine, to his brother Prince Yuri and to other kings and princes who would want to come into the Sovereign's grace, must be written as per this specimen, in accordance with local conditions.

Two letters of credence from the Sovereign addressed to King Alexander and to his son Prince Yuri.[3]

A letter to Prince Aristov of Soni, and a copy of that letter.

Three letters about escorts, addressed to Prince Solokh, to Kazy-murza son of Shepshuk,[4] and to Aytek, Araksan and Mundar murzas.

[1] Belokurov indicates that the manuscript has marginal notes to the effect that the drafts of these two documents were kept by dyak Afanasi Vlasyev in person; they have not survived.

[2] 'King Roston the son of Constantine'. The reference is to Rostom I, fourteenth king of Imereti, son of Constantine, brother of Giorgi II, thirteenth king. Rostom, born 1571; crowned 1590; married (1597) Tinatin, daughter of Manuchar IV, Atabeg of Samtskhe; died 1605 (see Brosset, *HG*, Vol. II/i, pp. 645, 263–5; Allen *HGP*, p. 159). Rostom was an insignificant personality, but the mention of his name shows the intention of the Russians to include Imereti in their diplomatic net.

[3] See pp. 413–14 below.

[4] Kazy (Ghazi) murza, son of Shepshuk or Pshaopshoka, belonged to a junior branch of the princely house of Kabarda (see Chap. 2, p. 108, n. 4 above, and Belokurov, *Snosheniya*, pp. 3 ff.). He was killed by the Nogays during their invasion of Kabarda instigated by Solokh's son Khoroshay. For Aytek, see Chap. 2 and Commentary 12. Araksan was a son of Alkas, see p. 426 below. Mundar was probably a member of the Mudarov family – see Commentary 18 (f).

Copies of Ivan Nashchokin's letter and of Suliman's petition, taken from the Department, over the seal of dyak Grigori Klobukov.[1]

Copy of the oath of allegiance taken by King Alexander and his son David.

(422) Copy of King Alexander's letter to the Sovereign brought by his ambassador the monk Kiril.

Copy of the record of the monk Kiril's visit to the Posolski Prikaz and to the boyars, and of Mikhail and Grigori's visit to the monk when they questioned him on where the forts ought to be built.

Inventory of the provisions issued to previous Georgian ambassadors and, in the last instance, to the monk Kiril.

Inventory of the Sovereign's bounty sent to King Alexander, to Prince Yuri, to King David's queen and to other royalty and princes. All the gifts listed in the inventory [are packed] in special chests with the seals of Treasury dyaks.

Five sheets of Alexandria paper,[2] with borders and initial words illuminated in gold.

The Patriarch's gift to King Alexander of an image of the Immaculate Mother of God with the Eternal Child, encased in silver; twice forty sables – arranged in a separate chest, sealed with the seal of Treasury dyaks. The Patriarch's letter is appended underneath the main instruction.

Sent in reserve: half a quire of large sheets of Alexandria paper; a quire of medium-sized sheets of Alexandria paper; a ream of writing paper; red sealing wax.

Such an inventory has been sent to Mikhail and to Andrey, sewn in paper and sealed with Afanasi's seal.

---

[1] Klobukov, Grigori: see Chap. 8, p. 379, n. 3.

[2] Name given to paper of very good quality. Most of the paper used in Russia in the fifteenth and sixteenth centuries was imported from France: from the end of the fifteenth century paper was also increasingly imported from Germany. Small quantities of Polish paper began to come in at the end of the sixteenth century (Brockhaus and Efron, *s.v.*)

And these instructions have been sent after the ambassadors:

On the 2nd day of May in the year 7112, the Sovereign Tsar and great Prince Boris Fedorovich of all Russia commanded the gentleman of the Privy Council and Lord Lieutenant of Mozhaysk[1] Mikhail Ignatyevich Tatishchev and dyak Andrey Ivanov to proceed on an embassy to the Georgian King Alexander on his own royal affairs and the affairs of the land ... Instructions have been sent by the Sovereign Tsar to Kazan, to Astarakhan and to [? the Terek], to the boyar, to the commanders and to the dyaks, to send 850 *streltsy* from Kazan, Svyazhski[2] and other towns of the lower Volga, who are to be stationed on the Terek, under two headmen, as an escort for the ambassadors between Kazan and Astarakhan ...

When they come to Kazan the ambassadors must take from (423) the boyar and the commanders the escort which they are ordered to give them, and must proceed from Kazan to Astarakhan without delay. And while journeying along the Volga they should take precautions and should camp carefully in strong positions, so that outlaw Cossacks or the men of Azov or Nogays from Kazy's *ulus* do not catch them unawares and do them no evil ...

And when, if God grants, they reach the Georgian land and (425) King Alexander bids them carry out their embassy, the gentleman of the Privy Council Mikhail Ignatyevich and dyak Andrey should send word to the king that no ambassadors or envoys from other sovereigns should be present at the same time ...

---

[1] The title of 'Lord Lieutenant of Mozhaysk' allowed to M. I. Tatishchev was purely honorific. It was customary to give ambassadors proceeding on important missions the title of Lord Lieutenant of a particular town – in order to impress the foreign ruler with the importance of the person whom the Tsar was sending to him. For further on M. I. Tatishchev, see Commentary 46.

[2] For these towns along the Volga route see Commentary 7.

(427)   And when they will have carried out their embassy, and King Alexander bids them attend on him again, the gentleman of the Privy Council Mikhail Ignatyevich and dyak Andrey should say to King Alexander and to the king's entourage: 'Our great Sovereign Tsar sent before now his envoys Ivan Nashchokin and Ivan Levontyev to King Alexander. And his royal Majesty's envoys wrote to our great Sovereign, and Ivan Levontyev – on his return – orally informed his royal Majesty's officials, that King Alexander had said much that was improper, enumerating the gifts which he had sent to his royal (428) Majesty and saying that he himself had received nothing from his royal Majesty and that the army had not yet come against Shevkal; and the king subjected the Sovereign's envoys to much dishonour and oppression, and gave orders for them to be quartered in forests and uninhabited places, and no provisions were given them so that many of their men died. Yet King Alexander honoured the Turkish *chaush* beyond measure and placed him at his side. And for such improper behaviour King Alexander brought upon himself his royal Majesty's wrath, for which reason his ambassador, the monk Kiril, was ordered to remain in Nizhni Novgorod, from where he was to have been sent back to the Iberian land; his royal Majesty did not want to send his ambassadors to King Alexander in the future nor to listen to the king's petition. But our lord Prince Fedor, his royal Majesty's son, begged our great Sovereign . . . not to deprive King Alexander of his mercy, but to order the monk Kiril to be brought to Moscow and questioned about everything.[1] And our great Sovereign

---

[1] Tsar Boris Godunov's son, Fedor Borisovich, was being schooled by his father for ceremonial occasions as early as 1595 – three years before the death of his uncle, Tsar Fedor Ivanovich (cf. Platonov, *Ocherki*, p. 195). In December 1598, when Boris Godunov was already Tsar, Fedor Borisovich deputized for his father in negotiations with the Polish ambassador, Lew Sapieha, who did not disguise his annoyance (cf. Solovyev, Vol. II, col. 698). Fedor was then ten years old, according to

Tsar . . . commanded the monk Kiril to come to Moscow and allowed him to see his most luminous royal eyes. The monk Kiril handed [the Tsar] King Alexander's letter. King Alexander wrote in his letter to his royal Majesty, and the monk Kiril informed him in his speech and letter, that our great Sovereign's envoys Ivan Nashchokin and Ivan Levontyev themselves committed many improper acts not in accordance with his royal Majesty's instructions when they were with King Alexander in the Georgian land, and subjected the king's men to violence and insults. And our great Sovereign and his royal Majesty's son, our lord Prince Fedor, following their royal merciful custom and in their graciousness towards King Alexander, did not believe anything that their own ambassadors had written and said to them but – instead – believed what King Alexander wrote in his letter to his royal Majesty, and what was notified orally and in writing by his ambassador the monk Kiril. They commanded that Ivan Levontyev be executed for that. But King Alexander's ambassador, the monk Kiril, begged his royal Majesty to be merciful to Levontyev for King Alexander's sake and to give orders not to execute him. And his royal Majesty, at the monk Kiril's supplication, did not pass sentence of death on him for King Alexander's sake, but sentenced him to be punished publicly

Purchas, Vol. xiv, p. 134, who wrongly gives the date as 1586. In this connection, see B. S. Izhboldin (Ischboldin), 'Tsar F. B. Godunov', in *Novik*, New York, 1956, p. 3, who gives his date of birth as 1589 – for which indication I am indebted to Professor George Vernadsky. A youth of promise, Fedor Borisovich had little chance of showing his true form for he fell victim to the partisans of the False Dmitri, shortly after his father's death in 1605. Tsar Boris seems to have liked to appear to encourage his son's liberal and moderating interventions in public affairs. The boy was an amateur of cartography; and the first draft of the map of Russia, published by Hessel Gerritsz in 1613 and dedicated to Tsar Mikhail Fedorovich Romanov, bears the autograph of Fedor Borisovich (cf. Map 1, *Tabula Russiae*). As an 'unfulfilled' historical personality, Fedor Borisovich merits comparison, perhaps, with his contemporary, Henry Prince of Wales, eldest son of King James I and VI.

and to be cast into prison for life; the monk Kiril has since been witness to this. And as for Ivan Nashchokin, he died on his return journey from King Alexander's land; had he been alive he would have suffered the same fate. His royal Majesty has sent with us, his ambassadors, 500 rubles in cash for those of King Alexander's men who were subjected to violence by Ivan Nashchokin and Ivan Levontyev, in order (429) to compensate them for the dishonour they suffered, as well as for the relatives and kin of those who were killed by the envoys' men. When, before now, King Alexander's ambassadors Prince Suliman and dyak Levan were on an embassy to his royal Majesty, his royal Majesty commanded that they be issued with a sufficient quantity of food and drink; yet the seal-bearer and Posolski Prikaz dyak Vasili Shchelkalov,[1] without the Tsar's command and at the ambassadors' request, had given them money instead of food. When his royal Majesty learnt about this, he gave orders to take 300 rubles from Vasili Shchelkalov and give this money to Suliman and to dyak Levan; Suliman was given two hundred rubles and dyak Levan one hundred.'

Having delivered this speech, they should ask the king's entourage to send to them the people who had been wronged. And when these men or their relatives are brought to them, Mikhail Ignatyevich and Andrey should distribute the Sovereign's bounty to them, at the rate of one hundred rubles for each case mentioned in the monk Kiril's supplication: for the murder at Morkanch of two women and a man by Ivan Levontyev's men they must give three hundred rubles, one hundred for each person; the ambassadors must also give one hundred rubles for the peasant's wife at Shuvamtez who had been taken by Ivan's men and by Terek Cossacks, led into the woods and violated, as a result of which assault this woman died; and they must also pay one hundred rubles for

[1] For Vasili Shchelkalov and his brother, Andrey, see Commentary 54.

the incidents at Zagem, when the Russians stole the clothes of merchants from many lands, and robbed them by force of their money, and dishonoured women and local inhabitants, and knocked the hats off their heads and sold them for drink in the taverns...[1]

And a memorandum for the gentleman of the Privy Council (436) Mikhail Ignatyevich Tatishchev and dyak Andrey Ivanov: If, when they come to the Iberian land, King Alexander is no more or if he has entered a monastery, and if his son Prince Yuri has become king in his stead in the Iberian land, and the new King Yuri bids them carry out their embassy, Mikhail Ignatyevich and Andrey Ivanov should go to the new King Yuri... They should present to him the gifts which had been sent for King Alexander; and as for what has been sent for Prince Yuri, the ambassadors should not hand them over but hold them for other expenses – except for the falcons, which they should give to the new king...

And should the ambassadors be asked: 'What are the (437) Sovereign's present relations with Caesar Rudolf and with the Roman Pope and with the Lithuanian king?' Mikhail Ignatyevich and Andrey should say: 'The Roman Caesar Rudolf entertains friendship and love for our great Sovereign Tsar, and frequent messages are exchanged between the two sovereigns.[2] His royal Majesty has a truce with the Lithuanian

---

[1] See Chap. 8 above, pp. 391–3.

[2] Belokurov notes that this sentence was followed by another, subsequently crossed out, which read 'And our sovereign has helped the Roman Caesar Rudolf with his royal treasure against the Turkish Sultan' – presumably a reference to the large quantity of furs, valued by merchants in Prague at 400,000 rubles, which the Tsar had sent to the Emperor in 1595. Two years later the furs were still unsold, and the Austrian ambassador, Abraham Burggraf von Donath, asked the Tsar to send bullion instead of furs; the request was not received favourably (cf. Solovyev, Vol. II, col. 597).

Rudolf's 'friendship and love' for Boris Godunov was relative. During the years 1593–8 – and notably after the death of Tsarevna Fedosia Fedorovna, only child of Tsar Fedor Ivanovich and Irina Godunova –

king Zhigimont. The Lithuanian king sent his great ambassadors to our great Sovereign Tsar – the chancellor of the grand duchy of Lithuania Lew Sapieha and his assistants – with the request that our great Sovereign Tsar should be at peace, friendship and love with King Zhigimont. And our great Sovereign Tsar, following his merciful royal custom, (438) and in his grief over the shedding of Christian blood, has listened to the supplication and intercession of his son Prince Fedor and has commanded for the sake of peace in Christendom to effect a truce with the Lithuanian king Zhigimont.'[1]

And should they be asked anything about the Swedish land ... the ambassadors should say: 'There was peace with the Swedish land in the time of the great Sovereign Tsar and great Prince Fedor Ivanovich, and there is peace now. The Swedish land is at present governed by Artsi-Karlo, a ruling and hereditary prince of the Swedish realm; he sent his ambassadors Yuri Klaus and his comrades to our great Sovereign Tsar asking that his royal Majesty our great Sovereign, should extend his grace to him, Artsi-Karlo, and to the Swedish land,

somewhat indiscreet conversations took place between Andrey Shchelkalov and the Austrian envoy, Nicholas Varkoch, on the possibility of sponsoring the Archduke Maximilian as successor to the ailing Tsar Fedor Ivanovich. This idea became known to Lew Sapieha, Christopher Radziwill, and some Italian diplomats (cf. Platonov, pp. 212 ff., 227 ff.). Boris got wind of the intrigues through his own secret agents. The mistrust engendered led to the dismissal of Andrey Shchelkalov in 1594 and may have been a factor in stimulating the desire of Tsar Boris to arrange Danish or Georgian marriages for his son and daughter. The removal of Vasili Shchelkalov from the Posolski Prikaz in 1601 may, perhaps, be connected with Tsar Boris's pursuit of these later matrimonial alliances (see further, Commentary 54).

[1] In 1600, when Poland and Sweden were at war, Chancellor Lew Sapieha was sent to Moscow to negotiate an alliance between Poland and Russia. The negotiations dragged on until August of the following year because, in the meantime, a Swedish embassy had also come to Moscow and the Tsar was trying to play the two contending countries off against each other. The Polish negotiations ended with the conclusion of a twenty year truce (cf. Solovyev, Vol. II, cols. 697 ff.).

and command that the peace status be ratified. These ambassadors of his have been sent back, and the peace status is in accordance with the former treaty; but the matter has not been completed, and the treaty not ratified.'[1]

Should King Alexander or his officials ask: 'What are the present relations of the Sovereign Tsar with the Turkish Sultan?' the ambassadors should say: 'The Turkish Sultan Murat before now sent his envoys to the great Sovereign Tsar Fedor Ivanovich of blessed memory, with the request that the Tsar should live in friendship and love with him. But his royal Majesty the great Sovereign – for the sake of his brother, his Majesty Abbas-shah, and of Caesar Rudolf and of King Alexander – did not wish to be in friendship and love with the Turkish Sultan Murat, and he sent his envoys back empty-handed; he only sent his own courier along with them for trade questions. There has been no fresh exchange of messages between the great Sovereign Tsar and great Prince Boris Fedorovich autocrat of all Russia and the Turkish Sultan Mehmet.'[2]

Should they then be asked 'What are the present relations of the Sovereign with the Crimean king Kazy Girey?'[3] the

---

[1] *Artsi-Karlo* (Herzog Karl) reigned as Charles IX of Sweden, 1600–11. Sweden and Russia had signed 'an eternal peace' in 1595 under the terms of which the latter regained possession of the towns of Ivangorod, Yam, Koporye and Korela. In 1604 Charles IX, who was the successful rival for the Swedish crown of his cousin Sigismund III (Vasa) of Poland, sent Tsar Boris an offer of military assistance against his enemies – which did not, however, come to anything (cf. *OI/PF/xv–xvii vv*, pp. 484, 564).

[2] For relations between Boris Godunov and the Sublime Porte, see Commentary 55.

[3] Kazy Girey (Ghazi Giray II, 1588–1608), called *bora*, literally hurricane, succeeded his brother Islam Giray II (1584–8): see Genealogical Tree in *IA*, cilt 4 by Halil Inalcik. Among the more gifted of the Girays, he took a prominent part in the Hungarian battles of the Long War. He was, too, an epicurean and a poet of distinction who passed the winter months of 1602 in Fünfkirchen composing a work in verse on the qualities of wine and coffee – a worthy pendant, according to von

ambassadors should say: 'The Crimean king Kazy Girey sent his ambassadors to our great Sovereign with the prayer that his royal Majesty should accept him into friendship and love, and with the complaint that Crimean people and men of Azov suffer constraint from the new forts built in the plain close to the Crimea[1] in accordance with his royal Majesty's command, (439) forts along the Donets and the Oskol such as Tsarev-Borisov, Belgorod, Oskol, Valuyki and many others close to the Crimea. His request was that the great Sovereign Tsar should command that forts should not be built close to the Crimea, so that Crimean people should suffer no constraint or losses from them . . .

(440) On the 2nd of May the Sovereign Tsar and great Prince Boris Fedorovich of all Russia sent off his ambassadors the gentleman of the Privy Council and Lord-Lieutenant of Mozhaysk Mikhail Ignatyevich Tatishchev and dyak Andrey Ivanov to the Iberian king Alexander.

Hammer, to Fuzuli's poem on wine and opium (cf. von Hammer, *HEO*, Vol. VIII, pp. 20–1, 149). His reign was a time of some intellectual florescence in Baghchesaray and numerous Tartar savants visited Istanbul (ibid., p. 50).

[1] The text has been amended to read *na pole* (in the plain) instead of *na Kole* since Kola is in the extreme north of European Russia and not 'close to the Crimea'. *Pole*, on the other hand, was the name given to the open steppes along the southern frontier of Russia. Purchas (Vol. XI, pp. 130–1), reports that in May 1598, shortly after the accession of Boris, 'the Crim Tartars had entered the borders thinking to find all things troubled with an interregne . . . But the Tartars hearing how things went, returned home and sent Embassadors to the Emperor's tents. Hee returned with them to Mosco'. Purchas erroneously dates the invasion May 1586.

The defences of the frontier over against the Crim Tartars were greatly strengthened by Tsar Boris by the construction of the forts of Belgorod and Oskol (both in 1598), Valuyki (1599) and Tsarev-Borisov (1600). Other fortified towns built in the area in the last two decades of the sixteenth century were Livny and Voronezh (in 1586), Elets (1592), Kromy (1595) and Kursk (reconstructed in 1597) – *OI/PF/xv–xvii vv*, pp. 480, 481.

And this was the letter of credence sent by the Sovereign Tsar to King Alexander, with God's name and the name of the Sovereign as far as 'of Vladimir' written in gold, and the great open-work seal in a paper cover.[1] The letters to King Alexander and Prince Yuri were written on medium-sized Alexandria paper:

We, the great Sovereign Tsar, send to you, King Alexander, ruler of the Iberian land, our gracious royal word and great bounty, and our royal authority's great protection for yourself, King Alexander, and for the whole of your Iberian land from all your enemies. You have sent, King Alexander, your ambassador the monk Kiril and the under-dyak Savva with a letter to us, the great Sovereign Tsar and to our royal Majesty's son. And we have become acquainted with the affairs about which you wrote to our royal Majesty and about which your ambassador spoke to us on your behalf. And we, the great Sovereign Tsar and our royal Majesty's son, in our bounty to you King Alexander, and your son Prince Yuri and all your Iberian land, have sent to you our ambassadors the gentleman (441)

[1] The words written in gold would be 'By the grace of God, the great sovereign Tsar and great Prince Boris Fedorovich, Autocrat of all Russia'; the rest of the Tsar's title consisted of the enumeration of his domains – beginning with 'of Vladimir'. In 1604 his full titles, according to Purchas (XIV, p. 134) included 'King of all Syberia and the North Coasts, Commander of the Countreyes of Iversky, Grysinsky and Emperour of Kabaadrivskey, of Chirkasky, and the whole Countrey of Garskey'(= *Gorskaya ʒemlya*, the mountain land = Tavlistan or Daghestan).

According to Kotoshikhin (pp. 36 ff.), the size of the sheet of paper on which the Tsar's letters were written varied according to the standing of the foreign ruler to whom a letter was addressed. Large sheets were used for correspondence with the Emperor, the Turkish Sultan and the Shah of Persia. King Alexander, to whom was sent a letter on medium-sized Alexandria paper, was treated on the same footing as the Kings of Sweden, Poland, England and Denmark. Belokurov (*O Posolskom Prikaʒe*, pp. 48 ff.), writes that the seals on letters to Georgian kings were enclosed in plain cases; these cases, in addition to protecting the seals, were also intended to indicate the importance of the recipient – thus, the seals on letters to the Emperor were enclosed in decorated cases.

of the Privy Council and Lord Lieutenant of Mozhaysk Mikhail Ignatyevich Tatishchev and the dyak Andrey Ivanov with full instructions on how you and your son Prince Yuri and the whole of your Iberian land should remain in our royal bounty and under our exalted royal hand in the future, enjoying protection and defence from all your enemies. You must believe everything which our ambassadors will tell you about our royal Majesty's affairs when they carry out their embassy to you, King Alexander – for those will be our speeches. Written at our court in our Realm's reigning city of Moscow, on the ... day of May in the year 7112 from the creation of the world.

CHAPTER 10

THE OLD ROAD TO SONI

To the Sovereign Tsar and great Prince Boris Fedorovich of all Russia, your servant Andryushka Ivanov makes obeisance. Sire, you have commanded me, your servant, to travel to the Georgian land with the gentleman of the Privy Council and Master of the Horse Mikhail Ignatyevich Tatishchev; and I, your servant, was sent off from Moscow three days after him. And, Sire, I arrived at Kolomna on the 9th of May; Mikhail accompanied by the Georgian ambassador had left Kolomna in boats three days before my arrival. And I, your servant, left Kolomna by boat on the 9th of May; travelling without stopping day and night I passed the Kizilbash ambassador at Kasimov.[1] I arrived at Nizhni on the 19th of May, but your Majesty's gentleman of the Privy Council and Master of the Horse Mikhail Ignatyevich Tatishchev had left Nizhni for Kazan on the morning of that same day, the 19th of May. And I went after Mikhail on the same day without delaying in Nizhni even for an hour.

[Brought on] the 29th day of May, 7112, by the inhabitant of Kazan Nikifor Vorontsov.

... And,[2] Sire, such people as come here to Astarakhan from the Terek have told us, your servants, that news of your

(420)

(445)

---

[1] For Kasimov, see Commentary 7(a). Veselovski (*Pamyatniki*, Vols. I and II) has no reference to the presence of a Persian ambassador in Moscow in 1604; but see Chap. 8, p. 399, n. 2, above and cf. Commentary 61. Persian ambassadors usually called at Kasimov on their way home to buy German and Livonian slaves – presumably because Christian slaves who could not be sold openly in the Russian towns could be discreetly marketed in Kasimov which was, in theory, a Tartar Moslem kingdom.

[2] This is a fragment of a report sent by Tatishchev from Astrakhan.

Majesty's army has long been known on the Terek, and the Cherkesses also know that your Majesty's army is marching against Shevkal. And, Sovereign, the commander and the dyak (446) at Astarakhan have told us, your servants, that the fact that your Majesty's army is on its way against Shevkal is known by people besides themselves in Astarakhan, too. This news has been spread by the petitioners from local towns who have been to Moscow. And as for the men whom the monk Kiril has sent to King Alexander we, your servants, asked them to find out in the land of Soni the true news about King Alexander and his son Prince Yuri and King Simon's son King Yuri, and, also, what the present relations are between King Alexander and his son Prince Yuri on the one hand, and King Simon's son King Yuri and King Roston on the other. We have asked them to let us know what they find out by sending us a message to the Terek by the men who have been sent to escort them. We, your servants, were ordered in your Majesty's instructions to proceed overland from Astarakhan to the Terek and to send our stores off in boats across the sea; and the instructions were that 500 mounted *streltsy* were to be sent to escort us overland from Astarakhan to the Terek. But, Sire, the monk Kiril did not want to proceed to the Terek overland, saying that his eyes and legs hurt and that because of his illness he could not travel to the Terek on horseback. And we, your servants, talked to the monk Kiril for a long time, asking him to come to the Terek overland with us. We wanted to have a cart made for him so that he could travel without hardship; but we could not persuade him to come. And your Majesty's commander Mikhail Saburov[1] and dyak Afanasi Karpov have told us that they had

[1] The Saburovs were descended from the same common ancestor as the Godunovs and the Velyaminov-Zernovs – Chete murza of the Golden Horde. The patronymic derives from the nickname *sabur*, aloe. Two members of the family held boyar rank in the second half of the sixteenth century and the third was the wife of Ivan IV's elder son, Ivan. Mikhail Bogdanovich, her brother, was *voyvode* of Astrakhan in 1605 when he was

sent off on your Majesty's affairs all the mounted *streltsy* whom they had at Astarakhan: to the Yaik and towards the saltings and elsewhere, and up the Volga because of the Cossack outlaws who had been wrecking merchants' boats; and to meet the Kizilbash ambassador in order to protect him from outlaws. Therefore they had no mounted *streltsy* to send with us overland. We, your servants, did not dare travel separately from the monk Kiril; and on the 26th of June we set off in ships from Astarakhan for the Terek by sea. As for our poor men, thirty-five have left Astarakhan with me, Mikhalko, and seven with me, Andryushka, as well as six falconers and interpreters. And, Sovereign, the 550 *streltsy* from Kazan and Svyazhski who had been with us have been sent to escort us from Astarakhan. The commander and the dyak have sent one hundred mounted *streltsy* and one hundred *yurt* Tartars to escort our horses as far as the Terek ...

To the Sovereign Tsar and great Prince Boris Fedorovich (448) of all Russia your servants Mikhalko Tatishchev and Andryushka Ivanov make obeisance. We reached the Terek on the 1st of July, and, Sire, the commanders Nikifor Trakhaniotov and Prince Vladimir Mosalski[1] told us that they had sent two Cherkesses, settlers on the Terek, to the Avar and the Black Princes to get news.[2] They said that these Cherkesses returned on July 1st and on being questioned reported that they had

handed over by the inhabitants to the partisans of the False Dmitri. In the following year he was killed in Tsarev-Borisov (*RBS*, under name).

The difficulties recorded in this paragraph reflect the conditions of anarchy which had been spreading since the famine and cholera epidemic which had followed the bad harvests of 1601–3 (see *RBS*, under Boris Godunov). For the Kizilbash ambassador, see above, Chap. 8, p. 400, n. 2.

[1] Prince Vladimir Koltsov-Mosalski was the son of Prince Vasili Semenovich, nicknamed *Koltso*, the ring. He had been commander at Orel, 1582, and later at Pronsk. The Mosalskis claimed descent from Rurik (*RBS*).

[2] For the Avar and Black Princes, see Introduction, Section 8 and Chap. 2, p. 105, n. 2.

heard from the Black Prince's son that the Georgian King Alexander had gone to the Kizilbash Shah Abbas some four months previously.[1] They did not know how many troops had gone with him and where Shah Abbas was. They said, Sovereign, that King Alexander's son Prince Yuri is now in the Georgian land. And, Sire, these same Cherkesses brought a letter from the Avar Prince to the commanders, who have sent a translation of this letter to us. The Avar Prince Natsal wrote in that letter to the commanders on the Terek that the Georgian King Alexander had gone from Georgia to the Kizilbash Shah Abbas and that he is no longer alive.[2] And we, your servants, asked the commanders Nikifor Trakhaniotov and Prince Vladimir Mosalski whether there are on the Terek any merchants from the Georgian land. They said that the Georgian Aley, son of Magmet, came to Terek-town with merchandise from the Koysu on the 21st of June and brought them a letter in Persian characters from the Georgian King Alexander; they said that they had nobody to translate that letter.[3] And, Sovereign, on being questioned, this Georgian said that it was the sixth week since his departure from the Georgian land. When he was still there, about a month before his departure, King Alexander had gone to the Kizilbash Shah Abbas to the

[1] i.e. at the beginning of March 1604. Abbas had been besieging Erevan since 16 November 1603 – with 6,000 Persians and 3,000 Kurdish irregulars called *Tulunki* or *Gök-Dolak* (cf. von Hammer, *HEO*, Vol. VIII, pp. 40 ff., and our Commentary 32). In a letter dated 7 September 1963, Professor V. Minorsky has kindly suggested that *gök dolak* can mean 'those who wear blue puttees' or 'clad in homespun'. It is likely that they were not an ethnic but rather a social group of common people wearing 'blue homespuns'.

[2] This would seem to be a reference to the maltreatment and imprisonment of King Alexander by his son David during the course of the year 1602. David had died after six months and Giorgi (Yuri) had assumed authority on behalf of his father (cf. Brosset, *HG*, Vol. II/i, pp. 156 ff., 375 ff.).

[3] From his name 'The Georgian Aley son of Magmet' would appear to have been a Moslem in the service of King Alexander.

town of Erevan.[1] He added that one thousand *aznaurs* and five thousand soldiers had gone with the King. And, Sovereign, he said that the Shah had these soldiers turned back to Georgia, except for the *aznaurs*.[2] The Shah ordered King Alexander's son Prince Yuri to await the news of his army marching on Shemakha; Yuri should then also advance to Shemakha with his troops. And, Sovereign, he said that King Alexander's other son Constantine is with the Kizilbash Shah near the town of Erevan. And we, your servants, ordered this Georgian to come to us, and we questioned him about King Alexander and his son Prince Yuri and asked him where he was. We also asked him whether Prince Aristov had seceded from King Alexander or whether he is obedient to him under his hand as of old. And, Sire, this Georgian told us, your servants, in reply to questions, that King Alexander had gone to the Shah a month after Easter,

[1] From the text here it would seem that Aley son of Magmet left Kakheti about the first week in May 1604. 'A month before his departure' would date King Alexander's march to Erevan to the beginning of April rather than March – as indicated by the Cherkess report (see p. 418, n. 1 above).

[2] As subsequent events indicate, it is probable that the Shah retained the *aznaurs* in his camp round Erevan with the intention of depriving the Kakhians of local leadership. On the other hand, his dismissal of Alexander's 'five thousand soldiers' may have arisen from his distaste for the employment of large numbers of half-trained troops: see Sir Anthony Sherley's Relation, printed in E. D. Ross's *Anthony Sherley: his Persian adventure*, p. 232, citing the Shah's opinion that 'multitudes are confusers of orders and devourers of time'. Again, Sheref Mehmet's garrison of six thousand had been reduced to five hundred fighting men when he surrendered on 28 May 1604, and Abbas may have found these Georgian peasant levies superfluous and unsuitable for the siege operation. The living and supply conditions of the besiegers were difficult: when Sheref Mehmet was received by the Shah he found him sitting in a dilapidated tent on a carpet of poor quality (von Hammer, *HEO*, Vol. viii, p. 59). From the following text, it would seem that the Shah preferred to send the five thousand Kakhian troops back to Prince Giorgi for use in later field operations against Shemakha.

According to *Suite des Annales* (Brosset, *HG*, Vol. ii/ii, p. 374) the corps of Georgian *aznaurs* distinguished themselves in the final attack on the citadel of Erevan.

(449) taking 400 *aznaurs* and 5,000 soldiers; and the Shah ordered that the soldiers be turned back. King Alexander's son Prince Yuri is in Georgia.[1] And, Sovereign, he also said that the Prince of Soni obeys King Alexander and is under his hand as of old...

We have delayed on the Terek, Sire, because of our poor horses; they were driven to the Terek from Astarakhan on the 8th of July and because of the heat many of them sickened and some died. We, your Majesty's servants, have bought horses on the Terek. And following your Majesty's instructions we, your servants, will be escorted from the Terek by thirty-eight boyars' sons, and by 320 mounted Terek *streltsy* under headman Pavel Shironosov, and the fifty *streltsy* under the *sotnik* Mikhail Semyshkin who will be with us in the Georgian land, and seventy-three newly christened Okok men[2] and Cherkesses; so, Sovereign, a total of 481 horse will accompany us from the Terek; the commanders have told us, your servants, that there are no more horsemen on the Terek. It was commanded in your Majesty's instructions that we should be escorted by 600 men or more, according to the news; and there are many reports here that the Kumyks intend to plunder and attack your Majesty's forts. Nikanor Shlyugin and Mosey Komynin wrote from the Sunzha to the commanders on the Terek in a letter

---

[1] According to Turkish sources, Alexander II of Kakheti and Giorgi X of Kartli were sitting on the left of Shah Abbas – while Persian and Kurdish notables were on his right – when Sheref Mehmet made his surrender (von Hammer, *HEO*, Vol. VIII, p. 59; Danişmend, Vol. III, p. 233). By the latter, *Dokuzuncu Görkin* (here referred to as Giorgi IX) is described as the father-in-law (*kaynata*) of Shah Abbas – through the latter's marriage to his second daughter Tinatin (Peri, Leila or Fatma-Sultan-Begum): cf. Commentary 67. Alexander's fourth son, Constantine – who later was to play the sinister role of parricide – is not mentioned in this context although he had for long been under the protection of Shah Abbas. He was twelve years old in 1579 when he was sent to Persia as a hostage (Brosset, *HG*, Vol. II/i, p. 634) and brought up as a Moslem (ibid, pp. 154, 157; but see Chap. 12, p. 465, n. 1).

[2] For these 'Okok men' (= Akki Chechens), see Commentary 14.

received on the 6th of July that the Kabardan Achekan Murza had come to them from the Kumyk land and said on being questioned that such Kumyks as had gone to Shemakha have returned. He said that he had heard from Kumyks that Shevkal and his sons do not want to complete their submission to you, Sovereign, but that they are awaiting the Turks; Saltan Magmut has stayed behind in Shemakha for that purpose: as soon as the Turks arrive he would bring the news direct to the land of the Kumyks, and having joined up with Kumyks and Turks he would march against your Majesty's forts. He said that the Kabardan princes Shepshuk's son Kazy and Solokh are in the same plot with the Kumyks; as soon as the Turks come they, Kazy and Solokh, would also march against your Majesty's forts. And there are rumours among the Kumyks about your Majesty's army. If your Majesty's army comes before the Turks, they would not oppose it but would flee into the (450) mountains. And, Sovereign, in a letter received on the 8th of July, Nikanor Shlyugin and Mosey Komynin wrote from the Sunzha to the commanders on the Terek that Kushakan, an *uzden* from Solokh's settlement who was travelling from the Kumyk land, told them on being questioned that on the 3rd of July the Kumyk princes – Shevkal's son Alkas, and Surkay Shevkal's son Alidar, and Andey's son Ali-Saltan, and Smagil's son Budachey – and some five hundred men or more with them, set out from the Kumyk land, taking the upper road to Sunzhiki.[1] And we, your servants, must proceed to those parts to the Sunzha and from the Sunzha to Kabarda; we shall travel with great care, in accordance with your Majesty's in-structions . . .

To the Sovereign Tsar and great Prince Boris Fedorovich of all Russia, your servants Andryushka Velyaminov[2] and

[1] See Commentary 56 for opinion among the chieftains of Daghestan in 1604.
[2] Of Tartar origin, the Velyaminov-Zernovs were related to the

Yakushka Molvyaninov do homage. Sovereign! Couriers come to Vladimir from Astarakhan and the Terek with your Majesty's secret affairs; and we, Sire, do not dare send them to your Majesty without copying them on to new paper. And in September of the present year [7]113, the boyar's son from Suzdal Fedosey Tepritski came as a messenger from Astarakhan bringing reports from Mikhail Tatishchev on the Terek; and it is written in the superscription that they are your Majesty's secret affairs. And we, your servants, gave orders that these reports be copied in our presence; having copied them and having sealed them in a sheet of paper, we have sent them to your Majesty. We have also sent to your Majesty reports from other towns of the lower Volga and from Siberia. And, sovereign, we have ordered Fedosey Tepritski to stay on at Vladimir until instructions are received from your Majesty. Command, Sire, that your royal instructions be given to us, your servants: should we copy out reports on your Majesty's (451) secret affairs or not? And, Sovereign, we have questioned the couriers who have come to Vladimir from Astarakhan and the Terek and from Kazan and from Nizhni whether horses have been dying of any disease or whether there are epidemics among men. And the couriers have told us, your Majesty's servants, that it is healthy at Astarakhan and on the Terek and in Kazan and in Nizhni – thank God – there are no epidemics among horses or men, nor have men been stricken down; there had been an epidemic among horses in Nizhni before the Day of St Elija but it has passed since St Elija's day and now, thank God, it is healthy.[1]

Godunovs and the Saburovs (see p. 416, n. 1 above). Several members of the family served as governors and commanders in Russia during the sixteenth and seventeenth centuries. Andrey's son, Miron, played a distinguished part in the resistance to the Poles during the Time of Troubles (Platonov, pp. 123 and *passim*).

[1] Probably glanders, a contagious disease in horses, the chief features of which are swellings beneath the jaw and discharge of mucous matter

[On the reverse]: [Brought] on the 8th day of September [7]113 by Gordeyko Artemyev, a sworn man from Vladimir.[1]

From the Tsar and great Prince Boris Fedorovich of all Russia to Andrey Ignatyevich Velyaminov and Yakov Molvyaninov: You have written to us that couriers come to Vladimir from Astarakhan and the Terek . . . And you asked us to give you orders for the future whether you are to copy out our secret affairs or not. You sons of a whore, you hinds and fools! Your behaviour is improper. How do you dare, you village boors, to break the seals and copy such great secret affairs of ours? Mikhaylo expressly wrote on top that those secret affairs of ours were not to be read without our command; and you read them and have had them copied by goodness knows whom.[2] After you have received this letter of ours, you should not break the seals on our secret affairs and should not read them, when couriers come to you at Vladimir with letters from Astarakhan or the Terek or from any other place from our gentleman and Master of the Horse Mikhail Ignatyevich

from the nostrils; a disastrous infection in cavalry and transport units. Literary references to this disease date from the fifteenth century (cf. *NED*, Vol. iv).

[1] *R. tselovalnik*: These local elected officials, first mentioned in 1497, performed legal, financial and police duties. Sometimes they were paid a salary. They lost their independence after the Time of Troubles and became mere functionaries (see Brockhaus and Efron).

[2] Belokurov notes that the original draft of the Tsar's letter differed from the final version in that 'brigands' had been used instead of 'sons of a whore' and in that two sentences were later left out. The first of these came after the words 'to break the seals and copy such great secret affairs of ours'; it read as follows: 'You instructed an unknown muzhik, a hind, a pen-pusher to copy these secret affairs of ours, whereas it was unfit even for you, fools, to be acquainted with them'. The second insertion followed the words 'by goodness knows whom' and was as follows: 'And because of that, you hinds, because of your crime, you nearly incurred the death penalty'.

It is likely that Tsar Boris's temper was inflamed by the fact that the secret correspondence from Tatishchev contained references to the proposed negotiations for the marriages of his son and daughter with members of the Georgian royal family (see below, Chap. 14).

Tatishchev, or from any others of our commanders, and there is a superscription to the effect that they contain our secret affairs. You should write to us in Moscow exactly from where and from whom by name these secret affairs of ours arrive, and you should keep these secret affairs by you in secret, without breaking the seal, until our instructions reach you. And as for Mikhaylo's present reports which you have copied, you should give orders for the original to be burnt in your presence, so that you should not retain it. And you should tell that scribe of yours who copied our secret affairs that should these affairs of (452) ours become known through you or through him, you will suffer the death penalty. And you should report to us the name of the scribe who did the copying for you, and how and for what reason you had the letters copied. You should give instructions that the report be given to our dyak Afanasi Vlasyev at the Posolski Prikaz. Written in Moscow on the 9th of September, 7113.

The commanders on the Terek Nikiforka Trakhaniotov and Volodka Koltsov-Mosalski *wrote in a report brought to Moscow* on 18th September, [7]113, by Fedor Tyrkov that the ambassadors Mikhail Ignatyevich Tatishchev and dyak Andrey Ivanov and the Iberian ambassadors with them, reached the Terek in ships from Astarakhan on the 2nd of July . . . And as soon as your Majesty's ambassadors arrived on the Terek we, your servants, issued light *strugi*[1] to carry your Majesty's treasure which your Majesty's ambassadors have with them as well as their own ambassadorial belongings, and sent them off from Terek-[town] up the Terek river to the Sunzha. We sent the Cossack headman Ivan Khomyakov with 200 *streltsy* and Cossacks as an escort in the boats. And your Majesty's ambassadors Mikhail Tatishchev and dyak Andrey Ivanov, after waiting for the arrival of their men and horses from Astarakhan, left Terek for the Sunzha overland on the 15th of July. We have

[1] For these *strugi*, light flat-bottomed river craft, see Commentary 7.

sent Yanglych's son Sunchaley murza and his cousin Mam-
stryuk's son Aley-murza with fifteen of their *uȝdens*,[1] together
with the Terek cavalry headman Pavel Shironosov with two
sotniks and 300 mounted *streltsy*, and forty-three boyars' sons[2]
from towns on the upper and on the lower reaches of the Volga,
from Arzamas, Nizhni Novgorod, Lukhovichi, Cheboksary,
Kurmysh,[3] who are serving for one year on the Terek, and sixteen newly christened Terek inhabitants, and fifty-eight Okok
Cherkesses serving on the Terek, to escort your Majesty's
ambassadors and the Iberian ambassadors from the Terek...
And we, your servants, have written in our name to the
Cherkess princes that Prince Solokh with his brothers and
children, and Kazy murza with his brothers and Aytek murza,

[1] For these Kabardan personalities, see Commentary 12.

[2] 'Boyars' sons': *deti boyarskiye*. The boyars' sons were a class of
squires and small landowners who held their estates from the Tsar – in
return for which they were liable for military service; the earliest reference
to them (in Novgorod) was in 1259. While some of them were literally the
descendants of boyars, others were descended from noblemen's retainers.
Kotoshikhin (pp. 26–7) reports that some were former peasants and serfs
(and their descendants) who had been raised above their former station
and given estates by the Tsar in reward for services; others were descended
from impoverished gentry (cf. Chap. 3, p. 133, n. 3, on the sometimes
comparable caste of *aȝnaurishvilni* in Georgia; also Baddeley, *RMC*,
pp. lxxxiii-lxxxiv).

[3] Arzamas (founded in 1578) was built at the site of a Mordvinian
village on high ground dominating the surrounding countryside, at the
confluence of the Tesha (an affluent of the Oka) and the Shamka. It was
fortified with a wooden wall and towers.

For Nizhni Novgorod, see Commentary 7: The towns along the
Volga route.

It is unlikely that Belokurov's Lukhovichi stands for Lukovitsy, a
village some ten miles south-east of Kolomna. They were probably men
from Lyskovo, a township on the right bank of the Volga, about halfway
between Nizhni Novgorod and the mouth of the Sura.

Cheboksary, a town built on three hills on the right bank of the Volga,
138 versts upstream from Kazan, was fortified in 1557 and garrisoned by
streltsy.

Kurmysh, on the left bank of the Sura, was founded in 1372 in Mordvinian and Chuvash territory (Brockhaus and Efron; *BSE*).

and Alkas's sons and Kudenek murza, the son of Kanbulat, together with his brothers, should show their service to your Majesty by meeting your ambassadors and escorting them as far as Soni...

(435)   To the Sovereign Tsar and great Prince Boris Fedorovich of all Russia, your servants Mikhalko Tatishchev and Andryushka Ivanov make obeisance. We, your servants, and the Iberian King Alexander's ambassador the monk Kiril reached the mountains, the settlements of Aytek murza and those of Alkas's sons and the defiles on July 26th. Aytek murza and Alkas's sons Araksan murza and Mundar murza came to us, your servants... And Aytek murza and Alkas's sons told us that they are your Majesty's servants and are ready to escort us. And, Sire, Alkas's sons also said that Aytek murza's settlements lie in the mountains along this route to the land of Soni, and that it is the responsibility of Aytek murza to see about the road and the bridges; they did not interfere in that and would not relieve him of it... And, Sovereign, Prince Solokh and Kazy murza did not send anyone to us, your servants, while we were on our way to Aytek's settlements. But when we got there, Solokh's cousin Ibak murza, and Solokh's son Khoroshay murza, and Prince Yansokh's son Topchyuk murza who is cousin to Shepshuk's son Kazy murza, came to us your servants... And, Sire, Solokh's cousin Ibak murza and Kazy

(454) murza's cousin Topchyuk have told us with regard to what is written in your Majesty's letters to Prince Solokh and Kazy murza to the effect that they should send people to escort us, your servants, to the Georgian land or that of Soni, that the people living in the mountains do not obey them but that Aytek murza rules over them; they themselves do not dare penetrate into the mountains and the defiles, let alone escort us...[1]

[1] This paragraph reflects the rivalries and intermittent hostilities between the Kabardan princes and the Ingush clan of Aytek murza (who

And, Sire, on the 30th of July, the Terek *strelets* Ivashko Nogayev whom we, your servants, had sent from the Terek for news, met us on his way back from the land of Soni. He brought with him a short letter from Aristov's mother written in her hand in Georgian characters to the monk Kiril. We have had this letter translated and we are sending the translation to your Majesty, glued to the end of this letter. On being questioned, the *strelets* Ivashko Nogayev told us that King Alexander and Simon's son Yuri and Prince Aristov of Soni are with Shah Abbas, while Alexander's son Prince Yuri is in the Georgian land.[1] He added that Prince Yuri had forthwith sent on to his father, King Alexander, the men whom the monk Kiril had sent from Astarakhan to the Georgian land. And he also said that Aristov's mother immediately sent a message to Prince Aristov of Soni to let him know that you, great Sovereign, have sent us, your servants, to King Alexander. Nogayev added that Prince Aristov's steward Berezov[2] had told him that the Kumyks and the Turks had come to the Georgian land and had ravaged Zagem: that was the design of King Alexander's son Prince Yuri because the King loves his son Prince Constantine who is a Moslem and lives with Shah Abbas.[3] He said that Solokh's cousin Ibak murza with Cherkesses had attacked the land of Soni earlier this summer, ravaging a village in the marchlands and seizing common people. The men of Soni are not coming to meet us and will not build the bridges soon for this very reason – that they fear a Cherkess attack. And,

seem to have been the forerunners of the later Mudarovs or Dudarovs, descended, perhaps, from Mundar murza) who held Lars and the communes to the east of the defile in the nineteenth century.

[1] See pp. 418, n. 1 and 419, nn. 1–2 above. From the context it is clear that the Eristav Nugsar was in the suite of Alexander at Erevan.

[2] *Berezov*: this Russian form probably expresses the common Georgian surname Beridze (= *beri-dze*, son of a priest: cf. *R.* Popov, *Eng.* Parsons). The Mingrelian form is *Beri-a*. There was a noble family of Beridze in Guria (cf. Wak./Brosset, pp. 49, 417).

[3] For the activities of Prince Yuri (Giorgi) see p. 419, n. 2 above.

Sovereign, the monk Kiril has told us, your servants – having found this out from Cherkesses – that Solokh's cousin Ibak murza accompanied by Cherkesses had attacked the land of Soni this summer, had ravaged King Alexander's village of Kado[1] and had taken forty women and children into captivity.

(455) We have written to the commanders on the Terek asking them to send a message to Prince Solokh to the effect that King Alexander and Prince Aristov of Soni are in your Majesty's grace under your exalted royal hand. Yet Solokh and his men attack their lands. These are improper actions. Solokh should seek out all the prisoners captured by Ibak murza in the land of Soni and should release them or send them to the Terek. The Cherkesses should not behave in this way in the future and should not attack the land of Soni or other lands that serve you, the great Sovereign . . .

And, Sire, we set out from Lars settlement for the defiles on the 1st of August. Aytek murza sent his cousin Murza bek[2] and his son Magmet to escort us as far as the land of Soni. We ordered the boyars' sons, the *streltsy* and the Cherkesses from the Terek whom we had with us to turn back at the defiles, at Lars settlement, the spot at which your Majesty's ambassadors sent their escort back in the past . . . and to march to the Terek without delay, taking great care that Kumyks do not come upon them unawares and do not cause them any evil. And we instructed the foot *streltsy* whom we had left at Aytek's settlement with the headman Ivan Khomyakov, where they built a fort, to wait for the boyars' sons and the mounted *streltsy* . . . and then to proceed to the Terek all together with great care.

[1] 'King Alexander's village of Kado': probably the commune lying in the small valley of Kando, a right-bank affluent of the Aragvi, to the south of the ridge of Kandos-mta in Mtiuleti (cf. Wak./Brosset, p. 221 and Map 3).

[2] Murza bek was the eldest son of Aytek's elder brother Soporuko and was therefore Aytek's nephew and not cousin.

[On the reverse]: [Brought] on the 5th of December [7]113 by the boyar's son Afanasi Ragozin, an inhabitant of Astarakhan.

Translation of the letter brought by the *strelets* Ivashko Nogayev to the monk Kiril from the land of Soni and written by Aristov's mother the nun Anna in her own hand:[1]

To our brother Kiril. We thank God that by His mercy and the King's bounty you have reached these parts and that you are accompanying such a great ambassador; we thank God and rejoice at it. Let it be known unto you that the Shah summoned King Alexander and Simon's son King Yuri, and that my son Aristov is also with them. They went on an expedition together, to help the Kizilbash Shah. The Shah's army is attacking the land of Samsk which had previously belonged to the Georgian (456) kings. Before that the Shah had captured many forts from the Turkish king this side of Samtskhe of great Armenia, which is called Tripolis in Greek.[2] And now the Shah's great army is encamped near Tripolis. And the Shah himself is encamped in the land of Erevan together with King Alexander. They are waiting for news from the army of what it has done besieging the Turk's forts. And we have heard a rumour that the Turks are marching against the Shah's force and against King Alexander. Let it be known unto you that the Turkish king, the Sultan, has died for certain.[3] Oh that all the haters, those who hate the Orthodox kings, should perish in this way! And let all those who insult the Christian faith perish in the way that the Turkish king has perished now. Let God give his blessings to the great Sovereign Tsar and great Prince Boris Fedorovich of all Russia. The Shah has bountifully given to

---

[1] 'The nun Anna': The family name of Eristav Nugsar's mother was not identified by Brosset in his genealogical tree of the Eristavni of the Aragvi.

[2] For 'the land of Samsk', see Commentary 57.

[3] The death of Sultan Mehmet III occurred on 22 December 1603.

King Alexander and to Simon's son King Yuri and to Aristov, my son, and to the whole of Alexander's army an unusually large quantity of gold and silver and clothes and horses and camels; and all the soldiers, great and small, have received some. Be gracious and do not be despondent at not having received news from King Alexander forthwith, but King Alexander and Aristov my son and all the fighting men, great and small, are accompanying the Shah on his expedition. And all of us, by the mercy of God, are the servants of the Sovereign Tsar and great Prince Boris Fedorovich of all Russia, and all our land belongs to his Majesty. Mikhail Ignatyevich should set out for our land. And you will get news from Prince Yuri soon.

To the Sovereign Tsar and great Prince Boris Fedorovich of all Russia, your servants Mikhalko Tatishchev and Andryushka Ivanov make obeisance. We, your servants, set out from Lars for the land of Soni on the 3rd of August. And, Sire, at our first camp, there came upon us mountain people with a fiery attack, but we were protected by a stockade with a strong guard. The guard lay in wait for them and fought with them, firing their muskets; they repulsed them from our camp and wounded many of them. And, Sovereign, the men from Soni who came to meet us in order to build bridges said that the men who had come from the mountains were the Kalkan[1]; they used to obey Alkas murza but now obey Aytek murza.

And, Sovereign, when we were a day's journey beyond Lars we were met on behalf of Prince Aristov by his *aznaur* Elidli,[2] who said that he had been attached to us as attendant and would travel with us. He said that Aristov had been in the Shah's army but that the Shah has now let him go together with Simon's son Yuri. Aristov had called on Simon's son Yuri on the way home. Elidli told us that King Alexander had

---

[1] For Kalkans, see Commentary 44.
[2] Elidli: possibly represents a Georgian form Elidze.

come back to his land from Shah Abbas's army. And we, your servants, told him that we had with us your Majesty's letter for Prince Aristov, together with your Majesty's bounty and an oral message, and that he should send word to Prince Aristov (457) to see us without fail . . .

And, Sire, on the following day, Aristov's majordomo Shang,[1] sent by Aristov's mother, and two *aznaurs* with him, met us, your servants, at Berezuy settlement.[2] They told us: '. . . Prince Aristov has not come home yet but will arrive very soon . . . Should he not be in time himself, his son will come to you and will escort you through the land. Provisions will be supplied to you in the future; but now we cannot get them together. You can see for yourselves that the people are poor. All the well-off men are with Aristov in Shah Abbas's army.'

And we, your servants, have been making enquiries en route in accordance with your Majesty's instructions as to what the present relations are between Prince Aristov and the Iberian king Alexander . . . The attendant and other men have told us, Sovereign, that Prince Aristov is now under the authority of Simon's son Yuri, and that Simon's son King Yuri has betrothed his daughter to Aristov's elder son.[3] And, Sire,

---

[1] Shang: possibly *G.* Peshang.

[2] The *kabak* belonging to Berezov (see p. 427, n. 2 above). This may, perhaps, be identified with Beris tsikhe [= 'Beri's castle'] in the district of Jamuri, on a small affluent of the upper Ksani. [Cf. Wak./Brosset, p. 223 and his Map 3.]

[3] Gvritishvili, p. 181, has overlooked the evidence for the details of the relationship of Eristav Nugsar with the Kings of Kakheti and Kartli. After the fall of Erevan, in June 1604, Shah Abbas had taken Alexander of Kakheti with him to Persia. Giorgi of Kartli, who had been forced by Abbas to surrender the fortress of Lori (Brosset, *HG*, Vol. II/i, 43), returned in no good humour to Kartli where he arrived by the end of July 1604. He was accompanied by Eristav Nugsar – on his way back to his own country (Brosset, *EC/BHP*, Vol. II, Nos. 19/21, cols. 315–16). In the summer of 1602 David of Kakheti, shortly before his death on 21 October of that year, had mounted an expedition against the Eristavi;

Prince Aristov is at peace with King Alexander as well and, as a pledge of good faith in this, King Alexander has a son of Aristov living with him.

And, Sovereign, on the 10th of August Aristov's son Bavenda together with Aristov's majordomo Shang and other officials came to our camp at Aristov's settlement . . .

(458) Bavenda said that, when Prince Aristov comes home he, with all the land of Soni, will kiss the cross to you, the great Sovereign, and everything will be done in accordance with your royal command. He said that Prince Aristov is anxious to be friendly with and love King Alexander in accordance with your royal Majesty's command. He said: 'Simon's son Yuri is now a friend and kinsman of Prince Aristov. Aristov, my father, has now agreed with Yuri that I am to take his daughter in marriage'.[1]

Aristov's son escorted us, your Majesty's servants, some three versts from his home; and their majordomo and *aznaurs* escorted us for some five versts to the Georgian frontier while Aristov's attendant officer rode with us, your servants, as far as the camp beyond the frontier. No escorting officer came
(459) from King Alexander and his son Prince Yuri to meet us at the frontier and no provisions were given us. And we, your servants, told the monk Kiril . . . that we had used up our supplies; some were lost at sea or fell down the mountain-side,

and Alexander, after his restoration, was complaining of the reluctance of the Eristavi to pay tribute and to co-operate against the mountaineers (Brosset, *HG*, Vol. 11/ii, p. 338). It is likely that Nugsar was leaning again towards a Kartlian allegiance and that the proposed marriage of Giorgi's daughter Khorashan with his eldest son Bahadur (Baadour in Brosset's Genealogical Tree, *HG*, Vol. 11/i, p. 632) was discussed.

[1] 'Aristov's son Bavenda': Bahadur. For some references to details of his later life, see Gvritishvili, p. 182. He never achieved his royal marriage and, some years after succeeding his father, was killed by his younger brother Zurab, *c.* 1620. *Chronique Géorgienne*, pp. 33–4, states that Khorashan, eldest daughter of Giorgi X, who had been promised to the son of the Eristavi of the Aragvi, was married to Taymuraz of Kakheti in 1609 – when her brother, Luarsab II, was on the Kartlian throne.

we could not buy any and our horses were tired out. And, Sovereign, the monk Kiril said to us, your servants: 'I do not understand myself how it is that no one has come to meet us so far on behalf of King Alexander. The most likely reason is that the King has not yet returned home from the expedition and that Prince Yuri is waiting for his father to send him word.'

And we, your servants, together with the monk Kiril, marched from the frontier of Soni through the Georgian land for three days without escorting officer, buying provisions on the way.

CRISES IN KAKHETI

(459)   **O**N August 12th, at the third camp after the frontier, in
Uman's villages, the equerry Prosodan and the *aznaur*
Ivan[1] came to us, your servants, from King Alexander's son Prince Yuri . . . Prosodan enquired after our health
on behalf of the prince . . . He then said: 'Prince Yuri has learnt
that you, the great Sovereign's ambassadors, are on your way
from his royal Majesty to King Alexander his father. King
Alexander is not in his Georgian land now; he is with the
Shah's army. And Prince Yuri now occupies his father's place
in his realm.[2] He has sent me, Prosodan, to meet you and be
your attendant officer together with his good *aznaur* Ivan, and
he has given orders to give you as much provisions as can be
got together.' And we, your servants, said to them that no
attendant officer had been sent to meet us at the frontier; we
had travelled without an attendant officer as far as that place
and had received no provisions or carts; that was not as had
been the custom previously. We said that King Alexander's
ambassadors enjoyed your Majesty's great royal bounty.
Prosodan replied: 'As soon as Prince Yuri learnt about you,
the great Sovereign's ambassadors, he sent his gentleman
Keystrov[3] to meet you with orders to travel with you and issue
provisions. But, unfortunately, he missed you, having taken

---

[1] *Okolnichi Prosodan*: here translated 'equerry'; probably equivalent to
the Georgian *amirakhori*, originally Grand Falconer, later Grand Equerry
with the functions of assistant war minister (cf. Allen, *HGP*, p. 258).
Prosodan = *G.* Farsadan; Ivan = *G.* Ioanne.

[2] See Chap. 10, p. 419, n. 2 above.

[3] *Keystrov*: *G.* Khosro (= *P.* Khusran). This is doubtless the same
Khosrov, son of Uman to whom reference is made below, p. 436.

another road. Do not be angry with the prince about it. You will have sufficient provisions.' But, Sovereign, the provisions they began to give us were poor and scanty – and even those (460) we did not always get; Prosodan told us that the land was without a sovereign, that nobody obeyed and that they gave us whatever could be got together.

We travelled three days to the locality of Shunta[1] where Prince Yuri was encamped; when we were some three versts from the camp, Prince Yuri's groom Zugrap[2] came to us, your servants, with three saddled horses – two horses to mount us, and the third horse for the translator . . . And he had our camp pitched about one verst from the prince's camp.

On the 18th of August Prince Suliman, who had been on an embassy to your Majesty in Moscow, came to us in our camp . . .[3] He said: 'You, the great Sovereign's ambassadors, should come to the Prince and make his royal Majesty's command known unto him; and . . . he will do whatever he can; he will write to King Alexander, his father, about that which he cannot do himself.' And we, your servants, told Suliman that . . . we had a letter from you, the great Sovereign . . . but that we had been commanded to hand it to Prince Yuri in King Alexander's presence; now that King Alexander was not in his realm, how could we go to the Prince in the King's absence?

[1] Shunta: From the context this appears to be a distortion of the name Shilda rather than of Shua-mta. Ten versts south of Gremi, Shilda was in the circle of prosperous villages spreading round the capital; and, when in the last quarter of the fifteenth century, King Giorgi I organized Kakheti into prefectures (*mo'uravates*), Shilda became one of them (cf. Brosset, *HG*, Vol. II, i, p. 148). Shilda seems to have been chosen as military head-quarters by Prince Giorgi (Yuri). It lay roughly halfway between the northern border in Tianeti and the south-eastern march in Eliseni, where, in October 1604, he routed a Turkish force with the help of the forty *streltsy* loaned by Tatishchev (cf. pp. 445–6 below). For several refs. and description of the nearby basilica church of Vartsani, see Chubinashvili, *AK*, Vol. I, *passim*.

[2] *Zugrap* seems to correspond to Georgian Zurab.

[3] For Prince Suliman, see Commentary 36.

And Suliman said to us on behalf of the prince: 'If you do not go to him and do not inform him of his Majesty's affairs, he will have nothing to write to his father and his Majesty's affairs will remain stationary; but should you go to him, all such affairs about which you have his Majesty's command will be done.'

(461) And we ... told Suliman that we would go to Prince Yuri, adding 'Only tell Prince Yuri from us that, when we perform our embassy, he should have no ambassadors or envoys present at that time from the Kizilbash or the Turk or any other sovereigns.' There was to be no repetition of what had happened when your royal Majesty's envoys Ivan Nashchokin and Ivan Levontyev came to them and performed their embassy while the Turk's *chaush*[1] was in the tent. And, Sire, Suliman told us that he would tell the prince about it, adding: 'The prince will do as you tell him.'

And, Sovereign, on the 19th of August their councillors the treasurer[2] Surkan and Uman's son Khosrov and Prince Suliman came to us, your servants, in our camp. They said to us from the prince that we were to go to him and perform the embassy and that the prince had sent with his groom horses for us to ride on. And, Sovereign, he sent a saddled horse for each of us, your servants, and a horse for the translator. We told them that we were ready, but that we had sent a message to the prince earlier on, asking that there should be no ambassadors, envoys or couriers from other sovereigns present while we carried out our embassy. The king's councillors said to us, your servants: 'The Kizilbash Shah Abbas is the friend and brother of the great Sovereign. The Shah's ambassador is now here, and will be with Prince Yuri when you, his royal Majesty's ambassadors,

---

[1] For the Turkish term *chaush*, see Chap. 2, p. 117, n. 3.

[2] Here the Russian term *kaznachey* (Belokurov, *Snosheniya*, p. 461) probably corresponds to the Georgian *sadchurdchlis mdsignobari*, secretary, lit. 'booker', of the treasury. Surkan or Surkhay was a name common in the Shevkal's family (Brosset, *EC/BHP*, Vol. II, Nos. 19–21, col. 317, proposes the well-known Georgian form Sulkhan).

attend on him.' And we, your servants, said to them: 'Shah Abbas is the friend and brother of his royal Majesty, the great Sovereign, but it is not customary for ambassadors of other sovereigns to be present when his royal Majesty our great Sovereign's ambassadors perform their embassy. If the Kizilbash ambassador is with Prince Yuri now, we shall not go to him. Even if we do go and find that he is with the prince, we shall leave the tent without carrying out our embassy.' The treasurer Surkan and his comrades replied: 'Prince Yuri has bidden us talk to you about it. Can you do it? If it ought not to happen, the Kizilbash Shah's ambassador will not be present.' And, Sire, they immediately sent a message to Prince Yuri to command the Kizilbash ambassador not to attend upon him.

We, your servants, attended upon King Alexander's son (462) Prince Yuri in his tent on the same day. *The treasurer Surkan, and Uman's son Khosrov, and Prince Suliman and the groom rode in front of us. And when we arrived in the camp we dismounted not far from the prince's tent; we were preceded into the tent by those who had been riding in front of us. At that time the prince was seated in the tent on a cushion, with a golden carpet under him.*[1] Archbishop Basil of Kisik,[2] and three Archimandrites and

[1] Belokurov indicates that the account of the ambassadors' talks with Prince Yuri is to be found both in their *stateyny spisok* and in the despatches. The two versions are almost identical except that the former includes a few additional sentences which have been italicised here.

[2] For Kisik (*G. Kisiqi*) and its bishops (often referred to by the Russian envoys as 'Archbishops'), see Commentaries 29 and 30. The bishop's seat was at Bodbe and he was hence known as Bodbeli. In 1589, at the time of Zvenigorodski's mission, Zakhari is named as Bodbeli, see p. 161, above. By 1604 Basil seems to have emerged as his successor. But there is some obscurity here since, in 1604, Tatishchev refers to a Zakhari as incumbent of Nekresi (*Nekresel* at p. 456, below). This ecclesiastic is closely associated in the negotiations and in the court protocol with the royal *aznauri*, Abel, who is described as the brother of the 'Rustvel' (titular Bishop of Rustavi who occupied the important see of Martqopi). Both the Rustaveli and his brother Abel became casualties in the coup against King Alexander, see p. 458, below. The Rustaveli is named as one of the close councillors of Prince Giorgi, see Commentary 61 (a). It

abbots, King Alexander's councillors and some fifty *aznaurs* were in attendance on Prince Yuri; they sat on his right. His son Prince Yessey[1] sat next to Prince Yuri on his right. When we entered the tent, Prince Yuri and his son got up and advanced towards us halfway down the tent. And in accordance with your Majesty's instructions, I, your servant Mikhalko, saluted the prince on behalf of yourself, the great Sovereign, and of your royal Majesty's son, the great Sovereign Prince Fedor Borisovich of all Russia . . . Prince Yuri said: 'I hardly dare enquire after the Sovereign Tsar's health and that of his royal Majesty's son, and ask what their royal health is. What is God's mercy towards them, the great Sovereigns?' *. . . I gave the letter and presented the Sovereign's bountiful gifts according to the list. Prince Yuri said*: 'I make obeisance to the great Sovereign Tsar and to his royal Majesty's son for their bounty and for the royal gifts which they have bestowed upon me.' And, Sovereign, he advanced towards us and embraced us and did not allow us to kiss his hand.

After that we, your servants, delivered the speech in accordance with your Majesty's instructions; the prince remained standing at that time. Having heard the speech, he said that they were in great sadness and were oppressed but that he would speak to us about it some other time, if God grants. And, Sovereign, he invited us, your servants, to partake of

is difficult to decide whether the Russian envoys were referring to one and the same Zakhari who had been preferred from one bishopric to another (that of Nekresi was the more distinguished) or whether two different Zakharis were on the ground between 1589 and 1604. There is no indication of the family name of the Rustaveli and his brother Abel.

Prince Yessey: G. Yese, later became a Moslem under the name of Isa Khan: died 1615; for further details, see below Chap. 12, p. 459, n. 1. It is apparent that Yese was the son of an earlier marriage of Prince Giorgi with the daughter of Krym-Shevkal, sultan of Eliseni, and not by the daughter of Kai-Khusrau Pasha of Genzha: see above, Chap. 8, p. 384, n. 1, and Commentary 47.

food. He sat down and he bade us sit near him *on his left;* *and the noblemen and aznaurs sat below us.* He commanded that (463) cloths be spread and the food brought in. And we told the prince's noblemen that we had not known . . . that we were to eat with him, and we wanted to get up. But, Sire, having heard that from his noblemen, Prince Yuri told us, your servants, that such was their custom, adding: 'I am rejoicing now at his royal Majesty the great Sovereign's mercy. You will offend me if you do not eat with me. I am the Sovereign's servant, so I am inviting you myself; I did not dare send a messenger to invite you to eat with me, because you are the great Sovereign's ambassadors.' And we, your servants, ate with Prince Yuri. When we were partaking of the meal Prince Yuri spoke of the disloyalty of King David his brother to-wards his father King Alexander and towards himself; *he had made an attempt against his father and deprived him of his realm, and he wanted to put out the eyes of himself, Prince Yuri, and to have him pushed off the town wall; he had cast him into prison. But God avenged David's disloyalty; soon he died an evil death; and God gave the realm to King Alexander his father and to himself, Prince Yuri.*[1] And, Sovereign, halfway through the meal Prince Yuri got up and after walking to the tent-pole he drank a cup to the health of your Majesty and your royal Majesty's son. After the meal the prince himself and his noblemen accompanied us out of the tent.

And, Sire, on the 23rd of August Prince Yuri sent his nobles Uman's son Khosrov and Prince Suliman and his councillor Dzhezdam-bek and dyak Arekel to our camp.[2] They said to us:

[1] For these events, see above, Chap. 8, pp. 386–9 and Commentary 49.

[2] Brosset (*EC/BHP*, Vol. II, Nos. 19–21, col. 258 and n. 105) has identified this Dzhezdam-bek with Prince Iaram, see Commentary 61 (c). Brosset further observes that the name Arekel (Arakel) is Armenian and remarks (col. 318, n. 84), that the Armenians were numerous in Kakheti

'Prince Yuri has commanded us, his councillors, to reply to what you said to him from the great Sovereign Tsar and say: "We make obeisance to his royal Majesty the great Sovereign for what you have told me on his behalf about his royal mercy and bounty to King Alexander my father, and to me and to the whole Iberian land, in defending us from the Kumyks by sending his royal Majesty's army against them; and we, (464) together with all our land, pray to God for his royal health. And as my father came under his royal Majesty's hand with the whole of the Iberian land, we now want to obey in everything in the same way and be the Tsar's servants for evermore without seceding; it is in God and in him, the great Sovereign, that we place our trust. And as for what you have told me about the army – that when his royal Majesty's army comes to the Kumyk land I, Yuri, should march against the Kumyks at the same time with my army from my side – I and my army are ready; when news comes from his royal Majesty's commanders, I shall immediately march with my army against the Kumyks. As for what you have told me about swearing by the cross to his royal Majesty on the charter . . . when, if God grants, my father comes here to his realm . . . I shall have the charter written and I shall confirm it by taking an oath by the cross, and – after affixing my signature and seal to it – I shall give it to you, his royal Majesty's ambassadors. If my father does not return from the Shah soon, and if the Shah commands that you, the great Sovereign's ambassadors should go to him, I shall likewise write the charter and shall kiss the cross on it in your presence, and shall send the charter to my father who will give it to you . . . Now I am sending Archbishop Basil of Kisik to my father with all these affairs, and I shall write to him about everything at length. I am expecting my father to return soon." '

and enjoyed a certain credit, although no reference is made to this fact in Georgian sources.

The Prince has given us, your servants, quarters some two versts from Shemta,[1] in the house of the Metropolitan of Alaverdy, and provisions are being issued to us, your servants...

We, your servants, have had no news from Ivan Buturlin[2] and his comrades as of August 27th...

And, Sovereign, since Prince Yuri has sent us word by his (465) nobles that he cannot attend to your Majesty's affairs without his father, we, your servants, have not told him and his nobles that your bounty of five hundred rubles in cash has been sent with us with instructions to distribute the money to those who had been wronged by Ivan Nashchokin and Ivan Levontyev. But even if we were to distribute the money in the absence of King Alexander, it would be lost.

[On the reverse]: [Brought] on the 5th of December [7]113 by Afanasi Ragozin, a boyar's son from Astarakhan.

To the Sovereign Tsar and great Prince Boris Fedorovich of all Russia his servants Mikhalko Tatishchev and Andryushka

---

[1] For *Shemta=Shua-mta*, see p. 381, n. 1, above. According to Wakhusht (Wak./Brosset, p. 317), the Archimandrite of Shua-mta was known as 'the abbot of abbots'; and, in 1850, when Brosset visited there (*VA, Ier Rapport*, pp. 57–8), this splendid shrine still retained an icon in gold, said by Bakradze (*Akty*, Vol. 5, p. 1100) to have been a copy of the celebrated Virgin of Kakhuli, a great cross in gold and silver and other treasures. The Metropolitan of Alaverdi had a summer residence in the vicinity (where Tsar Boris's ambassadors were lodged). From here, according to Bakradze, the prelate could look out towards his own cathedral, some twenty miles to the north-east, and over the wide plain of the Alazani to the peaks of Daghestan beyond. To the south lay the mountains of Hereti, their ridges bare of forest, but rich in pasture and flowers. The lower slopes, Wakhusht recalls (Wak./Brosset, p. 317), were dotted with villages and farms in the midst of abundant vineyards and orchards.

[2] The Buturlins were a numerous family, many of whom served the Russian Tsars with distinction between the sixteenth and eighteenth centuries. The founder was said to have been of German origin and to have settled in Russia in the time of Alexander Nevski. Ivan Mikhaylovich had already twice held the post of *voyvode* in Astrakhan when, in 1604, he returned to take charge of the operations against the Shevkal (see *RBS*).

Ivanov make obeisance. Following your Majesty's instructions we, your servants, have been finding out in secret various news during our stay in the Georgian land. We have been told by Georgians and by prisoners that the Kizilbash Shah Abbas is taking the Turk's towns and ravaging his land. They said that he has captured the Turk's towns of Tevriz, Erevan, Nikchivan and some five–six other small localities.[1] And as for the towns such as Shemakha and others about which the Shah wrote to your Majesty by his envoy that he had taken them, they still belong to the Turk.[2] And now, Sovereign, Shah Abbas is encamped at Zengich,[3] five days' march from the Georgian land; it is said, Sire, that he has an army of some 30,000 men with him. He has sent his commander Loverdi Khan[4] with a greater number of men towards the Turk's towns in great Armenia. And we have been told that the Turk's men attacked Loverdi Khan's Kizilbash troops in the

[1] For these events, see Chap. 10, p. 419, n. 2.

[2] From the text here it is apparent that the Persians had not occupied Shemakha by the end of August 1604 – although there had been some raids into Shirvan (cf. Commentary 56).

[3] Zengich: this seems to be a reference to the Zangi-su (*Arm.* Hrazdan), which flows from Lake Sevan (*T.* Gökche) into the Aras. Erevan is built on its eastern bank. Lynch (*Armenia*, Vol. 1, p. 229) described 'the Zanga, diffused into many channels, and lost beneath luxuriant foliage' – ideal summer quarters for an army operating north against Akhaltsikhe and north-east towards Shirvan and Kakheti. For near-contemporary descriptions of Erevan and the river Zangi, see Evliya Chelebi (von Hammer ed., Vol. II, pp. 150–3) and Tavernier (Paris ed., 1679, Vol. I, pp. 37 ff., with engraving opposite p. 40 showing valley of the Zangi and western walls of the town). According to Tavernier, the grazing to the south of the town could attract more than twenty thousand nomad tents during the summer months. For the healthy climate and good pastures round Erevan, see also *Don Juan*, p. 169.

Emirguneh, 'by birth a Georgian', appointed Khan of Erevan by Shah Abbas in 1604, was still flourishing when Sultan Murat IV took the city in 1634 (Evliya, Vol. II, p. 152). Della Valle, Vol. III, p. 290, writing in 1618, described him as 'âgé à présent'.

[4] For 'Loverdi Khan' (Allah-verdi khan), a Georgian *ghulam*, in high favour with Shah Abbas, see Commentary 8.

month of July, that there was a great battle in the Armenian land, and that the Shah's men killed many of the Turk's men.[1] The Shah's coming to Shemakha, Derbent and Baku is awaited late in the autumn. And as for the small lands here, the Iberian and the Dadiani and others, all their rulers and their best men are with the Shah, and they have all gone over to the Shah. And, Sovereign, the Kumyks repeatedly raided the Georgian lands this summer; together with Turks who had come from Shemakha they took the Georgian king's best place, Zagem, in June, and killed many men, took others prisoners, seized much merchandise, ravaged the king's palace and captured all the ordnance at Zagem. And now, Sovereign, the Kumyks carry war into the Georgian land ceaselessly.[2] There is no one to oppose them because all the fighting men are in the Shah's army with King Alexander. The Shah will not let King Alexander and the Metropolitan of Alaverdy and others of the best Georgian men go, but is keeping them by him perforce. And, Sovereign, King Alexander is at peace with Simon's son Yuri; the Shah had let Simon's son Yuri (466) go home because he was ill, but now he is said to be again with the Shah. And, Sire, Prince Aristov is now at peace with the two of them, both with King Alexander and with Simon's son Yuri; the Shah let him go and he is now living in his land. Shah Abbas has ordered him to assemble an army and march together with Simon's son King Yuri against the Turk's town of Tiflis.[3] And, Sovereign, the Turk's town of Tiflis is near the land of Soni, five or six versts from the road which we, your servants, followed; before now, Sovereign, this

[1] This is a reference to Persian raids into Samtskhe – where an attack was made on the Turkish garrison at Akhaltsikhe – and Shirvan in the late summer of 1604; see Commentaries 56 and 57; von Hammer (*HEO*, Vol. VIII, pp. 60–1); Brosset (*HG*, Vol. II/i, p. 227).

[2] The raid by the Turks and Kumukhs on Zagem took place in June 1604, see Brosset (*EC/BHP*, Vol. II, Nos. 19–21, col. 316).

[3] For 'The Turk's town of Tiflis', see Commentary 58.

town used to be Georgian and belonged to King Simon ...

[On the reverse]: [Brought] on the 5th of December [7]113 by the boyar's son from Astarakhan Afanasi Ragozin.

(473)   On the 12th of November, [7]114, the ambassadors Mikhaylo Tatishchev and dyak Andrey Ivanov returned to Moscow from Georgia, and were received on the same day by the Sovereign Tsar and great Prince Dmitri Ivanovich of all Russia.[1] They submitted to the Sovereign the report on what they had done in Georgia. The following is written in it:

(475)   ... On the 18th of September the ambassadors attended on Prince Yuri at the monastery of Alaverdy and told him that he ought to swear fealty on the charter to the Sovereign Tsar and great Prince Boris Fedorovich of all Russia to the effect that his father King Alexander, and he, Prince Yuri and all the Iberian land, should be under the Sovereign's hand; the ambassadors gave him a specimen of what the charter ought to be. Having taken the charter the prince said that he would give instructions for it to be translated into the Georgian language; he would give his reply when the charter was translated. After that, Prince Yuri sent the lord of Zagem, Andronnik's son Elizbar[2] and the attendant officer Suliman to the ambassadors. ... They said that the Shah had allowed

[1] For 'the Sovereign Tsar ... Dmitri Ivanovich', see Commentary 59.
[2] 'The lord of Zagem, Andronnik's son, Elizbar' = Elizbar Andronikashvili or Endronikashvili. Wakhusht states that the family ranked third, after Abashidze and Cholokashvili, among the *tavadni* of Kakheti (cf. Wak./Brosset, 'Liste des Thawads, p. 488, col. 2). According to Toumanoff (*SCCH*, p. 271), the Andronikashvilis were High Constables of Kisiqi; they were descended from Alexius Comnenus, natural son of Emperor Andronicus I of Byzantium (1183–5), by his cousin, Theodora Comnena, Dowager Queen of Jerusalem and widow of Baldwin III. For the beauty and adventures of this lady, see Réné Grousset (*Histoire des Croisades*, Vol. II (1935), pp. 297–9, *et passim*); and Steven Runciman (*A history of the Crusades*, Vol. II (1952), pp. 378–9). For the sojourn of Emperor Andronicus in Georgia as the guest of King Giorgi III, see learned article by V. Minorsky, 'Khaqani and Andronicus Comnenus' in *BSOAS*, Vol. XI, No. 3 (1945), pp. 550–78.

King Alexander to go and that he would be in the Georgian land soon; as soon as his father arrived, he would have the charter written out and would swear fealty on it, and would do everything the Sovereign desired.

On the 28th of September the prince's councillors Dzhezdambek and Prince Suliman visited the ambassadors and enquired after their health. They then said that King Alexander had written to his son Prince Yuri to say that they should take great precautions from the Turks and should keep the animals inside the fortifications, so that the Turks should not come upon them and cause some evil. They added: 'The Sovereign's army which you said had come against the Kumyks has not arrived so far, nor has anything been heard about it. The Prince's message is that you should write to the commanders sent against Shevkal to march on Derbent and occupy the town: for Derbent is now empty; the Turks have fled from it. When the Sovereign's men hold the town, they will be able to protect the Georgian land from the Turks. And now the Sovereign's army is too far away. Even if it wages war on Shevkal and builds forts, it will be unable to help us during a Turkish attack, being too far away.'

And Mikhaylo Ignatyevich said: 'Had our Sovereign only wished it, he would have long ago taken not only Derbent but Shemakha and Baku as well. He has not taken them because they belong to the Kizilbash Shah. Has the Prince sent the present message on his father's instructions? If these are his father's instructions, has he sent the message with the Shah's knowledge? Will the Shah cede Derbent to the Sovereign?'[1] Suliman replied that the Prince had sent this (476) message himself, without the Shah's knowledge, and added: 'If Derbent may not be taken, you should now write to the commanders to send the Sovereign's men with firearms here to the Georgian land at the time when we can expect the Turks' attack.'

[1] For Russo-Persian relations in 1604, see Commentary 60.

Mikhaylo Ignatyevich said: 'So far there has not been such a request to the Sovereign from King Alexander, and we have no orders from the Sovereign about it. The Turk's forts are close to this land – only a day's or two days' march. If an attack on the Georgian land is launched from these castles, how can the Sovereign's army reach here in time? It cannot cross the mountains, and it would take too long to march through the gorges. Consider it yourselves.'

On the 1st of October the attendant officer Prince Suliman told the ambassadors on Prince Yuri's behalf: '. . . The Turks are on their way against us from Genzha and from Shemakha; they have been raised against us by Shevkal's son Saltan Magmut; and the Kumyks are marching from the other side, from the mountains. They want to capture our best place, Zagem, which is vital to us, and they want to build a fort there . . . You should now give me the Sovereign's *streltsy*, even if it be only a few of them – because when the Turks and the Kumyks learn that the Sovereign's men are with me, they will on no account attack. But, should there be none of the Sovereign's men with me, all of us will be ruined utterly by our enemies. My father King Alexander is with the Shah, and all the best men are with him. If the Turks occupy Zagem now, the whole of the Georgian land will fall to them and will secede from the Sovereign through your fault, if you do not let us have the Sovereign's men. And you, too, will not get away from the Georgian land because of the Turks. I can assemble some 5,000 Georgians or more. And I want to be the first to die for the Sovereign and for the Christian faith.'

The ambassadors reached the conclusion that if they did not then let Prince Yuri have *streltsy* to fight the Turks, the Georgians would lose faith in the Sovereign's bounty. So they sent to Prince Yuri the *strelets sotnik* Mikhail Semyshkin with forty *streltsy*, with instructions to remain with the Prince.

On the 7th of October Prince Yuri met the Turks a day's march from Zagem, and a battle took place. The Sovereign's (477) *streltsy* began firing their muskets first. The Turks, recognizing the Russians, fled and Prince Yuri with the *streltsy* and the Georgians attacked them, killed many Turks and took prisoners and four banners; he liberated all the prisoners whom the Turks had captured in the Georgian land. All the Sovereign's *streltsy* were hale and sound. And on the following day the Prince got news that the Kumyks were attacking the Georgian land from the other side; he marched against them taking the *streltsy* with him. And, having heard about the Prince, the Kumyks fled into the mountains. These events have become widely renowned in the Georgian land to the honour of the Sovereign's name.[1]

. . . On the 30th of December Prince Yuri sent the monk (478) Kiril to the ambassadors and commanded that the charter be written after the copy which the ambassadors had made.

On the 1st of January the Prince bade the ambassadors attend on him at his camp at Boatan;[2] he sent Prince Aram and Suliman to fetch the ambassadors. They said that the Prince wanted to swear fealty on the charter; the ambassadors were also to sup with him. And the ambassadors called on the Prince that day.

About half a verst from the Prince's camp the gentleman of

[1] Brosset (*EC/BHP*, Vol. II, Nos. 19–21, cols. 317–18, n. 85) observes that Georgian sources ignore this attack on Zagem by the Turks and Kumukhs – the second during the year 1604.

[2] Boatan: Wak./Brosset has Boethan (pp. 207, 483 and Map 4) marked as a large village just south of the junction of the Belakanis-tsqali with the Alazani. The country running south between the Belakani and the Gishis-tsqali (which formed the boundary stream with the khanate of Sheki) was Georgian Eliseni, Turkish Elisu, and had become the appanage of Krym-Shevkal (see above, Chap. 6, p. 216, n. 1 and Commentary 35).

In the winter of 1596–7 King Alexander was holding court at 'Buyutan', where he received the Russian ambassadors Sovin and Polukhanov (Belokurov, *Snosheniya*, Vol. I, pp. 295 ff.).

(479) the Prince's council, Uman's son Key Khosrov who is close to the prince, and the gentlemen Simon son of David and Kozman son of David, met the ambassadors on behalf of the prince. When they came to the camp, but some distance from the prince's tents, the ambassadors were met by the gentlemen of his entourage, Adam's son Essey, who is a kinsman to the Prince on his mother's side, and David's son Kurman and Abulaskar and some thirty other good *aznaurs* on horseback. Essey said: 'Prince Yuri wanted to meet you, the Sovereign's ambassadors, himself, but was late. He has sent us, his gentlemen, and has bidden us meet you.' And having ridden for a short while alongside the ambassadors they rode off. When the ambassadors entered the camp they dismounted at the guests' tent, which was pitched about half a gun-shot away from the prince's tents. The ambassadors waited for the prince in that tent, and the attendant officer Prince Suliman was with them. After some delay Prince Yuri joined the ambassadors; the Archbishop of Martukop, Rustvel, and Archimandrite Iona (? of the monastery) of the Immaculate (Mother of God) at Krym, and the prince's trusted councillors Prince Aram, and Adam's son Essey, and Dzhezdam-bek and Abulaskar were with him.[1] The ambassadors had the cross ready. The Prince said to them:

'I now want to swear fealty on the charter to the great Sovereign Tsar. My father is now with the Kizilbash Shah, and you should not make it known to the Kizilbashes that I have sworn fealty to the Sovereign; that is why I have brought with me only a few of my councillors, whom I can trust, so that the Shah should not come to know about this. If the Shah learns that I have sworn fealty to the Sovereign, my father and all the men who are with him in the Shah's army will not remain alive.' The prince affixed his seal and his signature to the charter, and kissed the cross on it, on behalf of

[1] For the identity of Prince Yuri's councillors see Commentary 61.

himself and of Prince Yessey his son. Before he kissed the cross the Prince said: 'I swear fealty to the great Sovereign Tsar and great Prince Boris Fedorovich of all Russia in everything written in this charter. The Sovereign Tsar is to hold my father King Alexander and me with all the Iberian land in his mercy, and is to defend us from our enemies, and is not to yield us to any of them.'

Having kissed the cross, he invited the ambassadors to eat with him. He said about his son Prince Yessey that he was too young to understand what he was to swear and that for that reason he had sworn fealty on behalf of his son; as for the councillors whose names were written in the charter, he would send them to kiss the cross at their camp. The prince went to eat in the cold cellar,[1] and bade the ambassadors accompany him. And they supped with the prince. During the meal the prince drank a cup to the Sovereign's health. After the banquet the ambassadors were accompanied as far as their horses by the prince's trusted gentleman, Essey son of Adam, by the equerry, Key Khosrov, and by the good gentlemen, Aprosey's son Zugrav, Rustam son of Adam and Rustam Miskun.

Before the oath taking the ambassadors told the prince's (480) councillors about the 500 rubles in cash of the Sovereign's bounty which had been sent with them to King Alexander as compensation for the improper acts committed in the Georgian land by the envoys Ivan Nashchokin and Ivan Levontyev. After the prince had sworn fealty and kissed the cross on the charter, the ambassadors asked him to give orders to find the men who had been wronged by the envoys and the relatives of those who had been killed, and to have them brought into his presence so that the Sovereign's bounty could be distributed to them. Prince Yuri said that those people were not in the

---

[1] 'The cold cellar': Persian, *serdab*, a grotto ice-house or underground chamber – used for repose during the heat of the day in many Oriental houses.

neighbourhood at that moment. 'The Sovereign has sent his bounty in his grace towards my father King Alexander, and you should give the money to me; I shall hold it until my father's return. And when my father is here he will himself distribute this money to the wronged persons. Now many of our men are assembled here, and they will see the Sovereign's bounty towards us and the entire Iberian land.' The ambassadors gave these 500 rubles in cash to Prince Yuri in the presence of many men; they proclaimed the Sovereign's bounty and protection according to their instructions, and the prince made obeisance and bowed to the ground.

On the 3rd of January the prince sent to the ambassadors' camp the members of his entourage whose names were entered in the charter, Badzhan[1] and his comrades, and the ambassadors Mikhaylo Ignatyevich and Andrey administered the oath to them according to the charter.

On the 8th of January the *strelets sotnik* Ivan Volkov and two *streltsy*, sent in a party from the new fort of Tarku in the Kumyk land by the equerry and commander Ivan Mikhaylovich Buturlin and his assistants and by the dyak Mikhaylo Shironosov, came to the ambassadors Mikhail Ignatyevich and dyak Andrey. The commanders wrote that by God's mercy they had come to the Kumyk land and had built a stone fort at Tarku; the Sovereign's men had ravaged Andreyevo village and Erpeli and the Karabulak settlements and many settlements near the Hot Wells, killed many men and took prisoners, and seized much grain, horses and cattle. The commanders also sent a letter to King Alexander . . . The ambassadors gave orders for it to be given to Prince Yuri. They made a copy of Buturlin's letter and added what Ivan Volkov had said to them . . . about the number of prisoners (481) and horses taken in Andreyevo village and other places, and

[1] Badzhan is clearly the Bejan mentioned in Brosset's fragment – see Commentary 61 (d).

about the attack launched by Shevkal's sons – who had joined with all the Kumyks and with other mountaineers – on the Sovereign's men who were on their way back to the Terek from Tarku. The battle lasted the entire day, and the Sovereign's men killed over three thousand Kumyks and mountaineers and wounded many, while by God's mercy the Sovereign's men themselves withdrew hale and sound.[1] The ambassadors informed Prince Yuri of this and gave him the letter . . . And the prince had copies of that letter made in Iberian; he distributed them in his presence and sent some to the *katalik* Dementi, who is called in Georgia Patriarch of the entire Iberian land; he lives in Simon's land of Kartli and comes to Alexander and Yuri from time to time.[2] He sent other copies to the see of Alaverdy, and to the archbishops and bishops and the archimandrites and abbots of monasteries and to cathedrals; and he gave orders that prayers be offered to God for the Sovereign's health.

The ambassadors told Prince Yuri that he should assemble

[1] This operation, in January 1605, was the first phase of Buturlin's offensive against Shevkal. The effect seems to have been to stimulate the Turks to send reinforcements to Derbent from Shemakha, where Shevkal's son, Sultan Mahmut, was in touch with Chighala-zade Mahmut Pasha, son of the Turkish commander on the Caucasian front. For Sultan Mahmut see also the article 'Shamkhaly Tarkhovskiye' in *SSKG* (Vol. 1 (1868), p. 58 (twice) and n. 8) – where he is stated to have led the attack on Zagem in 1604 and to have been killed in the fighting against Buturlin in June 1605.

[2] '*Katalik* Dementi' = The Catholicos Domenti. In his 'Liste des Catholicos dont on sait très peu de chose' Tamarati (*EG*, p. 365) gives Domenti I, 1557–60 and Domenti II, 1595–1602. Domenti I is also mentioned by Wakhusht in his *History of Kartli*, as having been installed by Simon I who only became King of Kartli in 1558 (Brosset, *HG*, Vol. II/i, p. 31). Salia (*BK*, Nos. 41/42) gives Domenti I, 1557–62, and again for the years 1599–1603. He names Domenti II (Kaihosro Moukhran-Batoni) for the years 1660–75. At any rate it appears that the Domenti who was Catholicos at the turn of the century was still living at the beginning of 1605 when Prince Giorgi sent a copy of the Russian letter to him. His seat was at Mtskheta in Kartlian territory, as is indicated by Tatishchev.

his men and march against the Kumyks at the same time, for the ambassadors knew that the Kumyks, having fled before the Sovereign's men, were living near the Georgian land, near Zagem; others had come to Zagem with their wives and children. Yuri should give orders for them to be killed.

The prince replied: '... I cannot march against the Kumyks now, and I have no men for this. When my father comes back from the Shah, we shall march against the Kumyks immediately, having assembled our entire Georgian army and the mountaineers who obey us, and we shall operate against (482) them as much as God helps us' ... And he added: 'Should there be forts with even a few Russians here in the Georgian land, and if some 20,000 of our men assembled in armour and mounted on *argamaks*, the Turk and the Kizilbash would not dare even look at us. You can yourselves see what our realm is like: it lies in a fastness between mountains and is covered with forests, and there are not many ways through it. If only Simon's son King Yuri of Kartli also came under the Sovereign's hand and made peace with us, no enemy would do anything to us for he has as many fighting men as we. You can yourselves see our land's riches: everything is plentiful. Silk is sent to many realms; grain grows well; there is abundance of grapes; horses like ours are nowhere to be had, and there are innumerable cattle. Such realms are usually contended for with great armies, and God gives it to the Sovereign free. The Turk and the Kizilbash have been fighting with us for many years, wanting to build forts in our country and to place their men there, and we have been resisting them with God's help. Even though we sometimes gave them tribute and our children, we have not allowed them to build the forts. The Sovereign should extend his mercy to us now, should not abandon us to the Moslem sovereigns, and should not allow the Christian faith to be destroyed and the holy churches to be ravaged. By the mercy of God and the prayers of His

Immaculate Mother, her portion, the Georgian land, has been preserved unblemished since the days of the faithful King Constantine and until now, in the true Christian faith.'[1]

And the ambassadors told the prince and his councillors that, if God should grant, they would inform the Sovereign of these statements, and that King Alexander and Prince Yuri should send their ambassadors to the Sovereign to petition him about it. They wrote to the Sovereign about all this in a letter sent by the *strelets sotnik* Ivan Volkov.

[1] Prince Giorgi's reply is specious and evasive and, as Brosset (*EC/BHP*, Vol. II, Nos. 19–21, col. 319) rightly observes, reveals 'un trait de caractère d'une vérité frappante'. Tatishchev had already reached a state of exasperation where he had threatened to build strong points at Zagem and Gremi 'with the object of depriving the King of Georgia of all means of escaping the Russians who now knew the ways into Georgia' and had emphasized that the Tsar had already spent 300,000 rubles on the operations against Shevkal (ibid., col. 318).

CHAPTER 12

PARRICIDE IN ZAGEM

(483) No news of King Alexander reached the Georgian land between the 17th of October and the 27th of January; but on the 27th Prince Yuri told the ambassadors that he had received news from his father from the Kizilbash town of Ardevil,[1] to the effect that the Shah and the Turkish sirdar had separated: the Turks went to Babylon and the Shah returned to his land; and there had been no pitched battle between them because the Turks were too strong for the Shah.[2] Having returned to his land, the Shah let King Alexander go; and he sent with him five khans and commanders with fighting men and his, Yuri's, brother Prince Constantine who lives with the Shah. After escorting King Alexander as far as his land these khans are to march against the Turk's town of Genzha; while Constantine, having come to the Georgian land with his father and collected Geor-

---

[1] For the city of Ardevil or Ardabil, see Commentary 62.

[2] In November 1604 Shah Abbas was in Tabriz while Chighala-zade Sinan Pasha, who had recently taken over command on the eastern front, retired to winter quarters at Van. When the Shah made a movement against Van, the Turkish commander retired by Adiljevaz to Erzurum. After blockading Van without success for forty days, the Shah returned to Persian territory (von Hammer, *HEO*, Vol. VIII, pp. 62–3). It must have been at the beginning of January that Shah Abbas allowed Alexander to leave his court and move to Ardabil. The Shah accorded the Kakhian king royal gifts, including a robe of honour, a crown and aigrette and a jewelled belt. The old king was accompanied by his son Constantine and other members of his family; but his eldest grandson, Taymuraz, son of the late usurper David, was retained as a hostage (Brosset, *HG*, Vol. II/i, p. 464, citing Iskander Munshi). Taymuraz was then sixteen years of age (ibid., Genealogical Tree, p. 635).

11. A Georgian noble (*tavadi*). After Castelli.

gian fighting men, is to march against Shemakha. Prince Yuri added that the Shah has given Shemakha to Prince Constantine.[1]

On the 22nd of February Prince Yuri sent his equerry Prosodan to the ambassadors; Prosodan had come from King Alexander bringing a letter from the king for the ambassadors. He wrote in this letter that he would be arriving in his land soon, in five or six days' time.

Later on, on the 8th of March, King Alexander came to his land, to Zagem; with him was his son Prince Constantine who lives with the Shah, as well as four of the Kizilbash Shah's khans and six sultans with some two thousand fighting men and janissaries. At first these Kizilbashes encamped at the frontier near the river Kapra,[2] while Prince Constantine came to Zagem with his father, accompanied by a few men. The attendant officers told the ambassadors that Prince Constantine had come for the Georgian force which was to accompany him against Shemakha, and that King Alexander wanted to give many fighting men to the Shah. Prince Yuri welcomed his father at the frontier, and there were some three thousand Georgian fighting men with him. After meeting his father, he returned to the village of Tog where the ambassadors

[1] This difficult march, planned for the early spring probably by the ford across the Aras above Aslanduz and through the eastern foothills of Karabagh to Sheki and the border of Kakheti, was clearly considered urgent because of the reports of the activities of the Russian embassy in Kakheti and the movement of Turkish reinforcements from Shemakha to Derbent. The expedition was three-pronged: it had to cover the installation of King Alexander and his Persophil son, Constantine, in Kakheti; the capture of Genzha from the Turks by 'the five khans' who were to be detached from Prince Constantine's column; and, later, a march, reinforced by Georgian contingents, by Constantine on Shemakha.

According to *Chronique Géorgienne*, p. 27, Shah Abbas had already decided on the destruction of Alexander and his replacement by Constantine before the expedition started.

[2] River Kapra: Brosset (*EC/BHP*, Vol. II, Nos. 19–21, col. 320, n. 92) states that Kapra is the Persian name for the Iori.

were encamped.[1] On behalf of his father he told the ambassadors that they were to proceed to Zagem where the king was and conduct their embassy there, because the king could not leave Zagem soon – until he had raised the troops and sent off Prince Constantine. Prince Yuri said: 'My father, King Alexander, wants to see you soon. Whatever message you have from his royal Majesty he wants to know and to attend to the Sovereign's affairs.'

The ambassadors had heard rumours from Kizilbashes and Georgians that the Shah had sent Prince Constantine with ulterior motives, and that he had given instructions to capture Prince Yuri by treachery and to have him brought to him, or else to kill him. And the ambassadors told Prince Yuri about (484) this plot, and repeatedly warned him to beware of the Kizilbashes and not go to them. But he did not listen and retorted that he knew the Kizilbashes and did not fear them. He rode off to his father at Zagem; and he sent to their homes the soldiers who had been assembled under his command.

When the ambassadors were on their way to Zagem they met the Kizilbash Shah's Alekham-sultan, and some five hundred fighting men of his tribe. The ambassadors asked the attendant officers: 'For what purpose is he here in the Georgian land?' They replied that the prince was a nomad and had been the Turk's subject. But he had left the Turk and had joined the Kizilbash Shah, and at the Shah's command King Alexander had given him land in his realm where he and his men could live, and he was on his way home. When the ambassadors reached Zagem they were met outside the suburb by Archbishop Zakhari of Nekresel[2] and by the

---

[1] For Tog = Torga, see Commentary 28. This corrects the statement in *Chronique Géorgienne*, p. 28, to the effect that Alexander and Giorgi 'lodged in Torga, each in his own palace'. From our text it is apparent that Alexander had remained in Zagem, where Prince Yuri and the Russian ambassadors joined him between the 8 and 12 March.

[2] For 'Archbishop Zakhari' see Chap. 11, p. 437, n. 2.

king's nobleman Abel-bek on behalf of the king. They enquired after the ambassadors' health in the king's name.
They came into Zagem and were quartered in houses in the
suburb near the king's court. The Kizilbash khans and sultans
had come to Zagem with many men before the arrival of the
ambassadors, and others had encamped beyond the suburb.[1]

On the 12th of March King Alexander bade the ambassadors come to him, and his nobleman Sholvey-bek came to
the ambassadors with the message.[2] Following the Sovereign's
instructions, the ambassadors sent word to King Alexander
that no ambassadors or envoys from other sovereigns should be
present at the time they would be conducting their embassy.
And Sholvey-bek rode off to the king with that message.
Within the hour the same nobleman and the attendant officer
Suliman came to the ambassadors and said on King Alexander's
behalf that he would have no ambassadors or envoys from
other sovereigns present, and asked whether his son Constantine could attend the banquet after the audience. The
ambassadors said: 'Let it be as the king wishes. Only the
prince should not be present when we conduct the embassy,
and no other ambassadors or envoys should be present either.'
They rode back to the king with the message. After a delay of
some three hours Archbishop Zakhari of Nekresel and the
nobleman Abel-bek came to the ambassadors from the king
and said: 'For our sins Prince Constantine came to King

[1] It is clear from the report of the Russian ambassadors that Prince
Constantine had accompanied his father as far as Zagem; he had not yet
undertaken any operation in Shirvan, as is indicated in *Chronique
Géorgienne*, p. 28. Wakhusht's statement that Alexander went to meet
Constantine at Bazar (Zagem) (Brosset, *HG*, Vol. II/i, pp. 157–8; ibid.,
pp. 375–6, *Suite des Annales*), more or less follows this version. Cf. also
Brosset's abridgment of Iskander Munshi who explains that Alexander
and his son Gurgin (Giorgi) were killed by Constantine because they
refused to take part in his operation against Shirvan (Brosset, *HG*, Vol.
II/i, p. 464).

[2] Sholvey = G. Shalva.

Alexander's court early in the morning, and with him un-invited came Kizilbash khans and sultans, and many Kizil-bashes. We do not know what they have in mind. They have occupied the tent where you were to conduct the embassy, and we cannot and dare not evict them. If you can come to the king and say a few words in their presence and sup with the king, leaving the other speeches for another day, then go to the king. If you cannot do that, you should go to the king tomorrow.'

(485)   Before an hour was up noise broke out at the king's court and muskets were fired. The Kizilbashes began massacring and pillaging the Georgians in the streets and houses of the suburb. And the Georgians who were fleeing from the king's court said that Prince Constantine and the Kizilbashes were fighting with King Alexander and with his son Prince Yuri. The ambassadors immediately sent the translator Svoyetin Kamenev to the king's court with instructions to tell Prince Constantine not to cause bloodshed. On returning to the ambassadors Svoyetin said that he had told Prince Constantine to cause no bloodshed. The prince had replied: 'This has come to pass for our sins. My father King Alexander and my brother have been killed, and the matter cannot be put right any more.' Svoyetin said that King Alexander's head was being held in front of Constantine, and that the Archbishop of Martukop Rustvel and his brother, King Alexander's noble-man Abel, and five other noblemen and eminent *aznaurs* had been killed with King Alexander, and that the Metropolitan of Alaverdy had been wounded.[1] He said that Prince Yuri's

---

[1] Cf. the account in *Chronique Géorgienne*, p. 28: 'The same year on the 12th March, Constantine invited his father Prince Alexander and the Prince Royal Giorgi, his brother: and they sat down to eat. Meantime, he had given an order to his men: "As soon as I make a certain signal, kill my father and my brother." In the middle of the meal, the renegades entered, bound Prince Alexander by the head and killed him at the age of sixty years [? strangled him with a bow-string after the Turkish

son Yessey ran to Constantine, fell at his feet and began to cry, and Constantine gave orders not to kill him.[1] He added that Prince Constantine had been proclaimed Georgian king.

Within the hour King Constantine sent his equerry Aydar-bek[2] to the ambassadors with the message that his brother Yuri-murza had been a traitor to the great Sovereign and to the Shah, that he had married into a Turkish pasha's family, exchanged messages with the Turkish *sirdar*, and wanted to give the Georgian land to the Turk. That is why such a fate had befallen him. King Alexander had tried to defend Yuri-murza, and had also been killed. Aydar-bek added that the Shah is the great Sovereign Tsar's brother and loves him: 'Whatever instructions you have from your Sovereign, he, King Constantine, will carry all out, at the Shah's command.' King Constantine sent the Kizilbash Magmet-bek to the ambassadors to act as attendant officer, and gave instructions that provisions should be issued to them.

Four days later King Constantine came to his father's court and settled in the tents. He gave orders that the bodies of his

custom; he was, in fact seventy or even seventy-eight, see Brosset, *HG*, Vol. II/i, p. 158 and Genealogical Tree, p. 634]: they did the same to Prince Giorgi. The corpses were put on a camel and sent to Alaverdi where they gave them a modest funeral.' Brosset, (ibid.) gives Wakhusht's version that they were cut down with sabres, together with the Rustaveli and his brother, Abel – for whom see Chap. 11, p. 437, n. 2.

[1] Giorgi's son, Yese, was brought up subsequently at the Shah's court where he became a Moslem under the name of Isa Khan (see above, Chap. 11, p. 438, n. 1). After the flight of Taymuraz I from Kakheti in 1615 Isa Khan was proclaimed King by order of Shah Abbas. There is a picturesque account of his enthronement 'on the royal carpet according to the Georgian practice' by Iskander Munshi (see Brosset, *HG*, Vol. II/i, p. 476). His anti-Christian fanaticism provoked a revolt and he fled to Ardabil – whence he went to pay his respects to Shah Abbas then in Karabagh (ibid., pp. 479–81). According to Brosset's Genealogical Tree of the Kakhian Bagratids, ibid., p. 634, Isa did not live out the year 1615.

[2] Aydar (Haydar), according to Brosset (*EC/BHP*, Vol. II, Nos. 19–21, col. 322) was one of Constantine's *mtavarni* – and presumably an apostate to Islam.

father King Alexander and of his brother Prince Yuri should be taken to the Alaverdy Monastery, and he sent their heads to the Shah. King Constantine sent a message to the ambassadors that he wanted to see them; he sent his equerry Prosodan to them about it. Prosodan said in his own name: 'You should now carry to King Constantine the Sovereign's bounty, the presents which you brought for King Alexander, because King Constantine is now the ruler of the Georgian realm.' The ambassadors retorted that King Alexander had been for (486) many years in the Tsar's grace under his royal hand, and that the Sovereign's bounty had been sent to him because of his service, while King Constantine had only newly become the ruler of the Georgian realm. 'Should he want to be in our great Sovereign's grace in the same way as his father and his brother were, he should send his ambassadors to petition the Sovereign, and his royal Majesty will extend his grace to him. Now it is not proper for us to give him the gifts which have been sent for his father.'[1]

The ambassadors attended on King Constantine at his father's court; and outside the tent they were met by the Kizilbash Shah's khan and sultans. King Constantine met the ambassadors halfway down the tent, and he made them sit on his right, while the khans and the sultans sat on his left.[2] The ambassadors told King Constantine in conversation, and not in the Sovereign's name, that the great Sovereign Tsar had sent them as his ambassadors to his father King Alexander, to make his Majesty's royal grace known unto him . . . : 'We have been waiting for King Alexander in his land for more than half a year and now, when he came, we have had no meeting

[1] Prosodan/Farsadan was the former equerry of Prince Giorgi and, after the assassination crisis, seems to have been able, conveniently, to transfer his allegiance to Constantine. He may well have been one of Constantine's sources of information while still in the confidence of Prince Giorgi.

[2] The Russian envoys were thus accorded precedence.

with him; by God's judgement he and his son Prince Yuri have been killed. And, King Constantine, you yourself know that your father King Alexander and his sons King David and Prince Yuri were in the Tsar's grace under his Majesty's exalted royal hand; his royal Majesty was gracious to them and defended them from their enemies and, at their supplication, sent numerous armies into the Kumyk land and commanded that many forts should be built for their sake on the Terek and on the Koysu and on the Sunzha and in the Kumyk land. Numerous troops are now in these forts. His royal Majesty has repeatedly written to the Shah about King Alexander and sent word to the Shah with his ambassadors that King (487) Alexander and his sons with the whole Georgian land are under his exalted royal hand and serve him, the Sovereign. The Shah truly knows this and he is at fault in this before the Sovereign. Even if King Alexander and his son Prince Yuri had been guilty of something in so far as the Shah is concerned, the Shah ought to have exchanged messages with our great Sovereign about it, and not behave in this way.'

King Constantine said to the ambassadors: 'It has so happened for our sins that my father was killed in the brawl. And my brother Yuri murza was killed deservedly, because he had been a traitor to your Sovereign and to the Shah ... My father had been disloyal to the Shah on many occasions in the past. And now he promised to give the Shah a Georgian army of 60,000 men, and the Shah sent me here for that reason. He had commanded me to march with that army against Shemakha in the land of Shirvan. When we came here they began holding out promises to us about the army; I asked them for an army of only 6,000 men but they did not want to give me even that.[1] And they were planning to kill me or to feed me poison. For this reason they suffered the fate they did. The

[1] This corresponds with the version given by the Shah's biographer, Iskander Munshi: see p. 457, n. 1, above.

Shah is the friend of your great Sovereign and of all Christian sovereigns and loves them. And he hopes that there will be no enmity between the sovereigns because King Alexander and his son Yuri have been killed for their disloyalty. I shall send you back to the great Sovereign with honour as soon as I have settled down in this land.' And the king bade the ambassadors proceed from Zagem to the village of Tog where they had been encamped previously; and they were given sufficient provisions.

Meantime the ambassadors went about finding out from Georgians and Kizilbashes whether King Alexander and his son had been killed at the Shah's command. The ambassadors were told by Georgians who had been with King Alexander in the Shah's army and by Kizilbashes that the Shah had given orders to kill King Alexander and his son Prince Yuri because they had been in correspondence with the Turks, and that letters sent by them had come into the Shah's possession. Others said that the king was killed because he had sought the Sovereign's grace and allegiance despite the fact that the Georgian sovereigns had been under the Shah's hand from old times. The ambassadors also made the attendant officer Magmet-bek drunk and questioned him as to whether Constantine had killed his father and his brother with the Shah's knowledge. Magmet said: 'How can a son kill his father and ascend his throne without the Shah's knowledge? Where has such a thing been heard of? On the night before King Alexander's murder Prince Constantine wept throughout the night and confided to me, Magmet – "I do not know what to do. If I kill my father I shall perish from God's hand, and if I do not kill him, I myself shall be killed by the Shah." King Alexander and his son have been killed on the Shah's orders.'[1]

(488)

---

[1] When, six months later, Constantine was killed in battle following a popular revolt inspired by Queen Ketevan, the widow of his elder brother David, Shah Abbas, irritated as he was, commented: "That is

On the 21st of March King Constantine visited Mikhail Ignatyevich in his quarters in the village of Tog. He was accompanied by the Kizilbash Shah's khans and sultans and by the foremost Georgian *aznaurs*. Mikhail Ignatyevich and Andrey said to King Constantine: 'Our great Sovereign Tsar and great Prince Boris Fedorovich of all Russia, being merciful towards King Alexander and in answer to his supplication, has sent a numerous army against the Kumyks, which fought them and ravaged the land, and which has built forts in the Kumyk land. And now, by God's judgement, King Alexander and his son Prince Yuri have been killed – and we do not know whether it was done at the Shah's command or not. And you, King Constantine, have ascended the throne. A large army of our great Sovereign's is now in the Kumyk land. Will you, King Constantine, need these forts and our Sovereign's army? If you need them, how do you intend to be in our great Sovereign's grace? You can yourself understand the magnitude of the expense which his royal Majesty has incurred in raising such forces. Our great Sovereign has done it for the sake of the Christian faith and in his mercy towards King Alexander.'

King Constantine said to the ambassadors: 'Shah Abbas entertains friendship and love and union with your great Sovereign. He graciously gave me the land of Shirvan and commanded me to raise an army here in the Georgian land and to march against Shemakha. And it has come to pass that my father and my brother have been killed; it happened not at

just. The man who kills his father should be treated even worse" '
(*Chronique Géorgienne*, p. 31). According to Iskander Munshi the Shah was then preoccupied with the offensive of Chighala-zade Sinan Pasha round Lake Urmiya (autumn of 1605) and could not give any attention to Georgian affairs (Brosset, *HG*, Vol. II/i, p. 467; cf. also von Hammer *HEO*, Vol. VIII, p. 86 ff.). (Chighala-zade was defeated by Shah Abbas near Selmas in August, and died during his retreat to Diyarbekir, 2 Dec. 1605.)

the Shah's command but because of the dissensions between me and my brother Yuri. This is nothing new in our family, but has been happening since ancient times; my father had put an end to the life of his father who was my grandfather, and he also killed his brother.[1] Now I have done likewise, and myself do not know whether it will lead to good or to evil. And I intend to serve the great Sovereign Tsar even better than my father did. Though I am of the Moslem faith, I am not a Moslem of my own free will: my father had given me to the Shah. Yet I, with all the Iberian land, want to be in your great Sovereign's grace more than in the past; I need the Sovereign's gracious mercy – the army and the forts set up in the Kumyk land. I shall send at a later date my ambassadors to supplicate the great Sovereign about it. The gifts which I shall start sending to the great Sovereign will not resemble those sent by my father. They did not know how to serve his royal Majesty, and I shall start serving the Sovereign better than they did.'

The foremost Georgian *aznaurs* and the Archimandrites had told the ambassadors that they, the Christians, were suffering great oppression from the Moslems; the churches were shut and there was no chanting anywhere; they did not dare, because of the Moslems.

The ambassadors spoke to King Constantine about it and said that he himself knew that here in the Georgian land the (489) Christian faith of the Greek rite had existed from ancient days. Churches and monasteries had been established, and there were Metropolitans, and Archbishops and bishops, and Archimandrites and abbots in the monasteries, and priests and deacons in all the churches according to the canons, as in Christian realms; now he had become the sovereign of the Georgian land, and he himself was of the Moslem faith. He

---

[1] For King Constantine's reflections on his own life and the record of parricide in his family, see Commentary 63.

should cause no hardships or oppression to Christians in the exercise of their faith, and he should instruct all Moslem fighting men who were with him not to profane God's churches and the Christian faith, and not to oppress the Christians, so as not to bring the great Sovereign's wrath upon himself, and so that enmity should not begin between the Shah and the Sovereign because of it.

King Constantine said: 'My father and my grandfather and my great-grandfather were Christian sovereigns since days of old; and I myself was also a Christian and still remember the Christian faith. My father delivered me to become a Moslem when I was seven years old.[1] It was not of my own free will that I have become a Moslem; God will judge my father for it. And now, without fail, I shall not subject Christians to oppression in the exercise of their faith, and I shall give strict instructions that the Christian faith should not be profaned and that no violence should be done to Christians. Whoever does so despite my command will be executed.'[2] And he commanded his crier to proclaim this to his troops in Zagem and in other localities. The king bade the ambassadors go to Krym and said that he would shortly send them home from there. The king himself with all his troops marched against the Kisiks; the

---

[1] According to Brosset (*HG*, Vol. ii/i, Genealogical Tree, p. 634) Constantine was twelve years old in 1579 when his father let him go as a hostage to Kazvin. But in the ambassador's report he himself states that he was seven. He would therefore have been about thirty-two in 1604.

[2] Constantine followed the policy of Shah Abbas in an effort to conciliate the Kakhians – a necessary step in view of the continuing presence of the Turks in Azerbaijan, Shirvan and Kartli. There was none of the harsh suppression of the Christian religion, destruction of churches and deportation of peasants which followed Abbas' campaign in 1615. Iskander Munshi mentions the curious fact that Constantine was at first advised by Hoja Ziad-ed-din Kochit, formerly a *vizir* of Alexander – and presumably either a Persian or a Georgian apostate to Islam. But even this Moslem turned against him in the plots which soon led to the new king's overthrow and death (cf. Brosset, *HG*, Vol. ii/i, pp. 464–6). For the name Kochit, cf. Turkish *koç*, a ram, hence a brave man.

Kisiks also live in the Georgian land, but they muster a separate army. They refused to surrender to the king and sent him word that he should embrace Christianity; and having mustered their forces they wanted to fight for it. But the king called over all their best men and commanders and showered great gifts on them; and they persuaded the Kisik men to submit to the king and to pay him tribute, and they promised to send fighting men against Shemakha. Having made his peace with the Kisiks, King Constantine returned to Krym.[1]

On the 31st of March King Constantine sent to the ambassadors in Krym his equerry Prosodan and the attendant officer Magmet-bek, with a message asking them to meet him and talk about affairs . . . King Constantine met the ambassadors on horseback about twice gun-range from his camp. He was accompanied by Kizilbash khans and sultans and by Georgian noblemen and foremost *aznaurs*. Many other men were drawn (490) up on either side on horseback and on foot. King Constantine said to the ambassadors: 'I have come to meet you. I want to do some shooting with my *aznaurs*. And you should watch it.' The ambassadors replied that they were acquainted with shooting, but that he was free to do as he wished. King Constantine and the *aznaurs* galloped about and shot upwards at a pumpkin.[2] And having done so for a short while, the king

[1] For the tough character of the men of Kisiqi, see above, Commentary 30. This 'separate army' was in fact the second 'banner' (*drosha*) in the Kakhian royal army – which had been under the command of Ketevan's husband, the dead King David (see above p. 161 and Commentary 29).

[2] The sport is illustrated by Castelli in a drawing reproduced in Allen, *HGP*, opposite p. 331. In the wealthier Middle Ages, the target had been, according to Wak./Brosset, (pp. 32–5) 'the royal cup of gold or silver, which served as a target for the arrows of the young boys; the one who knocked it down received it as a reward.' The same sport was practised by Shah Abbas and his courtiers in the Grand Maydan at Isfahan: 'They also shoot with bow on horseback, coursing at full speed; the target, of the size of a plate, is suspended on a tree and they often

said to the ambassadors: 'Come to my camp. We shall talk over with you whatever needs discussing' . . . The king himself met the ambassadors midway down his tent, and he bade them sit on his left, and the Georgian noblemen and foremost *aznaurs* sat below them; and Prince Yuri's son Yessey sat at the king's other side, and the Khans and the Sultans sat below him.[1] The ambassadors told King Constantine that his father and brothers had served the great Sovereign and had sworn fealty to remain under his royal exalted hand, together with the whole Iberian land, without seceding for ever after. They asked him whether he wanted to be in the Sovereign's grace in the same way as his father and brothers had been. King Constantine replied: 'My father and my brothers lied to your great Sovereign when they said that they were serving him. They favoured the Turk all the time. I am the Shah's servant, and in his letters the Shah calls me his son. Should your great Sovereign be as gracious towards me as the Shah, I am ready to be in the Sovereign's grace, and I shall serve him better than my father and brothers did; I shall send him gifts of *argamaks* and various fine things.' The ambassadors Mikhail Ignatyevich and Andrey told him that he would receive the Sovereign's bounty in the future, and that the Sovereign's army was in the Kumyk land to give protection to the Georgian land; he should therefore swear fealty to his royal Majesty, and should take the oath according to his faith, to the effect that he and all the Iberian land would be in the Tsar's grace. King Constantine replied: 'I cannot swear fealty to the great Sovereign now. But my word will not be false.' The ambassadors also told King Constantine that the Iberian

hit it and bring it down . . . I have seen the king exhaust seven or eight horses in such pastimes between noon and four or five of an evening' (Abel Pinçon in Ross, *Anthony Sherley*, p. 161).

[1] Here the new king Constantine was giving precedence to his Persian allies – perhaps as a result of their having protested when, at the first meeting, he had placed the Russians on his right (cf. p. 460, n. 2 above).

land had been Christian from old times and that Christian sovereigns had ruled over it until then; he himself became a Moslem under duress; he should now embrace the Christian faith. King Constantine replied that he was unable to do so then, because of the Shah, but that later on he would see what was best; he said that what was needed was for the Sovereign to provide a strong backbone on which one could lean and hold out hope. 'Now no damage will be done in any way to the Christian faith here,' he said. And he placed fruit in front of the ambassadors, and after that he invited himself to supper with Mikhail Ignatyevich, and he supped with him.

When King Constantine dismissed the ambassadors he accompanied them himself as far as Elon, about twenty versts (491) from Krym. He sent to the ambassadors gifts of horses and clothing in exchange for the gifts which they had sent him in their own names. He also sent clothing and horses to the interpreters and to the *strelets sotnik* and to the under-dyak; and he gave each *strelets* two pounds of silk.

CHAPTER 13

THE MOVE TO KARTLI

TRANSLATION of the letter from the Kartlian King Yuri, (469) sent to the ambassadors by the interpreter Nikita Tyutchev:

By the mercy of God, I, King Yuri, the son of Simon, of royal descent from the beginning,[1] am writing to you, lord Mikhail and Andrey, the ambassadors of the great Sovereign Tsar and great Prince Boris Fedorovich of all Russia, and of his son, the great sovereign Prince Fedor Borisovich of all Russia, sovereigns of all the northern land, to rejoice in the Lord. You have sent a letter to us by the interpreter Mikita, and we have received your letter, and have understood everything that is written in it. We are unworthy and unable to reply to this matter. And if you are bearers of such a great and most wondrous affair, where have you been until now or since? And now let it be known unto you that we are engaged in war, and suffer from much disorder and want. We have gone to Samtskhe to fight the Hagarenes; and we consider this an obstacle to your coming here before the summer.[2] If God

---

[1] 'I Yuri, the son of Simon': Giorgi X, King of Kartli, son of Simon I by Nestan-Darejan, daughter of Levan of Kakheti; *her* mother was daughter of the Shevkal Kara-Musal. On 15 September 1578, according to *Chronique Géorgienne*, p. 19, Giorgi had married Mariam (called also Tomar or Tamar) daughter of Giorgi Lipartiani, a younger son of the Dadian Levan I of Mingrelia (died 1572). In 1605 Giorgi was probably rather over forty; for characterization, see Chap. 8, p. 388, n. 2.

Mr. Terence Gray has pointed out that the drawing by Castelli, reproduced in Allen *HGP*, opposite p. 166, is probably that of Giorgi III of Imereti (for whom cf. Brosset, *HG*, Vol. II/i, p. 642) – since Giorgi X of Kartli died in September 1605 – years before Castelli arrived in Georgia in 1631 (cf. Tamarati, *EG*, pp. 520–1).

[2] For Samtskhe, see Commentary 57; for Hagarenes (i.e. Turks),

grants and we return by the good fortune of the great king, we shall send a man to fetch you . . . And you are not to travel without our man. Written in the month of November 7113 [1604]. King Yuri of Kartli and all Iberia.

(470) . . .[1] And, Sovereign, along with Suliman we sent the interpreter Svoyetin Kamenev and the under-dyak Druzhina Stepanov, having first sworn them in, and four *streltsy* with them. And we, your servants, wrote to Simon's son King Yuri that he should command us to come to him without delay, because we had your Majesty's instructions for him, King Yuri, regarding many great affairs, and because you, the great Sovereign, wished to be gracious to him and to make him your Majesty's kinsman. When we reached the land of Soni on our way here, we sent a message to King Yuri by Aristov's men, saying that we had your Majesty's royal letter and message about many affairs and your Majesty's bountiful presents for him, King Yuri; while we were in the land of Soni we had no news from him. After we came to the Georgian land we

Chap. 1, p. 94, n. 1. Giorgi was brother-in-law to Manuchar II, atabeg of Samtskhe, who had married Elena, daughter of Simon I in 1582. Following the capture of Simon by the Turks in 1600, Giorgi had continued his father's policy of sustaining his relatives in Samtskhe. After the Persian capture of Erevan, in the spring of 1604, the Georgians had the support of Emirguneh, the new Khan of Erevan, himself an apostasized Georgian (see Brosset, *HG*, Vol. 11/i, pp. 471–5); for interesting details from Iskander Munshi, see also Chap. 11, p. 442, n. 3 above. The leaders on the Turkish side were also apostasized Georgians – Yusuf Pasha of Akhaltsikhe, a son of Beka Jaqeli brother of Manuchar II; and Ferhat Pasha of Penek (cf. Brosset, ibid., p. 472, n. 3).

[1] Here begins the surviving fragment of a letter which Tatishchev sent to the Tsar from Georgia by the *strelets sotnik* Ivan Volkov who, in January 1605, brought the ambassadors news of Ivan Buturlin's offensive against the Kumukhs – undertaken in the autumn of 1604 in accord with the pledges given to Alexander of Kakheti. Buturlin led about ten thousand men into the field – including several regiments of *streltsy* and Volga, Terek and Greben Cossacks. He took Tarku by storm. The Shevkal, Andi Khan, fled to the Avar Khan – where his able son, Sultan Mahmut, began to organize a counter-attack to recover the Kumukh capital: for details see Potto, pp. 10–11.

12. A Russian *strelets*. After Castelli.

spoke to Prince Yuri (of Kakheti) about this on many occasions, but the prince did not allow us to go to King Yuri, nor did he let us send messengers. And we, your servants, instructed Svoyetin to ask the Archbishop of Golgotha, Theodosius,[1] who had been to Moscow and whom Svoyetin knows, what King Yuri is thinking and whether he wants to be in your royal grace; whether he is willing to send his daughter, the elder princess, to your royal Majesty, and what her looks are, and how tall she is, and how clever, and how old she is, and whether there are in his realm any other princesses or princes of his royal kin – and if there are, whose children they are, and what they look like, how tall they are and what their age is, and why it is that King Yuri has instructed us not to proceed to him before he bids us come, but has put it off for a long time, until the spring. We gave instructions for Archbishop Theodosius to be told secretly that Prince Yuri [of Kakheti] did not allow us to go to King Yuri or send a message because he is jealous and does not want such a great divine act to take place in King Yuri's family; Prince Yuri is in sorrow because he has no daughter and his son is still young. And we secretly sent the Metropolitan of Caesaria, German,[2] with a message to King Yuri about your Majesty's affairs. We, your servants, also instructed Svoyetin to tell King Yuri of Kartli, in the course of conversation, about your Majesty's royal mercy to King Alexander and the entire Georgian land: that on your royal orders your Majesty's commanders fought

[1] For 'the Archbishop of Golgotha, Theodosius', see Commentary 64.

[2] 'The Metropolitan of Caesaria, German': The Metropolitan of Caesaraea (Turkish, Kayseri – in central Anatolia) ranked first among the Metropolitans of the Greek Orthodox Church. The presence of this Greek prelate in Georgia is not mentioned in the Georgian sources. For other journeys of Orthodox ecclesiastics between Constantinople and Moscow at the turn of the sixteenth century, see above, Chap. 6, p. 210, n. 1 and Commentaries 39 and 40. Boris gave the monks of Mount Athos a house in the Kitay-gorod which served as a lodging for priests and other Greeks visiting Moscow.

and ravaged the land of the Kumyks, killed many men, captured innumerable prisoners, and erected forts in the Kumyk land, and that your Majesty's royal army is in the Kumyk land in great numbers now. He was also to say that many Nogays took part in the war in the Kumyk land together with your Majesty's commanders, and now have their nomad encampments about Kizlar, near Terek-town; they are ready to put in the field as many thousand men as necessary, wherever your royal Majesty orders them to serve you.[1] We instructed Svoyetin to come back with whatever news he gathers in the land of Kartli; and we ordered under-dyak Druzhina to proceed to the Mereli and Dadiani lands with Suliman.[2]

(471)

On the 9th of February, Sire, the interpreter Svoyetin and the under-dyak Druzhina returned from Simon's land of Kartli, and said that Simon's son King Yuri had not let Suliman through to the Mereli and Dadiani lands but turned him back. Svoyetin and Druzhina brought to us, your servants, a letter from Simon's son King Yuri written in the Greek script. We instructed Svoyetin to translate this letter, and we have sent a translation to your Majesty. In reply to questions the interpreter Svoyetin and the under-dyak Druzhina told us that they had been to see King Yuri of Kartli in his town of Gori[3]; having made obeisance to him on our behalf, they gave him the letter. They said that the King accepted the letter and instructed Archbishop Theodosius to translate it; and he enquired after our health. When Archbishop Theodosius had translated our letter, he took the translation to the King; and, Sire, Archbishop Theodosius later told them that your royal Majesty's wish, about which we, your royal Majesty's ambassadors, wrote in the letter, would be done. They said that, when he heard of

---

[1] For the Nogays, see Chap. 4, p. 174, n. 1.

[2] 'Mereli and Dadiani lands'; (I)mereli = adjectival form of Imereti; 'Dadiani lands' = Mingrelia of which the ruler bore the title of *Dadiani*.

[3] For the town of Gori, see Commentary 65.

the Tsar's mercy, King Yuri rejoiced, and had never been as joyous as he was then; they added that King Yuri was gracious to them, held them in honour and entertained them to meals four times. During the banquet the interpreter Svoyetin spoke of your Majesty's royal mercy to King Alexander and his son Prince Yuri and to the whole Georgian land, and of your Majesty's royal army sent against the Kumyks, and of the forts – as we, your servants, had instructed him. Svoyetin told us that King Yuri had said: 'I have heard that by the great Sovereign's good fortune his realm grows in every direction.' King Yuri was vexed with King Alexander's son Prince Yuri and said to them: 'Prince Yuri sent a letter to me by his *aznaur* Suliman, and it was as if he were ordering me about. He instructed me to procure for his royal Majesty what his royal Majesty requires, and he instructed me to let him through to the Dadiani. I am not Prince Yuri's servant. King Alexander is sovereign in his land, and I am master in mine. The chief king in the Iberian land is myself and not Alexander.[1] His royal Majesty's ambassadors are now with them. When they have finished their work and come to me, and I see his royal Majesty's letter about his Majesty's affairs, I shall have everything ready.' . . . King Yuri said we should come to him this spring (472) after Easter, when King Alexander and his son Prince Yuri let us go . . .

Translation of King Yuri of Kartli's letter sent to the ambassadors by the interpreter Svoyetin Kamenev and under-dyak Druzhina Stepanov:

I, the sovereign King Yuri of Kartli and the whole Iberian land, the son of King Simon, am writing to you, Mikhail Ignatyevich and Andrey Ivanov, the ambassadors of the great Sovereign Tsar and autocrat of all Russia, Boris Fedorovich, and of his beloved son Prince Fedor Borisovich of all Russia,

[1] For precedence among the kings in Georgia, see Commentary 66.

and I bid you rejoice. I have received your honourable letter, and have well understood what is written therein. And, as I wrote to you before, so I am writing to you now – you know about it, for it is a great matter. You say that there exists a royal command that we should be kinsmen. You appear to be vexed at us: you appear to want to do things in haste and say that we should enter into kinship. You want to do it in haste, but a royal alliance is a great affair, and therefore I am telling you: wait until great Easter, until the Glorious Resurrection of Christ, in the spring, when King Alexander will also be in his land.[1] And then, if God is merciful, I shall send to fetch you, and you will come to me. And when we meet, and see the Tsar's letter and read it – then God's will and the Tsar's wish be done! And as for these men – Svoyetin and his assistant – whom you sent to the Dadiani, I think that it is not good that they should proceed there, since the Dadiani has not got what

(473) you require. He is the Turk's subject, whereas it is fitting for all Christians to be the enemies of the Turk and not to love him. I have not allowed your men through so that the Dadiani, having captured them, should not send them off to the Turk in the way that he has done with the Shah's men, and so that your men should not be lost. And in time the Dadiani will be in our hands, and the best thing will be done.[2] Written on the 1st day of February, 7113 [1605].

(492) On[3] the 6th of May, 7112, the Sovereign Tsar and great

[1] Easter Sunday fell on 31 March in 1605 (cf. Brosset, *EC/BHP*, Vol. II, Nos. 19–21, col. 324, n. 99).

[2] At this time the Dadiani was Manuchar I (1590–1611). It was he who had defeated Giorgi's father, Simon I, in Odishi, 1590 (Brosset, *HG*, Vol. II/i, pp. 40–1, 263–4; Allen, *HGP*, pp. 159–60). In 1591 he had married Nestan Darejan, a daughter of Alexander II of Kakheti, who died the same year in childbirth. There are references to this marriage in the reports of Sovin's embassy (Belokurov, p. 311). The Dadiani had a long coastline and he was always exposed to Turkish pressure from the sea.

[3] This is the beginning of Tatishchev's second *Stateyny spisok* in which he dealt with the 'secret affairs' entrusted to him by the Tsar (i.e. the marriage negotiations).

Prince Boris Fedorovich of all Russia commanded the gentle. man of the Privy Council Mikhail Ignatyevich Tatishchev and dyak Andrey Ivanov to busy themselves in the Georgian and Kartlian lands with a view to selecting a prince and a princess of the Georgian royal house suitable for his son and his daughter, in accordance with the instructions. The monk Kiril, on an embassy from the Georgian King Alexander, had told the Sovereign that the King had grandchildren, the children of King David, the seventeen-year-old Prince Teymuras and the twelve-year-old princess Helen, and that Simon's son King Yuri of Kartli had a daughter, aged about twelve, all of goodly countenance, and that the Georgians hoped that they would prove suitable. Kiril also said that there were other princes and princesses in the Georgian, Kartlian and Mereli lands, and that it would be possible to select from among them such as would suit the Sovereign's affair; King Alexander would attend to that.[1]

Two months before Mikhail Ignatyevich and dyak Andrey reached the Georgian land Shah Abbas's ambassador Magmet-bek had come to the Georgian land to fetch King David's children, the prince and the princess. King Alexander had written to his son Prince Yuri to send off to the Shah King David's children Prince Teymuras and Princess Helen together with their mother, adding that, if Yuri did not let them go, the Shah would not permit him to return to the Georgian land. The ambassadors Mikhail Ignatyevich and Andrey wrote in detail to the Sovereign from the Georgian land, in a dispatch sent by the Terek *strelets sotnik* Miney Sonin, about their attending on King Alexander's son Prince Yuri and asking him not to let King David's children go to the Shah but, instead, to let them go with them to the Sovereign; they also reported what Prince Yuri had said in answer to their arguments, as to why he was sending King David's children to the Shah. On his father's

[1] For the Bagratid royal children see Commentary 67.

orders Prince Yuri sent off to the Shah King David's children together with their mother; and the Shah took King David's daughter for himself.[1] And there were no other princes or princesses in the Georgian land.

The ambassadors Mikhail Ignatyevich and Andrey asked Prince Yuri to give them leave to go to Simon's son, King Yuri of Kartli, because of his daughter Princess Helen; but the Prince would not let them go in his father's absence . . .

(493)   When the ambassadors were received by King Constantine, Mikhail said to him in secret about King David's son Teymuras: 'Our great Sovereign gave us a message for your father King Alexander to send his grandson, King David's son Teymuras, to the Sovereign, because he wanted to give him his daughter in marriage. But Teymuras's uncle, Prince Yuri, lacking in friendship towards the Sovereign, did not let him go; instead he sent him to the Shah. We carry our great Sovereign's letter and oral message to the Shah about him, asking the Shah to command that King David's son be returned to King Alexander. We sent an interpreter to the Shah's Majesty with the prayer to command us to attend upon him. His Majesty Shah Abbas wrote to us that he had moved far away from the Georgian land because of the coming of the Turks, and that we, the ambassadors, could not go to him; but when he came close to the Georgian land and attacked the town of Genzha he would forthwith send messengers to fetch us. And so far

[1] According to Wakhusht's *History of Kakheti* (Brosset, *HG*, Vol. ii/i, pp. 375–6), following the death of David, Queen Ketevan herself took the initiative in sending Taymuraz, together with his younger brother Keshish, to the court of Shah Abbas, under the charge of Shermazen Cholokashvili. See also version of Iskander Munshi, for the year 1604 (Brosset, *HG*, Vol. ii/i, p. 463). There is no mention in the Georgian sources of a daughter of David being sent to Shah Abbas as early as 1604 – although Brosset (*HG*, Vol. ii/i, p. 635) in his Genealogical Tree of the Kakhian Bagratids, shows one nameless daughter of David 'laissée auprès de Shah Abaz I après 1610'. And see below, Chap. 14, p. 490, n. 2.

we have not been called by the Shah. Now, King Constantine, . . . you should show your service to the great Sovereign by writing to the Shah to send back this prince, King David's son, and to command that he be allowed to go to the Sovereign with us, his ambassadors. And should the Shah command us to attend upon him, we are ready to go . . .' King Constantine replied that Teymuras was in his hands and that he would give his reply about him another time. He said that King Alexander and Yuri-murza held out hopes to the great Sovereign, but did not know how to attend to his Majesty's affairs; they gave King David's son Teymuras to the Shah needlessly, and even asked that he should be turned into a Moslem.

After that King Constantine twice visited Mikhail Ignatyevich in the village of Tog; and Mikhail asked about his intentions with regard to Teymuras. King Constantine repeated his earlier words, that his father King Alexander and his brother Prince Yuri had acted disloyally towards the Sovereign in not letting Teymuras go to him; they feared that he would be (494) honoured as a great man at the Sovereign's court, and would take revenge for their enmity;[1] that is why they sent him to the Shah with instructions to turn him into a Moslem – but he was not a Moslem yet . . . King Constantine would give no definite answer about the prince, but said that he would do so some other time.

When Mikhail Ignatyevich and Andrey were received by King Constantine in farewell audience at Krym, Mikhail told the King that he had given no answer about Teymuras. King Constantine replied: 'I want to serve your great Sovereign better than my father and my brother did. If the Sovereign wants my nephew, King David's son Teymuras, I shall send

[1] Cf. later, King Giorgi of Kartli's own hesitations about allowing a prince of his house to become a son-in-law of the Tsar. Prince Constantine, himself, was an example of the risk which faced Georgian dynasts of a member of the royal house becoming a Moslem and enjoying the special patronage of the Shah.

to the Shah asking him to give leave to Teymuras to come to me; when he sends him to me, I shall let him go to your great Sovereign together with my own ambassadors – after your departure. Now I am sending you away at the Shah's command. If the Shah does not release David's son to me, I shall send my most prominent *aznaur* to the Shah with the message that the great Sovereign had sent you, his ambassadors, to fetch King David's son, and that the Shah should send him to your Sovereign with his own ambassadors; I expect that – because of his love for your Sovereign – the Shah will not insist on keeping the prince.'

When King Constantine dismissed the ambassadors, they proceeded from the Georgian land to the land of Kartli, to Simon's son King Yuri, to ask for his daughter Princess Helen. Bodradin, Master of the Gates[1] of Simon's son King Yuri, had just come to King Constantine bearing a letter, and had visited the ambassadors. They sent a letter by him to King Yuri, recalling that he had written to them by the interpreters and had sent an oral message that they should come to his land of Soni after Easter,[2] and that they would be met there . . . They gave the day on which they would reach the land of Soni, and asked that King Yuri should send an officer to meet and accompany them.

The ambassadors questioned King Yuri's Master of the Gates in every way about King Yuri's daughter Princess Helen: Had he seen her? what were her looks and stature? Did

---

[1] Bodradin, Master of the Gates: *R. kapychey* from *T. kapuji*, gate-keeper. At the Sublime Porte the *Kapuciler* were originally guards drawn from the lowest grade of the Janissaries. They came to be used as messengers to carry to the grandees of the empire or foreign princes invitations to festivities or documents of state. The commander of the gate-keepers was the *kapuciler bashi*, a kind of chamberlain (cf. article by Babinger under *Kapuci* in *EI*, 1st ed). The post evidently corresponded to that of *amirtchkari = amir* of the gate, at the Georgian courts (of Allen, *HGP*, p. 258). Bodradin = Badr-ed-din, a Moslem name.

[2] See p. 474, n. 1 and above.

King Yuri want to let her go with them, the ambassadors?
And the Master of the Gates Bodradin said that he often saw
the princess on her way to church with her mother; Princess
Helen was very beautiful and not of small stature. He had (495)
heard from King Yuri that he would show his daughter to the
Sovereign's ambassadors and would agree to send her at a
later date; the king would not let her go then, because he was
afraid of the Shah, who had ordered the killing of King Alexander and his son. And not only the Master of the Gates, but
also *aznaurs* from Simon's land, whom they met in Aristov's
land, told the ambassadors that King Yuri did not want to let
his daughter go with them . . .

On the 15th of April Prince Aristov of Soni met the ambassadors in his land, close to the Georgian frontier, and said that
Yuri, King of Kartli and head of all the Iberian land, had commanded him to meet them, the Sovereign's ambassadors, and
to give them provisions.[1] After travelling some fifteen versts
from the frontier, Aristov had the ambassadors' camp pitched
near his villages, and gave them adequate provisions.

On the 16th of April Archbishop Theodosius came to the
ambassadors from King Yuri of Kartli and enquired after their
health. He said to them: 'You should not be angry with King
Yuri because he has bidden you not to come to him at once.
It is the first time that ambassadors from the great Sovereign
have come to him, and he wants to gather things together and
to get ready. You stay here, in Aristov's land, for a little while.
And the King will soon send messengers to fetch you.'

Mikhail Ignatyevich and Andrey questioned Archbishop
Theodosius in the course of conversation; they asked: What

---

[1] Here 'the Georgian frontier' is evidently the frontier between Kakheti
and Aristov's land of Soni. The exact route followed by the ambassadors,
'fifteen versts to Aristov's villages', and then a further two days' march to
King Giorgi's camp on the Mejuda river, is not made clear but it was
probably from the Atchkhoti valley, over the ridge of mount Tini to the
crossing of the Ksani near Akhal-daba.

are the looks, the stature and the age of King Yuri's daughter Princess Helen? Is King Yuri ready to let her go to the Sovereign now? What princes of King Yuri's family are there in the land of Kartli? What are the looks, the stature and intelligence of each, and how old are they? Archbishop Theodosius said that King Yuri's daughter Princess Helen was very beautiful and of good intelligence; she was ten years old, but well grown. He did not know it for certain whether the king would let her go then, because he would not share his thoughts on this matter with anyone. He said that there was a prince from the Mereli land, called Alexander, beautiful of countenance and not small in stature, and that they would see him themselves.[1] King Yuri also had other princes related to him, but the Archbishop did not specify to the ambassadors their names (496) nor whose children they were. He added that King Yuri did not trust them, for fear that they should begin plotting to get the realm away from him. And Theodosius rode off to King Yuri.

[1] 'A prince from the Mereli land called Alexander': In the view of Brosset (*EC/BHP*, Vol. II, Nos. 19–21, col. 329 and n. 114) this Alexander was the son of Bagrat of a cadet line of the Imerian Bagratids – whom Simon I had taken prisoner in 1590 or 1591. 'L'histoire ne dit plus rien de Bagrat, dès le moment où il quitta l'Iméreth, mais sa famille put se perpétuer dans le Karthli'. As will be seen in the following chapter, the ambassadors did not agree with Theodosius's flattering description of this prince.

CHAPTER 14

A PLETHORA OF PRINCES

ON the 25th of April King Yuri again sent Archbishop Theodosius to the ambassadors in Aristov's land, together with a member of his entourage, Aslamaz-bek, bidding them come to him. Archbishop Theodosius and Aslamaz travelled with them.[1]

On the 27th, when they were some three versts away from King Yuri's camp, the ambassadors were met on his behalf by two Archbishops and two bishops from the land of Kartli, and by German, the Greek Metropolitan of Caesaria; a processional cross encased in silver was carried in front of them; some one hundred of King Yuri's noblemen and leading *aznaurs* came with them to meet the ambassadors. The Archbishops enquired after the ambassadors' health on King Yuri's behalf, and rode with them as far as the camp. King Yuri was encamped in his village of Mezhzheskov[2]; the ambassadors were quartered in this village near the King's camp, and adequate provisions were given to them.

On the 28th King Yuri bade the ambassadors conduct their embassy. Mikhail Ignatyevich Tatishchev and dyak Andrey sent word to King Yuri by the attendant officers – according to their instructions – that no ambassadors or envoys from the

[1] Aslamaz seems to represent the Georgian forename Ilamaz – 'Beau'.

[2] 'His village of Mezhzheskov': Brosset (*EC/BHP*, Vol. II, Nos. 19–21, col. 327) proposes Mejudis-khevi on the Mejuda river, one of the left bank affluents of the Greater Lyakhvi. 'In fact, the village formerly called Nadcharmagevi, a royal residence, later called Karaleti, was situated in the valley of the Mejuda.' Conveniently near to Gori, it was fine country for the chase: 'Plains, woods, game, birds, all sorts of attractions are combined' (Wak./Brosset, p. 251). At Mejudis-khevi was a demesne of the *eristavs* of the Ksani (letter from A. G. Tarsaidze).

481

Turk, the Kizilbash or other sovereigns should be present while they conducted their embassy. The ambassadors also sent word to King Yuri that they had the Sovereign Tsar's secret instructions about great affairs concerning him: only members of the entourage whom he trusted should be present when they conveyed the secret message. King Yuri sent word to the ambassadors that no other sovereigns' ambassadors or envoys would be present when they had their audience of him; first they should conduct their ordinary embassy and sup with him, and he would bid them come again on the following day, when he would listen to their secret message. The ambassadors conducted their embassy on that day; Archbishop Theodosius, and Prince Aristov of Soni, and Aslamaz-bek, and the nobleman Aval,[1] and the equerry Vardan[2] and the queen's chamberlain Agatan,[3] were sent by the king to the ambassadors' quarters to fetch them. When they came to the king's camp they dismounted, and some seventy feet from the king's tents they were met by King Yuri's uncle Prince Vakhtan,[4] and by his son Prince Potata[5] who was with him; in front of the tents

[1] Aval: doubtless a member of the ancient family of Avalishvili, *tavadni* of the Kartlian kingdom; there were also branches in Kakheti and Samtskhe (cf. Wak./Brosset, pp. 45, 47, 51, 487, col. 3; also Toumanoff, *SCCH*, p. 270).

[2] Vardan: The Vardanidzes were an ancient family of *tavadni* – from a branch of which the Gurielis, rulers of Guria, were sprung (cf. Wak./Brosset, pp. 31, 49).

[3] Agatan: this name does not correspond to any of the more distinguished Georgian family names; it resembles the old Kakhian royal name Aghsartan (cf. Allen, *HGP*, pp. 91, 94, 98). The Georgian equivalent of chamberlain is *ejibi* (cf. Allen, *HGP*, p. 259).

[4] For 'King Yuri's uncle Wakhtang', see Commentary 68.

[5] 'Prince Potata' = G. Paata. The name is not included in Brosset's Genealogical Tree of the Kartlian Royal House. The mention of this prince as son of Simon I's brother Wakhtang seems to distinguish the latter clearly enough from Wakhtang of Mukhrani, father of the Princes Taymuraz and Kai Khusrau: see further Commentary 68. See also p. 498, for further reference to Prince Paata as being younger than Giorgi's son Luarsab.

the ambassadors were met by King Yuri's son Prince Lev
Varsap.[1] They walked in front of the ambassadors, and when
they entered the tents King Yuri met the ambassadors in the
third tent from his seat. He walked back into the second tent
and bade the ambassadors conduct their embassy. He himself
remained standing.

Mikhail Ignatyevich saluted him on behalf of the Sovereign
Tsar and on behalf of Prince Fedor, his son, according to his
instructions, and presented the letter. King Yuri took the (497)
Sovereign's letter and kissed the seal, and enquired after the
Sovereign's health, saying: 'Do I dare or do I not dare enquire
after the health of the great Sovereign Tsar and great Prince
Boris Fedorovich of all Russia and his son Prince Fedor
Borisovich of all Russia? What is God's mercy towards them?'
Mikhail Ignatyevich replied in accordance with his instruc-
tions.[2] He then presented the Sovereign's bountiful gifts; and
King Yuri made obeisance for the Sovereign's bounty.

After that Mikhail Ignatyevich and dyak Andrey delivered
to King Yuri the speech in accordance with the Sovereign's
instructions on the ordinary affairs, to the effect that King
Yuri and the whole of his land of Kartli should be under the
Sovereign's hand. The ambassadors had also written a letter to
King Yuri about his daughter Princess Helen and about a
prince, if he had one living in his land – using as pattern the
specimen letter sent to the ambassadors about King David's

[1] 'Prince Lev Varsap': the elder son and heir of Giorgi X; born 1595;
in September 1605 succeeded his father as Luarsab II of Kartli; married
1610, the sister of Giorgi Saakadze, whom he afterwards repudiated
(see Commentary 68); incarcerated by Shah Abbas, 1616; killed by order
of the Shah, following a Russian *démarche* for his release, near Shiraz,
1622. A gallant youth, but rash and rather feckless in his politics; for
details of his life and reign, see Brosset (*HG*, Vol. II/i, pp. 44–51) and,
for a dramatic account of his death, *Chronique Géorgienne*, pp. 55–6.

[2] According to Kotoshikhin, p. 50, ambassadors were instructed to
say that when they last saw the Tsar, before they set out on their embassy,
he was in good health.

children, as well as the Sovereign's secret instructions. For the sake of the Sovereign's affairs the ambassadors brought with them the Tsar's presents which had been sent for King Alexander, because King Yuri of Kartli is the principal king in all the Iberian land, and it was the first time that ambassadors had come to him from a Muscovite sovereign, and on a great affair at that. Furthermore, the archbishops and *aznaurs* who had fled to King Yuri from the Georgian land told him of the Sovereign's bounty which used to be sent to King Alexander.

When the ambassadors had delivered the speech the king said: 'I have heard the Sovereign's message with joy, and I want to be in his Majesty's grace: my head, and my children and the whole of my realm belong to God and to him, the Sovereign. I have sinned before the Sovereign, for not having hitherto sent ambassadors to do homage. Yet his royal Majesty has extended his grace to me, has sought me out in his mercy and has sent you, his ambassadors, to me. I thank God for this. I shall listen some other time to the secret message which you have. And now is the occasion for you to sup with me.' The King sat down and bade the ambassadors be seated; he made Mikhail sit next to him on his left, and he made his uncle Prince Vakhtan sit below Mikhail; Mikhail did not want to sit above Prince Vakhtan, and the king bade him sit down against his will. The king bade dyak Andrey sit below Prince Vakhtan; and below Andrey, in another row, sat the feudal Prince Irakli and Prince Usein,[1] and Prince Aristov of Soni and other noblemen and *aznaurs*; and on the opposite side, on the king's right, sat his son Prince Lev Varsap and the Catholicos Dementi, whom they call patriarch; below him sat the Arch-

---

[1] 'The feudal Prince Irakli' was a son of Archil, brother of Wakhtang Prince of Mukhrani (see further Commentary 68). The reference to Usein remains obscure. It is a Moslem name (Husein): he was probably a brother of Irakli, possibly brought up as a Moslem after his father, Archil, had been sent to Persia in 1566 (cf. Brosset, Genealogical Tree, in *HG*, Vol. II/i, p. 626).

bishops and the bishops and Prince Alexander of the Mereli land; and *aznaurs* sat below him. And the ambassadors supped with the king.

On the following day the king bade the ambassadors attend upon him on the Sovereign's secret affairs; he sent to fetch them the persons who had been sent the first day; the ambas- (498) sadors' arrival at the royal court, and their reception were as on the previous occasion. The king met the ambassadors in the second tent, and sent away his men. There remained the king's uncle Prince Vakhtan, and Prince Irakli and Prince Aristov and the members of the king's entourage, Usein-bek, Aslamaz and Archbishop Theodosius. Mikhail Ignatyevich delivered the speech according to his instructions; having heard it, the king said that his royal Majesty's letter should be read out, and that the interpreters might explain it to him. Andrey read out the Sovereign's letter; Archbishop Theodosius explained it to the king in Kartlian after the translator Svoyetin Kamenev had interpreted it to the Archbishop in Greek. Having heard the letter, King Yuri said: 'What is written in the letter is the same affair as the one which you, ambassador Mikhail Ignatyevich, have conveyed orally on the great Sovereign's behalf. Having heard such a great and most glorious affair, it is fit for us to rejoice. Tomorrow, if God grants, we shall assemble all the clergy, the Catholicos, and the Archbishops, and the bishops, and our nobles and the members of our entourage; we shall think the matter over, and shall give you our answer on another occasion.[1] Now you will sup with me.' The king sat down and bade the ambassadors sit as on the previous occasion. And the ambassadors supped with the king. The king then invited himself to sup with Mikhail Ignatyevich, and was entertained to supper by Mikhail on the following day.

On coming to the land of Kartli, the ambassadors enquired

---

[1] It is interesting to note this comparatively representative composition of the King's Council.

from many of the king's officials and courtiers about the looks and the stature and the intelligence of Princess Helen, and about her age. They all praised the princess saying that she was very beautiful and not of small stature and that she was ten years old.

On the 2nd of May King Yuri sent to the ambassadors' camp Archbishop Theodosius, Prince Aristov of Soni and Aslamaz, who said in the king's name: 'The name of your great Sovereign Tsar is renowned in all kingdoms, for being the Sovereign of such great realms. Until now neither he nor previous Russian sovereigns had sent messages either to my great grandfather, or to my grandfather, or to my father; nor did our ambassadors ever go to the sovereigns of your country. Now the great Sovereign has extended his grace to me, has sought me out and has sent you, his ambassadors; he desires to make me a kinsman of his and to defend me and all my land from my enemies, and is asking for my daughter as bride for his son Prince Fedor. In this matter I have placed my trust in God and in the Sovereign's will: my head, and my house, and my children and all my realm stand before God and before the Sovereign. I expect that the great Sovereign knows how my grandfather and my father defended this land and the Christian faith from the Turks and the Kizilbashes.[1] My father gave his head for this – he is now held prisoner by the Turk, and my children are with him.[2]

[1] The grandfather of Giorgi X was Luarsab I, 1534/5–1557; his father was Simon I, 1557–69 and 1578–99. For discussion of the chronology of the reign of Luarsab I, see article by A. Gugushvili, 'The chronological-genealogical table of the Kings of Georgia' in *Georgica* (Vol. 1, Nos. 2–3, p. 133, n. 2). Luarsab I was the son of David VIII, who retired to a monastery about 1526. David was succeeded, first, by his brother Giorgi IX, who also entered a monastery, 1534/5 (cf. Brosset, *HG*, Vol. II/i, Genealogical Tree, p. 626; also Berdzenishvili, *Istoriya Gruzii*, Vol. I, p. 320, n. 1).

[2] In 1605 Giorgi's father Simon remained a prisoner in *Yedi Kule*, the Ottoman state prison called the Seven Towers forming part of the outer walls of Istanbul to the west of the Adrianople Gate. In an effort to arrange his ransom, Giorgi had sent a delegation of nobles to Istanbul, including his younger son David, who may have been proposed as a

Now I remain by the tombs of my ancestors, for the sake of the (499)
Christian faith, and I oppose the Moslems to the best of my
ability. Strong enemies, the Turk and the Kizilbash, neighbour
upon our realm. And before now we sometimes opposed them,
and sometimes made our submission and sent presents. But
now, when I shall carry out his royal Majesty's command and
shall be in his royal grace, I shall secede from them and shall
be their enemy. These enemies, on hearing about it, will attack
me and my land forthwith. Let us know your opinion: what
is to be done?'

The ambassadors Mikhail Ignatyevich and dyak Andrey
told them that King Yuri was afraid of the Turk and the
Kizilbash, but should give the matter no thought. 'Should the
great thing be accomplished – after King Yuri has shown us his
daughter Princess Helen and she has proved suitable for his
royal Majesty, the king lets her go with us, and God permits
her to become the wife of our great Sovereign's son – his royal
Majesty will raise his armies in defence of King Yuri and will
not abandon him to any of his enemies. The Kizilbash Shah is
the friend and the brother of our great Sovereign; he would not
act contrary to any message that our Sovereign might send him.
So the king should not be in doubt about this.'

The Archbishop, Aristov and Aslamaz went to the king.
They returned to the ambassadors within the hour and said:
'We have informed the king of what we had heard from you
and the king rejoices at it. He bade us say to you: "What you

hostage for his grandfather; cf. *Chronique Géorgienne*, p. 26, where it is
indicated that the boy was retained a prisoner after his father's death;
also for Wakhusht's account, Brosset (*HG*, Vol. ii/i, p. 42 and n. 6);
and ibid., p. 422, for Arakel of Tabriz's ref. to the boy's death. Simon was
still alive in the Seven Towers in 1606 – evidently enjoying some ameni-
ties, since Iskander Munshi gives a curious account of an attempt to open
peace negotiations between Istanbul and Isfahan through Simon's
Georgian mistress Gulchareh; she had been in the confidence of Sultan
Mehmet III's mother, the Venetian Safiye, and had access to the new Grand
Vizier, Dervish Pasha (cf. Brosset, ibid., p. 470).

have said about his royal Majesty's compassion and assistance against the Moslems is a great mercy on the part of the Sovereign towards us. But our realm is far away from your great Sovereign, and his Majesty's help is far away. Should my enemies now hear that I, King Yuri, have come under your great Sovereign's hand and have done according to his Majesty's wish, they will take up arms against me. Even though the Moslem sovereigns pretend to some that they are their friends, one should not believe them. You yourselves know what has befallen King Alexander and his son Prince Yuri. You should now leave in our realm some 500 *streltsy* with muskets so that I need not fear my enemies; if you do not leave *streltsy* to protect me, I shall be unable to attend to the Sovereign's affair." '

Mikhail Ignatyevich and Andrey spoke at length and used all arguments that the king should send messengers to petition the Sovereign about the troops; since they were altogether unable to comply with his request.

The Archbishop and his assistants went to the king. On their return they said: 'Unless you now leave the Sovereign's men to protect him, King Yuri does not want to attend to any of the Sovereign's affairs, for fear of his enemies: his enemies are near while the Sovereign's help is far away.'

(500)   The ambassadors held council among themselves: If they did not leave any of the Sovereign's men with King Yuri, none of the Sovereign's affairs would be done. And they took for comparison the fact that the Sovereign's commanders on the Terek send in the winter 500 and 600 *streltsy* to the Cherkess princes and murzas in Kabarda who serve the Sovereign to defend them from their enemies, and that *streltsy* from Astarakhan, too, are sent to the trans-Volga Nogays for their protection; furthermore, it was King Yuri's intention to come under the Sovereign's hand, together with the whole of the lands of Kartli and Soni.

488

So they told the Archbishop and the king's counsellors: 'If King Yuri carries out the wish of our great Sovereign Tsar and shows his daughter Princess Helen to us; if she is suitable and the king lets her go with us; if he chooses a suitable prince and sends him, too, to our great Sovereign; and if he swears on the cross that he, King Yuri, together with the whole land of Kartli will remain under his royal Majesty's hand without seceding – we shall forthwith write to the royal Majesty's commanders on the Terek asking them to send some 200 *streltsy*, and we shall leave them with King Yuri to protect him.'

The Archbishop and his comrades went to the king; they returned within the hour and said: 'The king has thought about it and has decided that he will give his daughter Princess Helen to the great Sovereign Tsar. And he has given her already, once he has given his word. However, it is impossible to let her go with you now. You yourselves know the age at which a maiden can be given in marriage in accordance with the rules of the Holy Fathers: she has not reached that age yet. She must be properly fitted out for the journey, so that she should not be exposed to shame but be sent off to the great Sovereign with honour, and not shamed in the eyes of foreign rulers.'

The ambassadors said that if the princess was still not of age, the happy event would not take place then. 'The journey to our great Sovereign takes about half a year, and she will spend another half year at the Sovereign's court, living with the great sovereign queen and great Princess Marya Grigoryevna of all Russia.[1] She will get used to the Sovereign's customs and to

---

[1] Boris Godunov had married the daughter of Grigori Malyuta Skuratov-Belski, a man of low rank who was raised to power by Ivan IV in the days of the Oprichnina. Malyuta was known for his bravery, ruthlessness and callous cruelty. William Parry, writing in 1600, gives an unattractive picture of the Tsaritsa Marya Grigoryevna: 'Next him (Tsar Boris) came the Queen, supported on either side by two old ladies; her face was thickly plastered with painting, as were the other ladies, according to the

the Russian language – and then it will be time. The king should not hold back because of that. As to fitting her out for an early start, we shall give 200 *tyumen* and more.' And in their country one *tyumen* is worth six rubles.[1] They also said that all kinds of attire would be sent by the Sovereign to the princess when she was on her way. In accordance with the Sovereign's instructions the ambassadors added: 'Is it a good thing for sovereigns in these parts to give their children to infidel rulers and destroy them body and soul? The Moslem potentates take them for nothing. Even now the Kizilbash Shah has taken King Alexander's grand-daughter – the daughter of King David – as well as the Guriel's daughter.[2] After dishonouring them, he has sent them away. Whereas his royal Majesty wants to extend (501) his grace to King Yuri, and to give the king's daughter in marriage to his own son, the great Sovereign Prince Fedor Borisovich of all Russia, so as to save the king's realm from the Moslems, and so that the true Christian faith should be firmly established in their Iberian land.'

The Archbishop and the king's counsellors said to the ambassadors: 'Our sovereigns give their children to the Moslems because they are forced to do so for the sake of their realms.

custom of the country; her body very gross, her eyes hollow and far into her head', cited from Ross, *Anthony Sherley*, p. 133.

Marya Grigoryevna, together with her son, Fedor Borisovich, was murdered on 10 June 1605, after Moscow had gone over to the False Dmitri. (On the same day Tatishchev had reached Terki on his return journey from Kartli.) For further detail, see Allen, 'The Georgian marriage projects of Boris Godunov' in *OSP*, Vol. XII, 1965.

[1] *Tyumen*: here the original Turkish pronunciation of the Persian unit of coinage *tuman*. About 1600 Raphael du Mans gives the value of the *tuman* as 40 French francs. Sir Thomas Herbert, 1630, and Fryer (1677) give the value as £3 6s. 8d. in English money (cf. article by Barthold in *EI*, Ist ed. under *tuman*).

[2] See Chap. 13, p. 476, n. 1 above for the daughter of King David of Kakheti. For the daughter of the Gurieli, whom Brosset assumes to have been Giorgi II, died 1600, see Brosset (*EC/BHP*, Vol. II, Nos. 19–21, col. 329, n. 112). Brosset finds that the statement of the ambassadors must have been based on sound information.

Had they not been forced to do it, they would not have behaved in this way.'

The ambassadors replied: 'King Alexander gave his son Constantine to the Shah. And what has befallen him? That son of his came and cut his head off. We look upon it as a sign given by God to the Christians, that Christian sovereigns in these parts should seek help from the great Christian sovereigns and not from Moslem rulers.'

Archbishop Theodosius, Prince Aristov and Aslamaz went back to the king. When they returned they said: 'The king bade us reply to you: How can he send his daughter with you now, without knowing the road or your great Sovereign's realm, since no man from this land, except for Archbishop Theodosius, has visited your great Sovereign? The king has decided that he will show his daughter Princess Helen to you; and having seen her you will report to your Sovereign. The king will send his ambassadors to your great Sovereign along with you; they will see him, the great Sovereign, and will hear his gracious words from his Majesty's own mouth. And when, in the future, the Sovereign sends messengers to the king to fetch his daughter, the king will send her off with honour, as befits the children of monarchs. It is altogether impossible to send her now, for such is not the custom in these parts. Even if the king brings the great Sovereign's grief and wrath upon himself, he will not change local customs, and will not send his daughter without honours with the first ambassadors as if she were a captive girl.'

The ambassadors replied: 'King Yuri wrote to us in the Georgian land, and he sent us an oral message by the interpreters, asking us to come to him when we had finished our affairs with King Alexander; he said that he had read what his royal Majesty our Sovereign desires, and that he would carry out the Sovereign's will. Following the king's letter and message, and relying upon them, we wrote to our great

Sovereign and we gave orders for a large body of troops to be sent to the gorges to meet us. We are expecting that the great Sovereign will send people with his royal bounty to meet the princess on the Terek and in Astarakhan, and that many troops will be sent to meet her. The Sovereign will be put to great expense thereby. Yet the king has not kept the promise he gave us in his letter, and does not now allow his daughter to leave with us. We do not know what we are to believe in the future.'

The Archbishop and his comrades said that the king was keeping the promise which he had given in his letter, adding: 'He has not disobeyed your great Sovereign's command and will carry out his royal wish. He will show his daughter to (502) you now. Should she, God grant, be found suitable in accordance with his royal Majesty's instructions, the king will send her to the Sovereign at a later date. But as for your wanting to take her now, that is altogether out of the question.'

The ambassadors argued with them in every way firmly, for several days, in accordance with their instructions, and as they themselves thought best, and they recalled the Sovereign's graciousness towards King Alexander and the Georgian land – but they were unable to persuade them.

The Kartlians said to the ambassadors: 'Your great Sovereign is renowned throughout the world, and we truly know about his royal mercy towards the Georgian king Alexander and his land, and about the protection accorded to him against the Kumyks. King Yuri is the sovereign in his realm and he is the first among sovereigns in these parts. He wants to send his daughter to the great Sovereign with honour; he will send her with his uncle Prince Vakhtan, and Catholicos Dementi and men of rank and noblewomen and maidens, the daughters of the foremost *aznaurs*. The king has given his word that he will send his daughter to the great Sovereign at a later date and he will keep the promise. He will even swear to it

on the cross. But as for the king letting his daughter go now –
that is altogether impossible.'

Mikhail Ignatyevich and Andrey also talked to them about
the other affair – about the prince. 'Our great Sovereign Tsar
has written to King Yuri, and he has sent an oral message by me,
Mikhalko, also to choose in his realm a prince of his blood for
our great Sovereign's daughter Princess Xenia:[1] a prince who
would be suitable for such a great matter. Having shown him to
us, the king should let him go to his royal Majesty. He should
thereby show his service to and love for the great Sovereign.'

Archbishop Theodosius, Prince Aristov and Aslamaz said
that they had no instructions about it from the king and that
they would report to him.

On the 4th of May the Archbishop and the king's counsellors Usein-bek and Aslamaz visited the ambassadors and said:
'What you told us yesterday about the prince, we have reported
to the king who bade us tell you: "The great Sovereign Tsar
has sent you to me about my daughter. And I am not refusing
the great Sovereign my daughter. I shall send her later, in
accordance with his royal Majesty's will. But as regards the
prince, you were sent to King Alexander to ask for King
David's son. King Alexander and his son Yuri did not give you
this son of David, but sent him away to the Shah; in that they
were disloyal towards the Sovereign. Although the great
Sovereign has written in his letter to me about the prince, and
although you told me about it orally – yet, I have not a prince
for such a great matter. My son Asey[2] is young and will not be   (503)
suitable because, if God grants, my daughter will marry his

---

[1] For Boris Godunov's daughter Xenia (Kseniya) see Commentary 69.

[2] 'My son Asey': there is no other record of Giorgi having had a son
named Asey (= G. Yese). Brosset (*EC/BHP/* Vol. II, Nos. 19–21, col.
329) has simply read the name as Luarsab. There may be some confusion
here with the name of Yuri of Kakheti's son Yese, see above, Chap. 12,
pp. 458 and 459, n. 1. The second son of the Kartlian King was David who
was with his grandfather Simon in Istanbul, cf. p. 486, n. 2 above.

royal Majesty's son. And as for my uncle Vakhtan's son, he is younger than mine – you can see it yourselves; and he, also, will not be suitable. There is also a foreigner living with me from the Mereli land, Pankrati's son whose name is Alexander: he lives as hostage with me, as security for the Mereli king Yuri.[1] He will not be suitable, either. Myself I know that a goodly prince is needed for such a great matter." '

And the ambassadors replied: 'Our great Sovereign Tsar sent us to King Alexander for King David's son, and he commanded us to inspect him; if he looked suitable we were to talk about him. But King Alexander and his son Yuri were disloyal towards the Sovereign and sent David's son away to the Shah; you yourselves know what has befallen them because of their disloyalty. King Constantine has told us that, if King David's son is needed, he would take him from the Shah and would let him go to his royal Majesty. But we did not want it because he is already a servant of the Shah. Nor would he be suitable for such a great matter, because he is not good-looking and is young. Our great Sovereign wrote in his letter to King Yuri and sent him an oral message that, if he desires his royal Majesty's bounty and love, he should select a prince of his blood and should show him to us; and, if the prince proves suitable, he should let him go with us.'

The ambassadors had seen Prince Alexander at King Yuri's court. He is ordinary-looking, his face is pitted with pock-marks, his eyes are small and, in addition, he is weak.[1] They found out that the king had two princes closely related to him: Vakhtan's sons Teymuras and Keykhosrov.[2] Vakhtan was the son of Pankrati who had been king of the Kartlian land, where Yuri is now king. Pankrati's younger brother was called David, and David's son was Varsap, and Varsap's son was King Yuri's father Simon. After Pankrati his younger brother David

___

[1] For this Alexander (of Imereti), see Chap. 13, p. 480, n. 1.
[2] For the King's view on these princes, see Commentary 68.

13. 'Levend-oghlu (= Alexander II of Kakheti), *r.*
and Lala Mustafa Pasha', *l.*
From the *Sheja'atname* of Asafi, MS. TY 6043, fol. 19*v.* of Istanbul University Library.

ascended the throne, and after David it was his son Varsap, and after Varsap it was Simon. Pankrati's son Vakhtan was given a fief, and Prince Irakli and Vakhtan's sons Teymuras and Khozdroy now live in the fief. Irakli is their cousin: their fathers were brothers; and Irakli's sister was the wife of King Alexander's son King David.[1] The ambassadors were told that Vakhtan's younger son Khozdroy was very good-looking, intelligent and young.

[1] The Pankrati of our text was a son of Constantine III (according to the numeration of Brosset, *HG*, II/i, Genealogical Trees, p. 626), who died 1505. Gugushvili, *Georgica*, I, Nos. 2–3, p. 127, following Javakhishvili, *Kartlis eris istoria*, IV (1924 ed.), part i, pp. 209–11, numbers Constantine as the second of his name. Brosset's Genealogical Tree indicates Constantine as son of Giorgi VIII, died 1469, but in *Sakartvelos Sidzveleni*, II, p. 40, there is published a seal which names Constantine and his son Bagrat (Pankrati) reigning in 1468; with the indication, p. 41, that Constantine was the son of Dmitri, a brother of Wakhtang IV and Giorgi VIII; this Dmitri had died in 1452. Bagrat received the appanage of Mukhrani in 1512 and became a monk in 1529, under the name of Barnabas. His brother, David VIII, had already entered a monastery, under the name of Damiane, in 1526; and Giorgi IX went the same way, under the name of Gerasime, in 1534. There was a fourth brother, Melchisedek, who was Catholicos, 1524–9. Although David was married three times, and Bagrat had numerous children, all these four brothers seem to have had a strong devotional bent. Their successor as King of Kartli was Luarsab I (the 'Varsap' of our text) – a man of different calibre, 'brave and strong and daring to attack . . . who would never submit either to the Sultan or the Qaen' (Khan) (cf. Allen, *HGP*, pp. 139–40; Manvelishvili, pp. 276–81). For discussion of the obscure point as to whether Bagrat was in fact senior in age to David VIII, see Brosset, (*EC/BHP/* Vol. II, col. 330, n. 2); also Gugushvili (*Georgica*, I, Nos. 2–3, p. 133, n. 2). According to the statement of the Russian ambassadors, primed perhaps by Prince Aristov, partisan of the Mukhranian princes, it would appear that such was the case – or at least that their claim was strong enough to prove disturbing to Giorgi X (cf. p. 486, n. 1 above and Commentary 68).

Bagrat of Mukhrani had a son Archil (sent a prisoner to Shiraz in 1569, and died 1582 – Brosset, *HG*, II/i, pp. 33, 34, 37 and n. 6) who was the father of the Prince Irakli mentioned in our text (cf. p. 484, n. 1 above). Ketevan, queen of David of Kakheti, was not Irakli's sister but his first cousin, her father being a brother of Archil, Ashotan who was killed in battle against the Pshavs in 1561 (Brosset, ibid., p. 32).

The ambassadors said to Archbishop Theodosius and to the King's counsellors: 'Our great Sovereign has written to King Yuri about the prince and has sent him an oral message, and he left the choice to him. We now know that the king has among (504) his relatives other princes in addition to Alexander. If King Yuri desires the Tsar's bounty and love, he will attend to the matter in accordance with the Sovereign's letter and message. If King Yuri does not carry out the Tsar's will and does not send with us a prince who would be suitable for such a great affair, and his royal Majesty learns that the king has princes whom he did not allow to go, King Yuri's disloyalty and lack of love will become manifest to our great Sovereign, and he will not experience the Sovereign's mercy in the future. We were expecting that King Yuri and the whole Kartlian land would rejoice at the fact that God has taken care of them and that such a great Sovereign has sought them out in his royal mercy, to the extent of wanting to become kin to King Yuri. And you seem to be putting us off.'

The Archbishop and his comrades said: 'The king has in mind that there are princes among his kin, the sons of Prince Vakhtan. The elder brother is plain-looking, but the younger brother Khozdroy is very good-looking and intelligent. However, the king is suspicious of him: once in the great Sovereign's grace, he may seek to deprive the king of his realm.'[1]

The ambassadors . . . argued that the king should not entertain such a thought. 'Should that prince be good-looking and suitable for such a great matter and the king let him go with us, he would be performing an act of love towards his royal Majesty, as if he had sent his own son to the great Sovereign. And should God grant that his royal Majesty's daughter marries him, our great Sovereign will not let him go anywhere but will establish him in his realm in accordance with his royal standing.

[1] 'The younger brother Khozdroy': this is Keykhosrov or Kay Khusrau, cf. p. 494, n. 2 above and Commentary 68.

Our great Sovereign will extend his royal mercy and love towards King Yuri, as towards his own kin . . .'

Archbishop Theodosius and the king's counsellors replied: 'When our enemies learn that King Yuri is in receipt of your Sovereign's bounty, and intends to give his daughter in marriage to your great Sovereign's son and has sent a prince from among his kin to your great Sovereign, these enemies will take up arms against him forthwith. Your Sovereign's help will not come quickly, and then what is the king to do against his enemies?' And they spoke to the ambassadors about *streltsy*, and said that before they leave the land of Soni they should provide *streltsy* to protect the king from his enemies.

The ambassadors Mikhail Ignatyevich and dyak Andrey said: 'If the king does not let his daughter go with us to our great Sovereign now, let him show her to us. Let him also show us the princes whom he has among his kin: and let him give leave to whoever is suitable according to our great Sovereign's (505) command to travel with us. Having seen them, we shall then start talking about *streltsy*. You come to us and do a lot of talking, but as for the princess – we have not yet even seen her. It is all empty talk.'

Archbishop Theodosius and his comrades said that they would report the ambassadors' words to the king.

On the 5th of May the Archbishop and the king's counsellors Usein-bek and Aslamaz came to the ambassadors and said: 'The king bade us say to you: ". . . Since the great Sovereign has entrusted such a great matter to me, I hold his command on my head.[1] My daughter will be suitable in the eyes of God and in the Sovereign's eyes. If God grants I shall send her to the great Sovereign at a later date. I have been thinking about the prince. My own son is young and, furthermore, he will be

---

[1] This is a literal translation of the Ottoman Turkish expression *baş üstüne*, a polite way of acknowledging the instructions of a superior.

497

unsuitable if my daughter is to be married to his royal Majesty's son. My kinsman, my uncle Vakhtan's son, is even younger than my son, and he also will be unsuitable.[1] There is also a foreign prince, called Alexander, living with me; he is from the Mereli land. I know myself that he is not fit for such a great matter. In addition to them I have among my kin the princes Teymuras and Khozdroy, two brothers, the sons of Vakhtan, who are related to me through my grandfather. And I believe that the younger, Prince Khozdroy, will prove suitable. In the army he is my right hand, and he is now opposing the enemy with an army in my stead. I shall have them fetched and show them to you. And if one of them is suitable, I shall let him go to the Sovereign for the sake of his royal Majesty's love. The only point is that he should not be sent to such a great Sovereign in a way that would expose him to shame: he must be equipped and supplied with everything." '

Mikhail Ignatyevich and Andrey said: 'The king is manifesting his service and love towards our great Sovereign by attending to his Majesty's affairs, by being willing to show us the princes who are his kin, and by intending to send with us the one who suits our great Sovereign. His royal Majesty will extend his royal grace and love to him for this. And when that prince comes to live with our great Sovereign, it will be an honour to King Yuri, it will enhance his prestige and will frighten his enemies. As regards your remarks about the preparations and the equipage for the prince, the king should send him off with honour and should supply him with everything. We, too, shall equip him for the journey with whatever (506) we happen to have . . . When – if God grants – we see him, we shall talk about it.'

On the 6th of May Archbishop Theodosius and the king's counsellors Usein-bek and Aslamaz came to the ambassadors and said: '. . . King Yuri will show his daughter to you . . . and

---

[1] Presumably Prince Paata ('Potata'): see p. 482, n. 5 above.

if she is suitable he will send her to the great Sovereign at a later date. He will also show you the prince about whom we have told you. He will then dismiss you and send his own ambassadors along with you. And you will tell his royal Majesty about the princess and the prince. If the Sovereign finds them suitable, he can send messengers to the king about it at a later date. The king will then send his daughter Princess Helen and Prince Khozdroy.'

The ambassadors replied: 'Our great Sovereign has sought King Yuri out with his great royal grace of which the king had not even entertained a thought. He wants to enter into kinship with the king. Many great sovereigns – his brother Caesar Maximilian, and the French king, and the Danish king and the Polish king – send messengers entreating to enter into kinship with our great Sovereign. But, for the sake of the true Christian faith, his royal Majesty preferred to enter into kinship with King Yuri rather than with one of those great sovereigns.[1] You are now proposing to put the matter off. This cannot be done. Our great Sovereign has many princes; and his royal Majesty will on no account let the year go by without giving his daughter in marriage ... You yourselves have told us that King Yuri wants to send Prince Khozdroy with us; and now you are telling us other things on the king's behalf, to which it is not proper even to listen.'

The Archbishop and his comrades told the ambassadors that the prince was the king's right hand and was fighting the enemy in the king's place. 'Should the king let him go now, and (507) should the Sovereign's help not come to us quickly' they said 'our enemies will learn about it and will take up arms against us, and will lay our land waste and will carry our women and

[1] 'Caesar Maximilian': for the Tsar's efforts to find a husband for the Grand Duchess Xenia, see Commentary 69. The Archduke Maximilian was a brother of Emperor Rudolph – whose interest in the Russian succession had been marked before the death of Tsar Fedor Ivanovich (see Chap. 9, p. 409, n. 2 above). The Archduke died in 1619.

children off into captivity. You have yourselves seen what befell King Alexander.'

And the ambassadors said to them: 'When we have seen the prince – and he proves suitable for his royal Majesty – we shall talk about what is to be done.'

CHAPTER 15

DISASTER ON THE TEREK

ON the same day, May 6th, King Yuri bade the ambassadors attend upon him. He met them in the courtyard in front of his tent. With him were his uncle Prince Vakhtan and Prince Khozdroy, about whom the ambassadors had been told. After greeting the ambassadors the king said: 'This is Prince Khozdroy about whom I sent word to you. He is my kinsman, not distantly related; my mother brought him up, we have grown up together, and he is like a brother to me.'

The ambassadors looked the prince over. He was not small in stature; his body was straight and he was of comely looks; his face was very dark and smooth, his eyes brown and not small; the nose was thin and somewhat hooked; the hair was chestnut and the moustache was not big. He shaved his beard. He was capable and intelligent in conversation; his speech was clear and he knew Turkish well. He was of the Christian faith of the Greek rite, and was literate in Georgian. He was 23 years old.

That day the ambassadors ate with the king; and Prince Khozdroy was seated on the king's right, next to the king's son Lev Varsap.

On the following day again the king sent to the ambassadors Archbishop Theodosius and his counsellors Prince Usein and Aslamaz, who said on the king's behalf: 'You have seen the prince. How have you found him? Is he suitable for his royal Majesty or not?'

And the ambassadors Mikhail Ignatyevich and Andrey said: 'We cannot disparage the prince. He is good looking but not outstanding. We do not dare say whether he is suitable for such

a great matter. Let the king send him to our great Sovereign –
and then let the will of God and of the Sovereign be done. That
would be an act of love by King Yuri towards his royal
Majesty. If the prince suits our great Sovereign, King Yuri will
enjoy the Tsar's bounty and great love for it; and if he does not
fit in with his royal Majesty's idea, and King Yuri requires
him back here, our great Sovereign will extend his royal
bounty to him and will dismiss him.'

The Archbishop and the king's counsellors said to the
ambassadors: 'The king is not holding him back, but will let
him go to the great Sovereign. But the king needs his royal
Majesty's troops quickly, to defend him from his enemies; and
he also needs the wherewithal to equip the prince and send him
(508) off. So you should leave at least 300 *streltsy* here with the king
and give whatever is suitable for equipping the prince.'

The ambassadors Mikhail Ignatyevich and dyak Andrey
said: 'We spoke about the *streltsy*. It was our intention to
leave them so long as the king sent his daughter with us. But
the king is not sending his daughter with us now. Let the King
send his ambassadors to our great Sovereign to petition him
about fighting men.' And they used all sorts of arguments about
the troops so as not to leave them. But they could not persuade
the royal counsellors in any way, because the king did not want
to send the prince if the troops were not left behind. And the
ambassadors said, 'We are taking it upon our own heads and
are acting outside the Sovereign's instructions by now leaving
with King Yuri 150 *streltsy* to defend him. The king should
give orders that they be fed; he should have them under his
protection and keep them by him. He should not send them
against the Turkish towns; and he should not begin war on the
Turk before he gets the Sovereign's command. For equipping
the prince we shall give the king fifty *tyumen* worth of sables
from our own funds.'

The Archbishop and the king's counsellors said at length

14. A Turkish archer. After Castelli.

that that number of men was too small, and that a greater
number should be left. And they also told the ambassadors
that there were mountaineers, known as Osintsy between the
Cherkess lands and the lands of King Yuri. There are some
200 of them in all. These people oppressed the Kartlians; they
raided them stealthily, killing and plundering. The counsellors
asked that the Sovereign's commanders should send troops
against those people from the Terek and should issue orders
to the Cherkesses to march against them. As soon as that part
was cleared, there would be a direct and comfortable road from
their Kartlian land to the Sovereign's patrimony, the Kabardan
land.[1]

Mikhail Ignatyevich and Andrey told the Archbishop and the
king's counsellors that when, if God granted, they came to the
Terek they would tell the Sovereign's commanders to send
troops against the Osintsy and to order the Cherkess Aytek
murza to take the field against them. They said about the
streltsy that it was not possible to leave a greater number with
the king.

These Osintsy had been subject to the Cherkess Aytek
murza, but they had seceded from him. And, when the ambassadors were on their way to the Georgian land, Aytek murza
spoke to them about giving him troops to fight these men; he
said that because of them the Sovereign's men travelling to the

---

[1] Osintsy: Georgian *Owsni*, plur. of *Owsi* = Os; Old Russian *Yasi*;
Modern Russian *Osetiny*, which incorporates the Georgian locative
suffix – *eti*. These people call themselves *Iron*. This is the earliest reference
in the Russian ambassadors' reports to Os elements in the immediate
neighbourhood of the Daryal Pass. Brosset (*EC/BHP*, Vol. II, Nos.
19–21, col. 331, n. 117) proposed a reading of 'two hundred families'
as it is evident that it was not always the same individuals who were
making the raids into Georgia and 150 *streltsy* would have been more than
adequate to deal with two hundred thieves. Settlements of Os south of
the Daryal were fairly widespread at the end of the sixteenth century and,
indeed, some of the noble families in Mountain Georgia claimed Os
(Alanic) descent (cf. Introduction, Section 7 and Commentary 19).

Georgian land across mount Shat suffered casualties. He added that it was possible to defeat them with the help of the Cherkesses, without needing many troops.

The ambassadors agreed with the Archbishop and with the king's counsellors to leave 150 foot *streltsy* with King Yuri and to hand them over in the land of Soni, the king under- (509) taking to feed them with his supplies. It was also agreed that the ambassadors would give fifty *tyumen* worth of sables for fitting out the prince. In their country one *tyumen* is worth six rubles.[1]

On the 8th of May King Yuri bade the ambassadors attend upon him, and the king's counsellors said that they were to visit the queens – the king's mother and his wife – and see the king's daughter Princess Helen. And the king's counsellors said to the ambassadors: 'It is a custom in these realms that when a sovereign asks another sovereign for his daughter's hand and sends his counsellors to view her, he sends with them gifts for the king, and for the queen and for the princess. Have you presents with you from his royal Majesty for the king's mother and for the queen and for Princess Helen? Even if no presents have been sent, you should not dishonour the queens and the princess thereby. According to our customs you cannot view the king's daughter without bringing the Sovereign's gracious presents for her mother and for herself.'

The ambassadors told them that the Sovereign had sent as presents for the king's mother and for his queen and for the princess sables in accordance with their royal rank. They took along forty sables each for them: for the queen's mother the forty sables which the Sovereign had sent for Prince Vakhtan; for the king's queen the forty sables worth forty rubles from

[1] For *tyumen* or *tuman*, see Chap. 14, p. 490, n. 1 above. The text indicates that one *tuman* was regarded as equal to six rubles in Georgia in 1605. The value of the silver ruble was declining during this period, as was the Turkish *asper*, a result of the flooding of the West European market with silver from the Spanish Indies.

the reserve sent with the ambassadors; and for the princess the forty sables sent for King David's queen. David's queen had been given forty from the reserve.

The ambassadors attended upon King Yuri in the queen's apartments; and the king showed Princess Helen to them. The princess was seated on a cushion embroidered with pearls, and golden carpets were spread. She was wearing an outer robe of gold-embroidered velvet, trimmed with lace, and underneath she had a robe of cloth of gold, girt like a *feryaẓ*.[1] On her head she was wearing a hat with a wide crown, made of plain purple velvet, like that for kerchiefs,[2] embroidered with pearls and precious stones. The princess's grandmother, King Yuri's mother Queen Tomar,[3] sat next to the princess on her right,

[1] *Feryaẓ*: From a Greek word meaning garment or frock. The name given to a long-sleeved, collarless coat worn by men and to a long, sleeveless garment with a belt worn by women. Dahl, *Tolkovy slovar*, suggests that a woman's *feryaẓ* was not unlike the sarafan, the traditional dress of Russian peasant women. For a Georgian lady wearing the *feryaẓ* (nineteenth century), see Baddeley (*RFC*, Vol. II, engraving opposite p. 12).

[2] By emendation of Belokurov's *uruẓ* to *ubrus*, kerchief, veil, embroidered cloth worn over the forehead (Dahl, *Tolkovy Slovar*). Kotoshikhin reports that *ubrusy* figured among items supplied to the Tsaritsa's workshop from two hamlets assigned to it. It was also customary for brides to make to the Tsaritsa and princesses gifts of 'taffeta *ubrusy* embroidered with gold and silver threads and pearls' (Kotoshikhin, pp. 117, 153).

[3] Here Tatishchev makes one of his rare slips. Tomar or Tamar was the name of Giorgi's queen. His mother, the queen of Simon I, was named Nestan Darejan; she was daughter of Levan of Kakheti by a daughter of the Shevkal Kara Musal. She was therefore a half-sister of Alexander of Kakheti who was borne by Tinatin, daughter of Mamia II Gurieli (Brosset, *HG*, Vol. II/i, pp. 26 and 634). Tomar had suffered at the hands of her half-brother whom she was now mourning. After Simon had been sent a prisoner to Persia in 1569, her private estates had been pillaged by Bardzim Amilakhori, father of Alexander's wife (cf. Brosset, *HG*, Vol. II/i, p. 34); and in 1580, following Simon's return to Georgia and his defeat by Alexander at Dighwam, the latter had ridden off after the battle with his half-sister's drawers on the point of a lance (ibid., p. 37); see also Allen (*HGP*, pp. 153, 157).

and her mother, King Yuri's queen,[1] was seated on her left; they were wearing outer robes of plain black velvet. And the king's counsellors told the ambassadors that the king's mother was in sorrow on account of King Simon's being held in captivity, and that her black clothes were for the death of her brother, King Alexander; and they also said that King Yuri's queen was wearing black for the same reason.

Mikhail Ignatyevich delivered the Sovereign's gracious bounty of forty sables for each one of them; and they made obeisance for it. The king bade the princess get up, and he removed her hat and her outer robe, and measured the princess with a rod, and gave the measure to the ambassadors. That measure was shorter than the one sent by the Sovereign, by a little under half a *vershok*,[2] or even less than that.

The princess is comely in appearance but not exceptionally beautiful; her face is white, but she whitens it, and her colour-
(510) ing is not remarkable; her eyes are black; the nose is not big; her hair is dyed red, but it is said to be black.[3] The princess's body is straight but thin, since she is young. King Yuri said

[1] 'King Yuri's queen' was in fact Tomar or Tamar (alternatively called Mariam) cf. Brosset, *HG*, Vol. II/i, Genealogical Trees, pp. 626 and 647. She was daughter of Giorgi I Lipartiani, lord of vast estates in Mingrelia to the west of the river Rioni. When her youthful son Luarsab became king, following the death of Giorgi X from a bee-sting at Mejudis-khevi, on 7 Nov. 1605 (*Chronique Géorgienne*, p. 31) she played a certain role, but in 1609 she told Giorgi Saakadze that she had no influence over her son and had tried in vain to attach him to the Dadiani – who seems to have been her uncle, Manuchar I (cf. *Chronique Géorgienne*, p. 41, and Brosset, *HG* Vol. II/i, Genealogical Tree of the Dadianis of Mingrelia, pp. 646–7). In 1614, when Taymuraz of Kakheti and her son Luarsab fled from Shah Abbas to the court of King Giorgi III of Imereti, Queen Tamar took refuge in Salipartiano, 'country of her birth where she was fêted and where she remained' (*Chronique Géorgienne*, p. 50).

[2] One *vershok* – 1¾ inches.

[3] Brosset observes (*EC/BHP*, Vol. II, Nos. 19–21, col. 332, n. 120) that the practice of dyeing the hair bright red still continued at the end of the eighteenth century; this artificial color, resembling gold, was supposed to emphasize youthfulness. In the twentieth century the custom still persists among some Kurdish tribes.

that she was nine years old. Her brother, King Yuri's son
Lev Varsap, is very goodly and remarkably handsome. The
princess is not as good looking as he is, and her face is not
plump.

When the ambassadors had seen the princess, King Yuri went
to another apartment and asked them: 'How have you found
my daughter? Will she suit your great Sovereign's son, Prince
Fedor Borisovich?'

The ambassadors replied that his daughter Princess Helen
was comely, thanks be to God, and that they were hoping for
God's mercy that she would be a suitable bride for his royal
Majesty's son; he should therefore let her go with them to his
royal Majesty.

King Yuri said: 'You have seen how young she is. According
to the rules of the Holy Fathers there are still three years to go
before she can be given in marriage. Let his royal Majesty be
gracious towards me, let him not command that my daughter
be taken away from me soon. I have but one son who is my
eye, and this daughter of mine who is my heart.[1] I rejoice in
them. It is a custom among us in these realms; if somebody asks
for a man's daughter in marriage, ambassadors come twice and
three times. You are but the first ambassadors of his royal
Majesty. How can I let my daughter go with you?'

When the interpreter Svoyetin Kamenev returned to the
Georgian land from the land of Kartli, he informed the ambas-
sadors that Archbishop Theodosius had told him that King
Yuri had other princesses, the daughters of Vakhtan and of
Kochey,[2] of fine appearance and not small in stature. The

[1] 'This daughter of mine who is my heart' recalls the Turkish expression *kalbimin güvercin* – 'pigeon of my heart' as applied to the youngest
and favourite wife of an ageing man. It will be noticed that the king
makes no reference to his eldest daughter, Khorashan, already promised to
Bahadur, son of Eristav Nugsar.

[2] Brosset (*EC/BHP*, Vol. II, Nos. 19–21, col. 333, n. 2) states that
there is no mention in Georgian sources of a daughter of Wakhtang,

ambassadors made enquiries about them and saw them themselves. They are plain-looking but, even if one of them had
been outstanding, the king would never have agreed to pass
over his own daughter, and he would not have attended to the
Sovereign's affairs in any other way, because he wanted to give
his daughter in marriage to Prince Fedor.

The ambassadors told King Yuri that he should swear fealty
to the Sovereign Tsar and should kiss the cross on the charter,
to the effect that he would remain in the Sovereign's grace
under his royal hand, together with the whole Kartlian land,
without seceding, and that he would let his daughter Princess
Helen go to the Sovereign at a later date – when the great
Sovereign sent to fetch her – and that he would let Prince
Khozdroy go with them. The ambassadors made out a copy
of what the charter should be like and gave it to the king.

King Yuri told the ambassadors that he would write out
such a charter . . . and added: 'And you should give me a
written undertaking that before you leave the land of Soni you
will leave 150 *streltsy* of the Sovereign's army, according to
(511) the agreement, and that you will have troops sent against the
Osintsy. You should kiss the cross on that.'

The ambassadors said that they would write such a charter
and would kiss the cross on it . . .

In accordance with this agreement, on the 9th of May the

Prince of Mukhrani; but in his Genealogical Trees of the Bagratids,
published twelve years later, Brosset (*HG*, Vol. ii/i, p. 626) indicates that
Giorgi's uncle, Wakhtang, younger brother of King Simon I, had a
daughter Tamar who married an Amilakhvari.

'Kochey' (= Gocha) is a diminutive of Constantine. The family of
Gochashvili were descended from Constantine, a nephew of David VIII
of Kartli, the grandfather of Simon I. Giorgi Gochashvili had his eyes
put out in 1638 during the reign of King Rostom; his son, Ioram, who
had pretensions to the kingship, suffered the same fate in 1664 (Brosset,
ibid.). In the same tradition David of Kakheti had been the victim of his
brother *Av* Giorgi; he was the ancestor of the Davitishvili family,
Russianized in the nineteenth century as Davydov-Bagration (cf.
Commentary 61 (e)).

ambassadors despatched two *streltsy* to the headmen who had
been sent towards the gorges to meet them near Aytek's
settlement; in the event that the troops had not reached
Aytek's settlement by then, the ambassadors ordered the
streltsy to proceed as far as the Sunzha or the Terek. They
wrote to the headmen that they had reached agreement with
King Yuri of Kartli to leave with him for the time being 150
foot *streltsy* armed with muskets . . . The headmen were to
choose a good *sotnik* and 150 good *streltsy*, skilled in the hand-
ling of fire-arms, who would not be inclined to drunkenness
and would not be badly turned out. They were to send these
men to meet the ambassadors in the land of Soni on the first
Wednesday after Ascension Day, without fail and without
argument. They were also to send 300 foot *streltsy* to Soni to
act as the ambassadors' escort, because King Yuri was sending
with them to the Sovereign his kinsman Prince Khozdroy and
his ambassadors, and they must be escorted in safety as far as
Aytek's settlement. The ambassadors also sent a written message
to the commanders on the Terek by the same *streltsy*, asking
for provisions for the prince and the ambassadors: wine and
honey, and white biscuits and rye biscuits, and groats and
vinegar and dried fish and caviar; and they wrote to the commanders how much they were to send of each type of provisions, having calculated the amount, on the basis of the number
of people, for fifty men.

On the 10th of May King Yuri sent to the ambassadors
Archbishop Theodosius and his clerk Surkay.[1] They read out
the charter written in the Greek language and in Greek characters, of what King Yuri's promise was to be; and the translator
Svoyetin Kamenev interpreted and checked the charter. In the
charter the Sovereign's name and title and affairs were all
written in the same way as in the draft; only they wrote it from

[1] 'His clerk Surkay': Probably 'The Chief of the Scribes' – *G. Mdseralta
Mtavari* Sulkhan.

their own specimen. The ambassadors read out to them the undertaking on which they themselves would kiss the cross. They wrote in their charter that they had agreed with King Yuri of Kartli to leave 150 *streltsy* with muskets with him until the Sovereign made his royal command known, and that they would give these *streltsy* to the king before they themselves left his land of Soni. They would also send the Sovereign's troops against the Osintsy in order to defeat them and open up a direct road to the Kartlian land. However, they did not write when the Sovereign's army would be sent against the Osintsy.

(512)   On the same day King Yuri bade the ambassadors attend upon him. His counsellors who came to fetch them said that the king wanted to kiss the cross to the Sovereign in accordance with the charter. At the king's court the ambassadors were received in the same way as before. The king met them in the second tent. Sitting down, he bade the ambassadors sit as before, and said that he wanted to swear fealty to the Sovereign Tsar and great Prince Boris Fedorovich of all Russia in accordance with the charter. And he commanded that the charter should be read out in the presence of the ambassadors, and Svoyetin interpreted and inspected it. Afterwards the king bade the ambassadors read out their undertaking in his presence; it was read out by Andrey, and interpreted by the same Svoyetin. When the charters were read, the King affixed his signature and seal to his charter, while the ambassadors affixed their signatures and seals to theirs. A processional cross encased in silver was brought in. The king got up and said: '... I am giving my daughter to the great Sovereign. The will of God and of the Sovereign be done to me and my children and throughout my house. However, I cannot let my daughter go with you now because she has not yet reached the proper age; I shall let her go later when, if God grants, his royal Majesty wants her ... And now I am sending with you to his royal Majesty my cousin,

Vakhtan's son Khozdroy, as if he were my son . . . I kiss the cross on all this, as it is written in this charter.' And the king kissed the cross on the charter, and the ambassadors kissed the cross on theirs, and they exchanged charters. Then the king bade the ambassadors sup with him.

On the same day the king gave the ambassadors leave to go.[1] He told them at the farewell audience that he was sending with them his own ambassadors – Archbishop Theodosius and his eminent *aznaur* Edisher.[2] They would go with the prince and meet the ambassadors on the way. On the same day the king sent Archbishop Theodosius to collect the sables which the ambassadors had said that they would give him for fitting out the prince. The ambassadors sent him four times forty sables from the Sovereign's reserves, their Moscow price being 110 rubles, and twice forty of the Patriarch's sables sent by him for King Alexander, at twenty rubles the forty: in all six times (513) forty sables for a value of 150 rubles. But they valued them at double that price and gave them as if they were worth 300 rubles. And King Yuri sent the ambassadors gifts in exchange for those which they had given him in their own name.

The ambassadors left the King and started off from the Kartlian land on the 11th of May. On the 18th they reached Berezov's settlement in the land of Soni. They were escorted as far as Berezov's settlement by Prince Aristov of Soni who gave them as much provisions as could be collected. Prince Khozdroy and King Yuri's ambassadors joined them in the land of Soni on the 29th of May. Twenty of his men had

---

[1] On this day, 10 May, Boris Godunov had been dead of a stroke three weeks. His unfortunate son, Fedor Borisovich, had been accepted as Tsar in Moscow. But on 7 May – three days before the final ceremonies at Mejudis-khevi – Basmanov, with some of the most notable boyars, the Galitsyns and M. Saltykov, had declared to their troops that the Pretender was indeed Dmitri, son of Ivan IV (cf. Pares, *A history of Russia*, p. 134).

[2] There is no record of the family name of this *aznaur* Edisher.

started out with the prince, but ten of them ran away en route, so that ten were left. There were also fifteen monks and men with King Yuri's ambassadors, the Archbishop and Edisher . . .

By the 4th of June the commanders on the Terek had not sent troops to Aytek's settlement to escort the ambassadors.[1] But they wrote to them that because of news of the Turks they had sent reinforcements to the blockhouse on the Koysu; the Turks and the Kumyks had come to the blockhouse with artillery and were bombarding it. If they captured the blockhouse, because of the Russians' sins, their coming to Terek-town was expected. The commanders wrote that they were short of men on the Terek and unable to send an escort soon to meet the ambassadors, nor had they any men to send.[2] They went on to say that the Cherkesses and the *streltsy* whom they had sent for news to Kabarda and Michkizy told them that there was a gathering of many Kumyks and Turks and that strong guards had been placed along the route which the ambassadors would have to follow, and that they intended to attack the ambassadors and the escort. The commanders could not therefore send a small number of troops to meet the ambassadors. They added that they had sent a message to the commander and the dyak at Astarakhan asking for men to be despatched to escort the ambassadors, but the commander and

---

[1] Three days earlier, on 1 June, Tsar Fedor Borisovich had been deposed and murdered; the Patriarch Job, familiar in the correspondence with Alexander of Kakheti, had also been deposed. News of these events cannot yet have reached the commanders on the Terek.

[2] See Commentary 70 for Buturlin's situation at Tarku. Prince Dolgorukov was forced to evacuate the forts on the Koysu (Sulak) and the Aktash which covered Buturlin's line of communications with Terki. Dolgorukov withdrew on Terki. His action, while isolating Buturlin, probably made it possible later for the Russians at least to retain Terki: cf. Potto, p. 11; also *RBS*, under Dolgorukov, Vladimir Timofeyevich (1569–1633) who was *voyvode* of Terki, 1604–6, and during the Time of Troubles supported first the Shuyskis, and later the Romanovs. In contrast to the old warrior Buturlin, Dolgorukov seems to have been a discreet soldier; he was a prisoner of the Swedes for two years, 1591–3.

the dyak at Astarakhan had not sent any men from there; they wrote that there were great disturbances at Astarakhan because of outlaw Cossacks, and they could not send troops to the Terek until they had reached a settlement with the Cossacks.[1]

The ambassadors saw that the commanders on the Terek were not sending men to meet them. Furthermore, the prince and King Yuri's ambassadors had been encamped for no short time in the land of Soni and were expressing annoyance that no army of the Sovereign had come to meet them. Prince Aristov was saying that the ambassadors had been encamped for a long time in his land; nothing was being done, no men (514) were being sent from the Terek in accordance with the agreement, nor were any troops expected later on. Therefore the ambassadors said to Prince Khozdroy and to King Yuri's ambassadors: 'It has become known to us that the Crimean king is marching with many men against the Kizilbash land to help the Turks, and that the Kumyks, who have joined the Turks, intend to attack our Sovereign's forts erected in their land. The Sovereign's army has been sent from the Terek to meet the Crimeans and prevent them from passing, while other troops have been sent against the Turks and the Kumyks. The commanders have written to us and sent strict instructions that we should proceed in haste to them on the Terek on the Sovereign's affairs. We shall therefore travel to the Terek ourselves without delay; and as soon as we get there we shall forthwith send to you in the land of Soni the 150 *streltsy* who are to stay with King Yuri in accordance with the agreement, and we

---

[1] With its variegated and turbulent population, Astrakhan became one of the worst centres of anarchy during the Time of Troubles which was beginning in Russia. Earlier in the year Buturlin and Pleshcheyev had sent back half their *streltsy* strength to Astrakhan, owing to shortage of local supplies in Tarku and, perhaps, to maintain internal security in Astrakhan. This reduction in strength proved fatal to their chance of beating off the growing forces which were gathering against them round Tarku.

shall also send an escort to Aytek's settlement. You should on no account go back from the land of Soni until you get news from us.' The Kartlian ambassadors agreed to wait in the land of Soni for a fortnight for their news.

On the 4th of June the ambassadors left the land of Soni for the Terek without escort. They ascended mount Shat with great difficulty; many pack-horses fell down the mountainside and the belongings were lost.[1] When the ambassadors reached Aytek's settlement he told them that the Turks and the Kumyks had captured the blockhouse on the Koysu and that they had come to Tarku and were bombarding the fort.[2] The Sovereign's commanders on the Terek had burnt the blockhouse on the Sunzha and withdrawn the men. It was altogether impossible for them to get through to the Terek because the Kumyks were waiting for them on the way. Aytek murza did not want to let the ambassadors through, having conceived the idea of handing them over to the Turks; and he sent news about them to the Kumyks and to the Cherkesses in Kabarda. The ambassadors devised various ways, spoke with Aytek about letting them through, and gave many presents to him and to his brother and to his son. It was with great difficulty that he let them go. They travelled to the Terek in haste day and night; and they reached the Terek on the 10th of June. From there they sent two *streltsy* to the land of Soni; they wrote to the prince and to the Kartlian ambassadors that, thank God, they had come to Terek-town without mishap and that they would soon send them an escort of the Sovereign's men as well as the troops who were to stay with King Yuri in accordance with the agreement. They told the commanders on the Terek that

[1] For mount Shat, see Commentary 18 (h).

[2] Aytek was a brother of Alkas, Prince of Little Kabarda, for whom see Chap. 2, p. 120, n. 1; also Commentary 12, p. 284 and Commentary 18 (f). There had been complaints about the unreliability of Aytek during Sovin's embassy to Kakheti, 1596–99: see Belokurov *Snosheniya*, p. 305.

they should send men to meet the Kartlian prince and King Yuri's ambassadors and escort them from Aytek's settlement, and that they should select the 150 men who were to stay in the Kartlian land and send them there. But the commanders did not send any troops to meet the prince and King Yuri's ambassadors, retorting that the people on the Terek would not obey them. At that time, for the Russians' sins, the Turks and the Kumyks captured the fort of Tarku, and the people were seized by panic, expecting the coming of the Turks to Terek- (515) town.[1] The commanders sent the ambassadors from the Terek to Astarakhan by sea. The ambassadors' horses were sent to Astarakhan across the steppe without escort: and all these horses were caught in the steppe by the Nogays of Yan-Araslan and Kanay-murza's *ulus*, who killed those of the ambassadors' men who were with the horses and took others captive.[2]

[1] For Buturlin's catastrophe at Tarku, see Commentary 70.

[2] The ambassadors finally reached Moscow on 12 November 1605, after an absence of eighteen months and six days. They were received in audience by the False Dmitri who was at that time installed as Tsar. After the death of the Pretender, (17 May 1606) the new Tsar, Vasili Shuyski, sent Prince Romodanovski as ambassador to Shah Abbas. His instructions covered the situation on the Terek and in Georgia. He was killed, in the general anarchy of the time, at Saratov on his way down the Volga (cf. Brosset, *EC/BHP*, Vol. II, Nos. 19–21, cols. 335–6). For a recent study of the career of Dmitri, see Philip L. Barbour, *Dimitry called the Pretender. Tsar and Great Prince of All Russia, 1605–1606* (London, 1967).

COMMENTARIES

COMMENTARY 45

The Posolski Prikaz (ref. Chap. 8, p. 379, n. 1)

The Posolski Prikaz, the Ambassadorial Office, came into existence as a result of administrative reforms carried out by Ivan IV in the mid-sixteenth century. In 1549 dyak Ivan Viskovaty was entrusted with the conduct of all correspondence concerning Russia's foreign relations and was given a house in which to set up his office. The new office and its head, the *posolski dyak*, gradually took over the administration of foreign relations from the Boyars' Council (*duma*) and the Tsar's Chancery. In 1565 grander premises were built in the Kremlin across a street from the church of Ivan the Great: these premises were the Posolskaya Palata. However, it is only in 1579 that the earliest documentary evidence occurs of the existence of a Posolski Prikaz as such. Despite the often stormy character of Russian history in the latter half of the 16th century, the terms of office of the *posolski dyaks* were very long: Viskovaty himself held the post for thirteen years; his successor, Andrey Vasilyev was *posolski dyak* from September 1562 until August 1570. Andrey Shchelkalov's term of office was from November 1570 until June 1594, and that of his brother Vasili from June 1594 until May 1601; Vasili was succeeded by Afanasi Vlasyev (until May 1605). Belokurov, *O Posolskom Prikaze, passim.*

On the rank of Yaselnichi (ref. Chap. 8, p. 379, n. 2)

The court rank of Master of the Horse (*yaselnichi*) was less exalted than that of *Konyushi boyarin* held by Boris Godunov in Tsar Fedor's reign. The *yaselnichi* was the nominal head of the oldest department of the Tsar's household, whose competence extended over the Tsar's stables and horses. From the point of view of seniority, a *yaselnichi* ranked together with a gentleman of the Privy Council.

Mikhail Tatishchev was appointed a *yaselnichi* in 1596. Two years later he was sent to Lithuania to announce Boris Godunov's accession and in 1600 he played a prominent part in the negotiations with Lew Sapieha's embassy sent to Moscow to conclude 'eternal peace' between Poland and Russia. In these negotiations he was rude to Sapieha and even went so far as to call him a liar; Sapieha retaliated by calling the *yaselnichi* a groom. On Tatishchev's return from Georgia he won the favour of the False Dmitri and became a frequent guest at the merry-making in the royal apartments. When the Pretender's position began to deteriorate, Tatishchev turned against his patron and went over to the anti-Dmitri faction. He played a prominent part in the plot which led to Dmitri's overthrow and was at the head of the mob which broke into the palace. He was killed in 1609 by the mob at Novgorod where he had been sent as commander in the previous year (*RBS* under name; see also article by Allen, 'The Georgian marriage projects of Boris Godunov', in *OSP*, 1965).

COMMENTARY 47

'*The Turkish Pasha of Genzha, Kaikhosr*' (ref. Chap. 8, p. 384, n. 1)

'The Turkish Pasha of Genzha, Kaikhosr'; this name is of Persian origin; it was uncommon among the Turks later than the Seljuk period but is frequently found as a Georgian personal name. The monk Kiril makes it clear that this Kay Khusrau was a Georgian of high standing in the Turkish service. It is possible that he may be identifiable as Kay Khusrau Jaqeli, second son of Kwarkware V, Atabeg of Samtskhe (*Sa-atabag-o*), died November 1582. This Kay Khusrau was a grandson of Atabeg Kay Khusrau II (died 1575) and of the celebrated Dedis-Imedi, daughter of Bagrat, first Prince of Mukhrani – of the cadet line of the Bagratids of Kartli (see Brosset, *HG*, Vol. II/i, p. 640, Genealogical Tree of the Atabegs). Kay Khusrau must have been born after 1564 when his father married Marekh, daughter of the Dadian Levan I. In 1588, he is mentioned as having been sent, with his grandmother, on an embassy to the Turkish Pasha of Akhaltsikhe – on behalf of his uncle, Atabeg Manuchar II, ally and son-in-law of Simon I of Kartli (cf. Brosset, *HG*, Vol. II/i, p. 227 and *Chronique Géorgienne*, p. 27). Following the political eclipse of Simon and Manuchar, it is possible that Kay Khusrau – like other members of his family – took service with the Turks. In 1602 he may have been about thirty-six years of age – old enough to have had a marriageable daughter of fifteen or sixteen.

COMMENTARY 48

Georgian coronation customs (ref. Chap. 8, p. 388, n. 1)

In his account of Georgian manners and customs, which prefaces his *Geographical description of Georgia*, Wakhusht states clearly that 'the bishop consecrated and crowned the

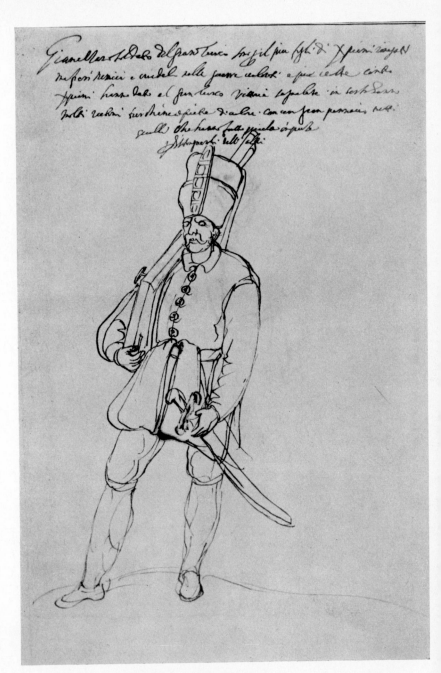

15. A Turkish musketeer (*tufanji*). After Castelli.

monarch; it was the function of the Catholicos when there was one ... After the division of the kingdom, the Catholicoses of Imereti and of Kartli each crowned their sovereign, and the Bodbeli (Bishop of Bodbe) him of Kakheti' (Wak./Brosset, p. 27). Nevertheless, when a candidate for the Kartlian or Kakhian thrones was nominated by the Shah, as accepted suzerain, the customary insignia, for a long time, had been a *khalat*, composed of a long sable robe and a belt and costume stitched with gold; a *taj* or Persian crown wound round with a turban of cloth of gold and decorated with twelve aigrettes; a sword, a dagger and mouthpiece of a pipe ornamented with pearls; gold horse harness enriched with precious stones; a vase and a cup (cf. Brosset, *HG*, Vol. ii/i, pp. 32 and 35, for the insignia given to David (1569) and Simon (1578) on their respective nominations by the Shah). From monk Kiril's account, it would appear that the Kakhians had adopted the Persian practice among themselves and that consecration and coronation by ecclesiastics had been abandoned; all this confirms Wakhusht's lamentations on Kakhian adoption of Persian customs.

For a beautifully preserved charter with miniatures showing members of the Kakhian royal house in the seventeenth century wearing these Persian insignia of royalty, see *MAK*, Vol. vii, plate iii, and text, p. 42.

COMMENTARY 49

The feud between the Kakhian princes (ref. Chap. 8, p. 389, n. 1; Chap. 11, p. 439, n. 1)

The account given of the feud between the two Kakhian princes is confirmed in general terms by Wakhusht, but differs in detail. According to Wakhusht's *Histoire de Kakheth*, David and Giorgi went to stay in Kartli as the guests of King Giorgi X. They were installed at Isani (Wak./Brosset, p. 185,

Isni or *Nisani*), the suburb of Tiflis lying on the left (northern) bank of the Kura (later called Avlabari). Here they were entertained with tournaments and feasts. The arrogance and irascibility of David had made him unpopular with the Kakhian nobles and some of them engaged Giorgi in a plot to kill his elder brother while he was drunk. The plot was revealed by Baram Cholokashvili; and David seized Giorgi and had him imprisoned in the castle of Torga in Kakheti (for which see Chap. 4, p. 159, n. 1 above and Commentary 28). Twelve of Giorgi's followers were decapitated and thrown from the walls of the castle of Dchoeti (ref. Brosset, *HG*, Vol. ii/i, p. 156; also ibid., 'Suite des Annales', pp. 374–5). It is interesting to note that the powerful Cholokashvili family, related to the blood royal through the marriage of Anna Cholokashvili to Alexander I (1492–1511) and of Helen Cholokashvili to *Av* Giorgi (1511–13), were partisans of David and, later, of his widow Ketevan and her infant son (afterwards Taymuraz I). On this family, see Iosseliani's *Rod Knyazey Cholakayevykh*. Also Wak./Brosset (pp. 30–2). Iosseliani (p. 5) believes them to have been of ancient Albanian origin.

COMMENTARY 50

The Gold Painted Hall (ref. Chap. 8, p. 390, n. 1)

The map of the Kremlin – 'Kremlenagrad, Castellum Urbis Moskvae' – in Blaeu's Atlas (Amsterdam 1663) shows the Posolskaya Palata on the north side of the rectangular Cathedral Square. To reach the Cathedral of the Annunciation the Georgian party would have had to walk across a street leading to the square and then past the Cathedral of Michael the Archangel. The Royal Palace stood west of the Cathedral of the Annunciation and could be reached by a staircase from the north porch of the Cathedral.

The Cathedral of the Annunciation was built in 1484–9,

during the reign of Ivan III, in the early Muscovite style; it was the Tsars' palace church. (For a recent description of the sixteenth century frescoes in the Cathedral see *Kreml Moskvy* (Moscow, 1957), pp. 130–8, and two plates.)

The Gold Painted Hall was built in the last decade of the fifteenth century, not far from the still extant Granovitaya Palata; in the first half of the seventeenth century it was incorporated in the Patriarch's Palace. The Gold Painted Hall was later pulled down to make way for the Winter Palace built by Rastrelli for Empress Elizabeth in 1752–3 (*Kreml Moskvy*, pp. 69, 88, 93).

COMMENTARY 51

The approaches to Tarku (ref. Chap. 8, p. 396, n. 1 and p. 400, n. 1)

For details on the Kumukhs and on Shevkal of Tarku and his dominions, see Introduction, Section 8. In the present context Koysu is the Sulak of Russian maps. Tuzluk is derived from *T. tuz*, salt. The saltings were essential to the well-being of the herds of the Kumukhs. (For the importance of salt in horse-breeding, cf. Commentary 22, ref. to the salt lake Tambi, near Besh-tau.) In the eighteenth century Reineggs/W. (Vol II, p. 67) explains that: 'Between the Koisu (Sulak) and the Urussai-bulak, the country is crossed by two rivers; namely the Oseni and the Manassa. Both rise in the highest of the Lesghaean mountains, sixty versts from the sea, and are uncommonly rapid; particularly in the month of May, when swollen by the melting of the snow. Between an arm of the Koisu and a salt stream called Bakas, they form, near the sea, large morasses covered with rushes. Between Oseni and the Manassa stands Tarki, on a declivity facing the plain, in a narrow glen abounding with springs and streams, some of which are salt.' From this description, it is clear that the Tuzluk saltings lay between the Bakas and the Sulak, to the north of Tarku and at the base of the Agrakhan peninsula (see Reineggs: map at end of Vol. II). Other - sulphurous - springs were at the mouth of the Bashli river, half-way between Boynak and Derbent.

In the eighteenth century the settlement of Boynak was the residence of Shevkal's heir where 'he may learn the art of governing' (Reineggs/W., Vol. I, p. 113 and Vol. II, map, where the author indicates a small river but does not show the place). It lay in the mountains south-east of Tarku on a ridge rising to about 2,000 m. In Khvorostinin's state of Shevkal's forces, it only furnished thirty horsemen, while the district of Kafyr Kumukh (in Reineggs, Ghyffr) as a whole provided one hundred and fifty, so Boynak must have been a comparatively small fief. The river of Boynak was not anything like the size of the Koysu (Sulak), as indicated by Kiril who seems to have confused it with the larger Osen of Reineggs's map and the Shura-Osen of Felitsyn's map. Overlooking the Osen was Shura or Temir-Khan-Shura, which name is interpreted by Baddeley (*RFC*, Vol. II, pp. 2–3, citing P. K. Uslar) as meaning 'the rock or lake of Timur', since Timur is said to have camped there after his victory over Tokhtamysh on the Terek in 1395. But there is a reference to a contemporary Temir Khan of Shura in Sovin's embassy (Belokurov, *Snosheniya*, p. 293). The name of Buinaksk has been given, under the Soviets, to former Temir-Khan-Shura, which is now the administrative capital of the Daghestan ASSR.

COMMENTARY 52

'Alexander's fort' (ref. Chap. 8, p. 396, n. 2)

The reference here is not to a fort built on the Caspian coast by Alexander of Kakheti but to the legend, so wide-spread in the Caucasus, that Alexander of Macedon had built Derbent and other fortifications in the Caucasian mountains (e.g.

Daryal). In the eighteenth century Reineggs, while recording this legend (Reineggs/W., Vol. I, p. 128) discounts it (ibid., p. 268) and recalls that it was controverted as early as Plutarch's life of Pompey. Cf. also, Baddeley, *RFC*, Vol. II, p. 62; and for full discussion see Andrew Runni Anderson, *Alexander's gate, Gog and Magog, and the inclosed nations*, Cambridge, Mass., 1932, particularly p. vii: 'The legend of Alexander's gate at the pass of Derbend . . . was apparently not established until the memory of Khosro I Anushirvan (A.D. 531–79), who finished the Iron Gate of Derbend and the Caucasian Wall begun by his father Kavadh, had faded out and become supplanted by that of Alexander.' (But for early history of the fortification of Derbent see Commentary 9; and for the Iron Gates, Commentary 38.) The references in Arrian to Alexander's campaign in the Caucasus apply to the Indian Caucasus (Hindu Kush); (cf. Arrian, Loeb ed., Book III, 28, i–v). Nevertheless, Alexander did receive from Pharasmanes, king of the Chorasinians (Khorazmians) a proposal to invade the Pontic Caucasus: 'Pharasmanes said that he lived on the borders of the Colchians and of the Amazon women; and should Alexander desire to invade Colchis and the territory of the Amazons and subdue all races in this direction which dwelt near the Euxine Sea, he promised to act as guide and to provide all the necessities for the expeditionary force . . . Alexander said that it was not just then convenient to make an expedition to Pontus . . . He said that for the time being he had India in contemplation; for by subduing India he would then have all Asia; but when he was master of Asia he would return to Greece, and thence in the direction of the Hellespont and the Propontis would make an expedition into Pontus . . . Pharasmanes must therefore reserve his promises which he now made to that future time' (Arrian, Book IV, 15, v–vi).

COMMENTARY 53

The route from Tarku to Zagem (ref. Chap. 8, p. 398, n. 1)

Tarkali seems to be the *Atlibojunn* of Reineggs/W., Vol. I, p. 105, *Atli-Bouyoun* of Baddeley, *RFC*, Vol. II, p. 2, = T. 'Horse's Neck' – a name appropriate to describe a low col at 563 m. above the level of the Caspian. According to Reineggs the tribe around spoke their own peculiar language and were 'famed for the size and beauty of the men'. This seems to have been the district of the Kafyr ('pagan') Kumukhs–who, as Reineggs/W., Vol. I, p. 73, indicates, had also been known by the older name of *Tallen*: possibly a remnant of Alans who are recorded in this region in the eleventh century (cf. Minorsky, *HSD*, p. 51 and *passim*). Crossing the Ghimri ridge into the valley of the Avar-koysu, it would be *more* than a day's march to the territory of the Ghazi Kumukh. From here there are several difficult mountain routes leading to Zagem and the valley of the Alazani. Kiril's estimate of four days march from Tarku to Zagem is certainly optimistic – some two hundred versts over very difficult mountain tracks. It might have been practicable for experienced raiders among the mountaineers, but hardly for Russian troops or the feudal levies of the Kakhian king.

There is evidence for the first half of the fourteenth century, during the brief revival of the Georgian mediaeval kingdom under Giorgi V Brtsqinwale ('the Brilliant'), that Georgian influence and, perhaps, occupation extended into Avaria down the valley of the Avar-koysu to Antsukh and, possibly, as far as Khuntzakh (cf. Genko, p. 729; and particularly n. 4, for bibliography of the celebrated inscription at Khuntzakh in old Georgian script). But the days of effective Georgian intervention in Daghestan were long past. The last attempts of Kay Khusrau Omanishvili (1612, Wakhusht, *Histoire de*

Kakheth in Brosset, *HG*, Vol. ii/i, p. 161) and of King Taymuraz I (1640, ibid., pp. 169–70) to assert Kakhian authority in Didoeti and Avaria proved abortive. The expedition of Taymuraz was intended to clear the route for a Russian mission which had been waiting in Terki for three years; it ended in a major disaster.

COMMENTARY 54

Vasili and Andrey Shchelkalov (ref. Chap. 9, p. 408, n. 1)

When Tatishchev was being given his instructions in 1604 Vasili Shchelkalov was no longer head of the Posolski Prikaz: he had fallen into disfavour and had been replaced in 1601. He was the younger brother of Andrey Shchelkalov, the all-powerful *posolski dyak* of the later years of the reign of Ivan IV and of the reign of Fedor (cf. Fletcher/Horsey, pp. 39, 194). His career is an interesting example of the vicissitudes of a Russian official of the period. The son of a dyak, he began as an under-dyak and rose to eminence by the later 1560s. In 1570 he was appointed head of the Razryadny Prikaz (a post he retained until 1575) and shortly after 1571 he became his brother's assistant at the Posolski Prikaz. In the 1570s he frequently took part in negotiations with foreign ambassadors. About 1579, he and his brother were the first dyaks to get the rank of 'Dyak of the Duma'. This promotion did not save either from being badly beaten by Semen Nagoy, one of the brothers of the last wife of Ivan IV (Fletcher/Horsey, p. 194).

For many years a close friend of Boris Godunov, Vasili does not seem to have taken part in his brother Andrey's intrigues against the latter in 1593–4 (cf. Platonov, *OIS*, pp. 212–13, 227). He succeeded Andrey as head of the Posolski Prikaz in June 1594 and retained the post until May 1601. Meantime, in 1596, he had been made Seal Bearer of the Council. After his dismissal from the Posolski Prikaz in 1601, he remained in disfavour until Tsar Boris's death. He was back at court with the rank of equerry during the reign of Vasili Shuyski but did not play any part in the conduct of affairs. He died at the end of 1610 or the beginning of 1611. He was less gifted than his brother Andrey (described by Jerome Horsey as 'a great bribinge officer' – ibid., p. 194) and his career was marred by cases of forgery, misrepresentation and insubordination (cf. *RBS*, under name). The False Dmitri, when in Poland about 1603, averred that his chief supporter (in Moscow) was a leading *dyak* named Shchelkalov. As Andrey had died in 1597 this can only have been Vasili who may have been acting as an agent for the proscribed Romanov faction (cf. Klyuchevski (Hogarth ed., III, pp. 26, 31) and *RBS* under names).

COMMENTARY 55

Relations between Boris Godunov and the Sublime Porte (ref. Chap. 9, p. 411, n. 2)

Murat III had died 16 January 1595. During the brief reign of his son and successor, Mehmet III (who was in blood three parts Venetian – see Allen, *PTP*, Tables of Rulers, VIII), the Long War on the Danube had continued with some notable victories for the Turks – Erlau and Keresztes, 1596, Kanisha, 1600. But popular revolts in Anatolia had weakened the régime; and in January 1603 there was a serious outbreak of military anarchy in Istanbul (cf. Kramers under 'Muhammad III' in *EI*, 1st ed.). On 22 January Mehmet died. In September of the same year the capture of Nakhichevan and Tabriz by Shah Abbas I marked the beginning of the end of Turkish hegemony in Eastern Caucasia.

Ahmet I (1603–17) departed from the imperial custom of fratricide on the succession of a new sultan by sparing his brother and only male heir who eventually followed him as

Mustafa I. It was a curious coincidence, not generally noted by historians, that the houses of Osman, Rurik, Tudor and Valois – and also the Abdulkhairids of Bukhara, were all on the verge of extinction at the end of the sixteenth century. Of these only the House of Osman survived through the seventeenth century.

In the present context the references to Russo-Turkish relations are cautious – doubtless in view of the discussions which had been proceeding between Boris Godunov and the Imperial ambassadors with a view to the formation of an anti-Turkish bloc during the years 1593–9. The last Ottoman mission to Moscow (Ridvan Chaush) had arrived in the autumn of 1593 and had renewed complaints of Russian military activities on the Don, Terek and Sunzha rivers. In July 1594 the *dvoryanin* Daniil Istlenyev and the under-dyak Tretyaka Abramov had been sent on a return mission to Istanbul with counter-complaints against the Turks of Azov. The Russians seem to have been stalling. Istlenyev's full report has not survived; but from Austrian reports it would appear that he was held under arrest by orders of the new sultan Mehmet III in 1595 (cf. Hammer, *HEO*, Vol. VII, p. 316; Smirnov, *RT*, Vol. I, pp. 150 ff.). Von Hammer cites a Venetian source that Istlenyev was intending to proceed to Georgia to negotiate an alliance with Simon of Kartli, Alexander of Kakheti and Shah Abbas. In 1595 fortune was favouring Simon in his effort to reintegrate a united Georgian kingdom; but the Russians had no direct contact with him. In the following year (June 1596), the embassy of Sovin and Polukhanov left Moscow for the court of Alexander of Kakheti; their instructions covered also the possibility of negotiations with Simon (Belokurov, *Snosheniya*, pp. 276, 303).

COMMENTARY 56

Opinion among the chieftains of Daghestan in 1604 (ref. Chap. 10, p. 421, n. 1)

From the text it is clear that opinion among the chieftains of Daghestan was restless and fluid and that they were waiting on events. The news of the victories of Shah Abbas had disturbed a situation in which Ottoman hegemony in Georgia, Shirvan and Daghestan had been accepted for a quarter of a century. Again, information about the deterioration of conditions in Russia must have reached the Shevkal from Astrakhan (cf. Chap. 10, p. 416, n. 1). The mountaineers, it would appear, were ready to attack the Russians on the Terek should the situation prove favourable enough.

After the conquest of Erevan, Shah Abbas had taken Kars and other Turkish strong points and was showing his strength in Samtskhe and Shirvan before returning to winter quarters in Tabriz (von Hammer, *HEO*, Vol. VIII, pp. 60–1). The undecided balance of forces between the Turks and the Persians was clear to Shevkal's son, 'Saltan Magmut' who – as our text implies – was remaining in Shemakha to maintain contacts. The concentration of a strong Turkish army in Erzurum under Chighala-zade Sinan Pasha (Scipione di Cicala, a Genoese renegade – see *EI*, 2nd ed., article 'Čighāla-zāde Yūsuf Sinān' by V. J. Parry) must have been known to him. (Sinan's son Chighala-zade Mahmut, had been appointed to the governorship of Shirvan in succession to Alaja-Atlu Hasan Pasha, Hasan of the Piebald Horse (cf. von Hammer, *HEO*, Vol. VIII, p. 60); and on 15 June, the father left Üsküdar for the Persian front – Danişmend, Vol. III, p. 223.) The Kabardan chiefs Kazy and Solokh were biding their time. Other minor chieftains in the triangle of mountainous country between the Sunzha and the Sulak were following the same course;

Shevkal's sons, Alkas and Surkhai of Tarkali, with his son Alidar; Ali Sultan son of Andi Bek of the Kafyr Kumukh, and Budachey of Erpeli – were all ready at the beginning of July to reconnoitre by the 'upper road' from the Sulak through Khasav-Yurt against Sunzhiki (Sunzhenski-ostrog or Old Terki at the junction of the Sunzha and the Terek. See Introduction, Section 5).

COMMENTARY 57

Samskaya ʒemlya= the land of Samsk (ref. Chap. 10, p. 469, n. 2)

Here the reference is to the land of Samtskhe, the great Georgian province known in the period of the united kingdom as *Zemo* (Upper) *Kartli*, covering the uplands between the middle valley of the Chorokhi (*T.* Çoruh) and the sources of the Kura. *Sa-mtskhe* has been anglicized by Marjory Wardrop, *The man in the panther's skin*, as 'The Meskhian land'. In Georgian *sa* – is a locative prefix, sometimes combined with the suffix - *o* (as in *Sa-baratian-o, Sa-wakhtang-o*), and is alternative to the suffix – *eti, eta* (as in Kakh-eti, Mtskh-eta). Sa-mtskhe, like Mtskh-eta, preserves the name of the ancient Mushki (the Meshech of Genesis). *Tripolis*, three towns, is a popular etymology derived from a play on the Georgian words *sami tsikh(n)e*, three castles. From the latter part of the fifteenth century, the Jaqelis, *atabegs* of Samtskhe, with their seat at Akhaltsikhe (new castle, T. form *Ahiska*) were virtually independent and Samtskhe was often known as *Sa-atabag-o*, the Atabeg's country. Ottoman ascendancy was gradually established during the Turko–Persian wars of the sixteenth century, but only after 1625 did the Jaqelis become Moslems and more or less hereditary pashas of Akhaltsikhe. Relations with the Bagratids and the Safavids were close. Dedis-Imedi, the famous regent of Saatabago towards the end of the sixteenth century, was the daughter of Bagrat Prince of Mukhrani;

her lover and adviser, Waraza Shalikashvili, was the brother of a wife of Shah Tahmasp who was his favourite during the latter part of his reign; and Castelli has left a drawing of 'Elena de Artabac', wife of Shah Safi II, grandson of Abbas I (for reproduction, see Allen, *HGP*, p. 169). Dedis-Imedi's son, Manuchar II (1582–1614), married, 1581, Elena, daughter of Simon I of Kartli and co-operated closely with his father-in-law against the Turks (Brosset, *HG*, Vol. ii/i, pp. 226–7). Manuchar sent his son to join Shah Abbas in front of Erevan, and arranged to hand over Khertvisi, covering the approaches to the Turkish stronghold at Akhaltsikhe, to the Persians (ibid.). After the capture of Erevan and Kars in the early summer of 1604, Abbas made an attack on Akhaltsikhe which was, however, successfully defended by Karakash Pasha (Brosset, *HG*, Vol. ii/i, p. 462, n. 1, citing Iskander Munshi). Further, on Samtskhe-Saatabago, see Wak./Brosset, and Wak./ Jan. for Wakhusht's detailed geographical description; Brosset, *HG*, Vol. ii/i, pp. 206–36, for Wakhusht's 'History'; and Allen, *HGP*, index. Also, below, Chap. 13, p. 469, n. 2.

COMMENTARY 58

'The Turks' town of Tiflis' (ref. Chap. 11, p. 443, n. 3)

Tiflis, the ancient capital of the Georgian kings and the greatest city of Transcaucasia, had been in Turkish occupation since 1578, when Lala Mustafa Pasha set a garrison of 2,000 (not 200 as stated in the article in *EI*, 1st ed.) in the old citadel of Tabor (Korchi-kala) on the hill on the right bank of the Daba-khana, a small southern affluent of the Kura. With Gori, Dmanisi, Lori and Akhaltsikhe it formed one of the quinquelateral of strongholds on which the Turks attempted to base a permanent occupation of Kartli. The maintenance of these strong points proved costly in relief expeditions (for details see article 'Tiflis' by V. Minorsky in *EI*, 1st ed.). In 1595, allied with the Persians, Simon I had managed to take Gori but he failed in attempts against the citadel of Tiflis. Nevertheless, the Georgians continued to occupy the suburb of Isani or Nisani (now Avlabari) on the left (northerly) bank of the Kura opposite the citadel. Here, Giorgi X of Kartli had entertained the Kakhian princes, David and Giorgi, in 1602 (see Commentary 49).

Evliya Chelebi (von Hammer ed. Vol. II, p. 172) states that the fortress remained in the hands of the Ottomans 'from the time of Sultan Murat III till that of Sultan Mustafa, when the Persians united with the Georgians took the castle by surprise and gave it to the Shah'. Sultan Mustafa would appear to be a mistake for Sultan Ahmet I (1603–17). Mustafa I only reigned one year, 1617–18. Minorsky in *EI*, 1st ed., states that Tiflis fell to Shah Abbas on 21 October 1603, but gives no reference. From our text, it is clear that the citadel of Tiflis was still in the hands of the Turks in August 1604 (Russian year 7112). It was only in 1606 that the Turks finally surrendered Tiflis to Shah Abbas (cf. Brosset, *HG*, Vol. II/i, pp. 469–70 citing Iskander Munshi; also Berdzenishvili, *IG*, Vol. I, p. 245).

There are near-contemporary descriptions of Tiflis by the Turkish travellers Katib Chelebi (his account referring to the years 1630–5) and Evliya Chelebi, 1648. The first detailed (and attractive) description by a European is by Chardin, 1673. His Atlas, pl. iii, gives a general view of Tiflis showing nineteen principal features. For Wakhusht's description, see Wak./Brosset, pp. 185–91. The Georgian geographer states that outside the citadel (with its six hundred houses) 'the Georgian population is less numerous than the Armenian[s]; but these latter follow the Georgian customs'. For many interesting details and excellent bibliography, see article by Minorsky in *EI*, 1st ed.; also Polievktov and Natadze, *Stary*

Tiflis (Tiflis, 1929) an otherwise slight work which is valuable for its inclusion of Wakhusht's plan of the city which is not reproduced among the maps in Wak./Brosset.

Asafi, f. 18r., gives what is probably the earliest surviving view of Tiflis, showing the capture by the Turks in the early autumn of 1578. In the right-hand bottom corner is the field commander, Özdemiroghlu Osman Pasha, with his mounted staff in armour. Janissary musketeers are attacking the old citadel of Tabor to the south of the Kura. A bridge leads over the river to the north bank where major buildings are already in flames. Here the Turks are attacking from the right flank. The Georgians, identifiable in their *bashliks*, continue the defence. For similar *bashlik* see Castelli's drawing of Giorgi Saakadze, reproduced in Allen, *HGP*, opposite p. 166; for exactly comparable uniform of a Turkish musketeer of the early seventeenth century, see below, pl. 15, opp. p. 519.

COMMENTARY 59

'*The Sovereign Tsar . . . Dmitri Ivanovich*' (ref. Chap. 11, p. 444, n. 1)

'The Sovereign Tsar . . . Dmitri Ivanovich': called *samozvanets*, impostor or pretender. He claimed to be Dmitri son of Ivan IV by Marfa Nagaya (which family was of Tartar extraction). Dmitri Ivanovich had died at Uglich in mysterious circumstances in 1591 during the reign of his half-brother Fedor Ivanovich, brother-in-law of Boris Godunov; and hostile elements attributed the death to Boris. The *samozvanets* was probably born Yuri Otrepyev, a lowly member of the household of the eldest Romanov. After many adventures, he procured the support of powerful Polish nobles and in October 1604 invaded Muscovy. He proved more fortunate than the Yorkist pretender, Perkin Warbeck, who had emerged in somewhat comparable circumstances. After the sudden death of Boris Godunov from a stroke, April 1605, Dmitri entered Moscow, 19 June 1605, and was proclaimed Tsar. 'He was ugly, awkward and red-haired, with a melancholy expression, but he was certainly possessed of great courage and much ability. He almost compels one to think that he believed in his own authority . . . Daily the young Tsar worked with his Council of Boyars, showing discrimination and resource. He was widely informed, and commented perhaps too freely on the ignorance of the boyars, saying that he would make it possible for them to travel abroad. The boyars, who appear never to have believed in him, were disgusted with his abandonment of the old stiff etiquette and his disregard of all formalities' (Bernard Pares, *A history of Russia*, pp. 134–5, following Platonov, *OIS*). On 17 May 1606, the Pretender was killed in a palace revolution organized by Vasili Shuyski, who for a short time succeeded him. For summary of varying views on the death of Dmitri of Uglich and subsequent events, see article by George Vernadsky, 'The Death of the Tsarevich Dimitry' (in *OSP*, Vol. v, 1954, pp. 1–19); he concludes that Boris Godunov was not responsible for the incident.

In seeking to avoid concessions to his Polish supporters, the False Dmitri 'found a substitute in a proposal for a united crusade against Turkey' (Pares, p. 135). In this connection, it is interesting to note that he received the ambassadors Tatishchev and Ivanov on the very day of their return – an unusual procedure at the Muscovite court.

COMMENTARY 60

Russo–Persian relations in 1604 (ref. Chap. 11, p. 445, n. 1)

It is unlikely that the Kakhians were taken in by the ingenuous explanation of the Russian failure to make any headway in Daghestan. Derbent, Shemakha and Baku were among the towns captured by the Turks in their campaigns against the

Persians between 1578 and 1584. By the treaty of 1590 the Persians had formally ceded them, along with other territories, to Turkey. In the meantime Shah Muhammad Khudabanda, the father of Abbas, had promised Derbent and Baku to the Tsar as a reward for Russian help against the Ottomans. The offer was repeated in the letter of Shah Abbas to Tsar Fedor, delivered by the ambassadors Butak Beg and Andi Beg in the summer of 1590 and, again, by a Persian messenger or *Kaya* (this is a rank and not a personal name as implied in Veselovski – see *EI*, 1st ed., under *Ketkhuda*) two years later.

In June 1595 Tsar Fedor and his Boyars' Council decided to send an embassy to Shah Abbas with the offer of an alliance in consideration for which the Shah was to be asked to cede not only Derbent and Baku but also Shemakha to the Tsar. This plan came to nought because the Russian ambassador died on the way. In October of the same year his successor, Vasili Andreyevich Zvenigorodski, reported from Persia that he had been told by the Shah that should the Russians be successful in their projected campaign to expel the Turks from Derbent and Baku he would not stand in their way. In 1597 the Tsar sent another ambassador, Vasili Tyufyakin, to Shah Abbas. Tyufyakin's instructions were to get the Shah's agreement to the cession of Derbent and Baku to Russia while 'Shemakha and all other towns which the Shah will seize from the Turk' were to be retained by Persia. But Tyufyakin also carried with him a draft treaty of alliance to be signed between Russia and Persia under the terms of which the Shah was to hand over Shemakha as well as the other two towns to Russia after he had taken them from the Turks. This treaty was never signed. Veselovski (*PTDS*) does not mention any Persian embassies or missions to Russia in the early years of the seventeenth century. One Andi Beg (perhaps the emissary who had appeared in Moscow in 1590), who was suspected by the Russians of travelling for his personal account, was sent back in September 1600 in the company of Prince Alexander Zasekin, Tsar Boris's last ambassador to Shah Abbas. With the party travelled also Pir Kuli Beg who had reached Moscow on a mission from the Shah in the autumn of 1599. Pir Kuli Beg had travelled from Astrakhan with a suite of three hundred, according to *Don Juan*, p. 239; or forty, among whom 'were several Persian merchants and a gentleman who was chief falconer to the Sophi', according to Abel Pinçon (Ross, *Anthony Sherley*, p. 170). 'He brought with him much merchandise, saying it belonged to his master, and this he wished to barter in Mosco for divers merchandise of Europe, such as woollen cloth, coats of mail, precious skins of animals – black foxes, sables and others – falcons and other birds for hawking, which sell for nothing in Moscovie. The merchandise which they brought from Persia consisted of satin, velvet, cloth of gold, many cotton materials and wide belts of silk.' (These last became very fashionable in Poland and, as 'Polish belts' could be found in the *Charshi* in Istanbul as late as the 1920s.) About the same period, the practice of merchants posing as diplomatic envoys, or of ambassadors engaging in trade, while enjoying the hospitality of the Sublime Porte, was causing irritation among officials in Istanbul.

In the first years of the seventeenth century – when the Ottoman power was weakened by the strain of the Long War on the Danube and by popular revolts in Anatolia, and when the serious social and dynastic crisis in Russia was becoming apparent – Shah Abbas, whose own strength was growing, lost interest in a Russian alliance; and in 1606–7 he regained possession of Shemakha, Baku and Derbent by his own efforts. For details of Russo–Persian relations, see Veselovski (*PTDS*, Vol. 1, pp. 24, 129, 162, 299, 322, 353, 372, 375).

COMMENTARY 61

The names of Prince Giorgi's councillors (ref. Chap. 11, p. 448, n. 1)

Brosset (*EC/BHP*, Vol. 11, Nos. 19–21, cols. 318–19 and n. 88) examined fragments of documents not published, and probably not seen by Belokurov; he states that we have only the end of the Act of the Kissing of the Cross, sealed and signed by Prince Giorgi, but he is able to give some further particulars of the councillors present at the ceremony. The names from Brosset's and Belokurov's versions may be identified as follows:

(a) 'The Archbishop of Martukop, Rustvel': the titular bishop of the ancient see of Rustavi – destroyed by the Mongol Khan Berke, *c.* 1260 – had his seat at Martqopi, for which see Commentary 33 (a) above. Rustavi formed part of the complex of ecclesiastical foundations round the shrine of St David of Garezhda, for which see Commentary 33 (d) and Wak./ Brosset, pp. 181, 305 (cf. further, Chap. 11, p. 437, n. 2).

(b) Archimandrite Iona = G. Iona = Jonah; for Krym (Gremi) see Commentary 25 above.

(c) For 'Prince Aram', Iram, Ioram or Iaram Dzhezdambek, see Chap. 11, p. 439, n. 2. In 1583 there was a certain Ioram in command of a Kakhian contingent fighting against the Turks outside Derbent (cf. Asafi, MS. fol. 179r.). Brosset (*EC/BPH*, Vol. 11, Nos. 16–18, col. 258, and also n. 105) states that in December 1592 Prince Aram, together with the monk Kiril, accompanied Pleshcheyev on his return from Kakheti, as head of the mission sent to Moscow by King Alexander. He returned to Kakheti with Vsevolodski's mission in June 1593; and he again appeared in Moscow together with Vsevolodski in December 1594 (Brosset, ibid., col. 260). He left Moscow with his companion, the Circassian Khurshit, on 6 June 1596 with the embassy of Sovin and Polukhanov (Brosset, ibid., col. 263; Belokurov, *Snosheniya*, p. 269).

In the exchanges at Shunta (Shilda) between Prince Yuri and

Tatishchev during August 1604 a certain Dzhezdambek appears as the principal representative of the Kakhian prince. Brosset identifies Dzhezdambek as Prince Aram: he would be the natural Kakhian choice with his earlier experience of the Posolski Prikaz and his knowledge of Russian language and mentality. But in the negotiations between Prince Yuri and Tatishchev at Buyutan in January 1605, the names of Prince Yuri's councillors include both 'Dzhezdambek' and 'Prince Aram'. There is an ambiguity here. However, in his account of the negotiations, Brosset persists in his identification; and, on balance, his view is acceptable. 'Dzhezdam-bek' is a territorial title – 'lord of Dzhezdam'. It derives from the name of the river Jegami, an affluent of the Kura, in Somkheti: cf. Toumanoff (*SCCH*, p. 485, n. 201) for discussion of the topography of this region. Prince Aram may well have come of a family of Armeno-Kartlian origin which had emigrated from the harried marchland of Somkheti and taken service with the Kakhian kings. (For the movement of population from Somkheti into Kakheti during the first half of the sixteenth century, see Introduction, p. 57.)

(d) The Adamishvilis and others: Brosset, in his summary of Zvenigorodski's embassy (*ibid.* col. 319) describes Yese Adamishvili ('Adam's son Yessey') as related through his mother to Prince Giorgi. The Adamishvilis were, it appears, a cadet branch of the Andronikashvilis.

Brosset includes also in his list Kaikhosro Omanishvili (for whom see above, Chap. 3, p. 135, n. 1). Abulaskar is a name of Arabic origin – *abu-al-askar* – 'father of the soldier'. Brosset adds to these names a certain Bejan, a common Georgian forename (see Chap. 11, p. 450, n. 1 above); and 'perhaps Zurab Aprosiev, Rustam (Rostom) Adamishvili and Rustam Miskun'. Zurab, who seems to have been the groom or equerry of the Prince mentioned in Chap. 11, p. 435, n. 2 above, can have been a member of the *tavadi* family of

Abashidze (see Wak./Brosset, p. 488, col. 2). Rustam Miskun (=Mishkuni) may have been a noble from the rich mining district of Mishkana of Kartli (cf. Wak./Brosset, p. 149); like Aram Dzhezdambek, he may well have been an Armeno-Georgian refugee from the devastations of south-eastern Kartli by the Turks.

(e) Brosset adds to these names 'Simon and Cozma (variant p. 488 – Kurman) sons of David'. These brothers would appear to have been members of the Davitishvili family, collaterals of the Kakhian royal line. They were also called *Twal-Damtswriani*='son of him who has had his eyes burnt out'. For this interesting family, see Brosset (*HG*, Vol. ii/i, pp. 573–7 with Genealogical Tree). From them descend the Davidov-Bagrations who became Russianized during the eighteenth century; but a branch remained in Kakheti as *aznaurni* directly dependent on the king (cf. Wak./Brosset, 489, col. 1); also Toumanoff (*SCCH*, p. 203, n. 299) for the family of Bagration-Davidov, still surviving.

COMMENTARY 62

The city of Ardabil (Erdebil) (ref. Chap. 12, p. 454, n. 1)

Erdebil is the Turkish pronunciation of Persian *Ardabil*. As the home of Shaikh Safi-al-din and the original centre of the Sufi order at the end of the thirteenth century, Ardabil enjoyed great prestige under the Safavids. With Tabriz and Kazvin it was one of the triangle of capitals of the earlier Safavids before Shah Abbas removed the centre of administration to Isfahan. On the west the city is dominated by the peak of Savalan (4800 m.). It lies at an altitude of 1370 m. in a circular plain surrounded by mountain ridges and is subject to extremes of heat and cold and formidable dust storms. In a near-contemporary description, Evliya Chelebi (von Hammer ed., Vol. ii, pp. 146–7) observes:

the climate much resembles that of Erzurum; hard winter and a fruitful soil, the corn multiplying eighty fold; there are no fruit-trees and vines, but gardens for vegetables and rosebuds ... Erdebil is famous for its immense number of mice which are great destroyers of cloth. Cats are therefore so dear that they are sold in cages by public auction; some of Divrigui fetch the price of a hundred piastres, but they are short-lived like all cats of Erdebil. The cryers at the auction call out: 'A good hunting cat, well bred, a good companion, an enemy to rats, which steals not'.

The most detailed near-contemporary description is by Olearius (Wicquefort, ed., Vol. I, pp. 523 and 629–42 with pictorial map of town between pp. 628 and 629). He found it rather larger than Shemakha. Much of the library of the shrine of Shaikh Safi and many art objects were removed by the Russians to St Petersburg after the campaign of 1827. A famous sixteenth-century carpet from the shrine is the pride of the Victoria and Albert Museum in London. For further details, article by R. N. Frye, in *EI*, 2nd ed.; and longer one with useful bibliography by Mirza Bala in *IA*.

COMMENTARY 63

King Constantine's reflections on his own life and family (ref. Chap. 12, p. 464, n. 1; cf. also Commentary 42: *King Alexander's account of his own life*)

Brosset (*EC/BHP*, Vol. II, Nos 19–21, col. 323, n. 96) comments that there is no record in the Georgian sources of Alexander's having killed his father Levan (1520–74), who, according to Wakhusht (Brosset, *HG*, Vol. II/i, p. 153) died at a very advanced age. However, Brosset (ibid., n. 1) observes that the fact may be true although the annals do not mention it. Alexander's half brothers were killed in battle against him, although the cause of death of his brother Yese who, according to some sources, was the elder and who died in a monastery, remains obscure. Constantine's great-grandfather *Av* Giorgi II

(1511–13) killed his father Alexander I and blinded his brother Dmitri. Brosset (*EC/BHP*, Vol. II, Nos 19–21, n. 96) remarks that there is only one other record of parricide among the Georgian dynasts; but on parricide as customary law among the Osetians and in Daghestan, see Baddeley (*RFC*, Vol. I, pp. 173–4). In the Ottoman imperial house fratricide became the accepted practice at the accession of a new sultan and it was not uncommon among the Safavids and Uzbeks. It occurred in Russia among the later Rurikovichi and in England brothers, uncles and nephews were frequently killed by the later Plantagenets. It is hardly necessary to recall the ruthlessness of the Tudors and some of the Scottish Stewarts towards relatives who were near the succession. Gvritishvili, in his study of the feudal houses of Kartli, finds fratricide a fairly common practice. It would seem, however, from the grim fates of both *Av* Giorgi and of Constantine that royal parricide really shocked opinion in sixteenth century Georgia. By contrast, we may note the laudable efforts which Giorgi X of Kartli made to ransom his father Simon I from the Turks, recorded by Wakhusht and in 'Suite des Annales' (cf. Brosset, *HG*, Vol. II/i, pp. 42–3 and 373–4).

COMMENTARY 64

'The Archbishop of Golgotha, Theodosius' (ref. Chap. 13, p. 471, n. 1)

'The Archbishop of Golgotha, Theodosius' seems to have been an adventurous, not to say pretentious, prelate, as his later history shows. In 1624 he appeared in Moscow as an envoy of Taymuraz I of Kakheti and Russian officials questioned him. Their conclusions were that he had been a bishop and not an archbishop for twenty years and that he had been in Jerusalem in the entourage of the Patriarch Sophron. Since then he had lived in Kisiqi but he could not show letters of installation to that important see. He had been in Moscow in the time of Tsar Fedor Ivanovich in the company of Bishop Theophanos who had been sent by the Patriarch to collect alms. From there he had returned to Georgia in the time of Tsar Boris. On his second visit to Moscow he was the bearer of letters from the Patriarch Cyril (Lucar) of Constantinople, asking for alms to rebuild the church of the Georgians in Jerusalem which had been burnt. Brosset observes that the Georgians possessed a chapel in the Temple of the Resurrection in Jerusalem on the very spot where the Cross of the Saviour had been set up. This chapel was called Golgotha and was a dependency of the monastery of which Theodosius was the abbot. Brosset believes that this monastery had been destroyed by fire about the time of the mission to Moscow in 1624 (cf. Brosset, *EC/BHP*, Vol. II, Nos. 19–21, cols. 325–6 and n. 104: and Vol. III, No. 4, cols. 66 and 67, also n. 49).

(For Georgian churches and monasteries in and near the Holy City, some of which had been established as early as the sixth century A.D., and for an account of the Georgian chapel on Golgotha, see Tamarati, *EG*, pp. 305–18; and p. 414 for illustration of a Georgian mosaic surrounding the hole where the Cross was planted.)

COMMENTARY 65

The town of Gori (ref. Chap. 13, p. 472, n. 3)

'His town of Gori': a town and fortress in the triangle formed by the junction of the greater and lesser Lyakhvi rivers with the Kura. Commanding the approaches from the Turkish base at Akhaltsikhe along the middle Kura to their garrison in Tiflis and also the ways over the Likhis-mta (Suram mountains) from Kartli into Imereti, it was a place of strategic importance. It was one of the strong points occupied by Lala Mustafa Pasha in 1578; twice besieged by Simon I, the Turks surrendered the place to him in 1599 (cf. Brosset, *HG*, ii/i, pp. 41–2; also *Chronique Géorgienne*, p. 26).

For description of the town and fortress, see Wak./Brosset, pp. 246–7; Wak./Jan., p. 85. 'The climate is delightful and the water good . . . The summer is fine and freshened by breezes . . . The inhabitants, Armenians and Georgians, are tall, handsome men, proud and full of boasting in their talk.' According to Wakhusht the fortress was ruined during the long siege operations of Simon I; in the middle of the seventeenth century King Rostom built a palace in Gori in the Persian style; but by the first quarter of the eighteenth century – following destructive occupations by Turks, Lesghians and Persians – the place had lost its importance. Castelli's fine view of Gori in the middle of the seventeenth century is reproduced in Allen, *HGP*, between pp. 130 and 131. (Gori was the birthplace of Joseph Jugashvili – Stalin.)

COMMENTARY 66

Precedence among the kings in Georgia (ref. Chap. 13, p. 473, n. 1)

Since the Russians had first been in political and diplomatic contact with the branch of the Bagratid family ruling Kakheti, they had been in the habit of treating them as the kings of 'Georgia' or 'Iberia'. But as the core of the old Georgian Kingdom – which remained united from the beginning of the twelfth to the middle of the fifteenth century with its capital at Tiflis – Kartli might be regarded as the surviving trunk of the Iberian monarchy. Simon I certainly held to this tradition in his attempts to assert his authority over Samtskhe and Imereti. Giorgi had his father's view in mind when he claimed that 'the chief king in the Iberian land is myself and not Alexander'. Terence Gray in an article 'Les Bagratides: la plus ancienne dynastie de la Chrétienté', in *La Science Historique* (XLI ann., Nos. 22–3, p. 10) puts the view that legitimately primacy lay with the Imerian kings; he notes that in Castelli's drawing of Alexander III of Imereti (1639–60), reproduced in Allen, *HGP*, opposite p. 348, he is described as *Rex Georgianorum* and *Il re di Giorgia*. For the complexities of the dynastic system in Georgia, see further Toumanoff (*SCCH*, particularly pp. 266–73).

COMMENTARY 67

The Bagratid royal children (ref. Chap. 13, p. 475, n. 1)

According to Brosset, (*HG*, Vol. 11/i, p. 635) Taymuraz (Teymuras) was sixteen years old when he was crowned King of Kakheti in 1605. He had a chequered career and was a leading personality in Caucasian politics during the first six decades of the seventeenth century.

In 1609, Taymuraz married (i) Anna, daughter of Mamia II Gurieli. She was described as a girl of remarkable beauty; but died of an ulcerated throat in the same year (for a curious and touching account of her illness, see *Chronique Géorgienne*, p. 34). Concerned to ensure the succession, Taymuraz married very soon afterwards Khorashan, eldest daughter of Giorgi X of Kartli, and sister of the new boy king, Luarsab II. (Khorashan had already been promised to Bahadur, eldest son of Nugsar Eristav of the Aragvi – and this breach of faith brought trouble to Luarsab in the following years.) In the same year, according to the Georgian sources, Luarsab's second sister, Tinatin, entered the *harim* of Shah Abbas, where a sister of Taymuraz was already installed. Tinatin is named in different sources Peri (Fairy), Leila (Dark) or Fatman-sultan-begum (cf. *Chronique Géorgienne*, p. 34 and Brosset, *HG*, Vol. 11/i, Genealogical Tree, p. 627, where he gives the date 1610 for the alliance with Shah Abbas). On the other hand, Danişmend (Vol. 111, p. 233) referring to the presence of *Dokuzuncu Görkin* (erroneously Giorgi IX) in the camp of Shah Abbas before Erevan in May 1604, refers to the king as the *kaynata* (father-in-law) of the

Shah. As Giorgi himself had been married as early as 1578, one is inclined to believe that his second daughter must have been already in her early twenties in 1604, and to accept the dating of the Turkish sources. Tinatin was subsequently given by Shah Abbas to a certain Pheikar Khan who was named governor of Kakheti in 1616, after the expulsion of Taymuraz by the Persians. (He was called in Georgian sources Pheiknis-Khan, and was perhaps named from the small settlement of Pheikrian in Garet-Kakheti on the upper Iora, to the east of Martqopi, where Wakhusht lists a chain of 'obas des Tartares', Wak./Brosset, p. 480, cols. 2 and 3.)

Theodosius of Golgotha, when he appeared in Moscow in 1624, told Russian officials that the wife of Pheikar-Khan was 'Elena daughter of King Giorgi of Kartli' and that as the former wife of the Shah she had the upper hand and protected the Christian religion. Theodosius, or the Posolski Prikaz clerk who recorded his report, seems to have confused Tinatin with the youngest daughter Elena, whose name might still have been a memory in the Posolski Prikaz; for discussion see Brosset (*EC/BHP*, Vol. III, No. 4, p. 67 and n. 51). Wakhusht, in his *History of Kartli* (Brosset, *HG*, Vol. II/i, p. 51) definitely calls the Shah's wife Tinatin and indicates that she proved a loyal friend to her brother, Luarsab II, during the difficult period which preceded his arrest and imprisonment in Astrabad in 1616. It was doubtless because of the bad relation with Luarsab – which ended in the tragedy of the king's execution – that Abbas discarded the Georgian Sultan-begum to Pheikar-Khan.

It is curious that Khorashan – who was not married until 1609/10 – is not mentioned in the negotiations between Tatishchev and King Giorgi in 1605; but she had recently been promised to Aristov Sonski (Eristav Nugsar) for his son Bahadur; and, as will transpire, Nugsar seems to have been the principal informant of Tatishchev on the affairs of the Kartlian royal family. It would seem that the elder girl was simply kept out of view of the Russian mission.

(For impression of Taymuraz and his queen Khorashan in later life, see reproduction of drawing by Castelli in Allen, *HGP*, opposite p. 172.)

COMMENTARY 68

'King Yuri's Uncle Wakhtang': and the Bagratids of Mukhrani (ref. Chap. 14, p. 482, n. 4; p. 484, n. 1; p. 494, n. 2)

There are several obscurities here. Brosset (*EC/BPH*, Vol. II, col. 327, n. 106) observes that Wakhtang (I) was not the uncle of King Giorgi, but the son of the uncle of the King's grandfather, Luarsab I. This was his view in 1844. However, in 1849 he was able to cite a charter of Luarsab I which establishes that there was a younger brother of Simon I named Wakhtang (*VA*, IVme rapport, p. 26). This Wakhtang is included in the Genealogical Tree of the Kartlian Bagratids which he published in 1856 (Brosset, *HG*, Vol. II/i, p. 626; see also ibid., p. 43, n. 2, for the sons of Simon I). Wakhtang was the father of 'Prince Potata' (Paata, see Chap. 14, p. 482, n. 5) and of a daughter, Tamar, who married an Amilakhvari.

Wakhtang (II), Prince of Mukhrani, who appears as the father of the eligible Prince Khozdrov, was the son of Bagrat, first Prince of Mukhrani, a brother of David VIII. This Wakhtang was, therefore, first cousin to Luarsab I. He had a sister, the famous Dedis-Imedi, who became the wife of the Atabeg Kay Khusrau of Samtskhe; and two brothers, Archil, who was sent as a hostage to Persia in 1566 and who was the father of the Princes Irakli and Useyn (see below); and Ashotan – father of the martyred Queen Ketevan of Kakheti. Born hardly later than 1510, Wakhtang, in the 1570's, must have been an elderly man with a late litter of infant sons. (He had first been married to the daughter of Bad George of Kakheti before 1528.)

The *Chronique Géorgienne* mentions Wakhtang Prince of Mukhrani as fighting against Lala Mustafa Pasha – p. 18; but later he was made prisoner by Simon I – p. 21. These incidents took place in 1578; and Wakhtang is stated to have died in 1580 – p. 22; but since his youngest son Khozdrov (Khusrau) was 23 in 1605 Wakhtang must have been living at least in 1581. According to *Chronique Géorgienne* – p. 13, Irakli, son of Wakhtang's younger brother Archil, was 'elected' Prince of Mukhrani (*Mukhranis-batoni*) as early as 1576. In May 1578 the new prince gave refuge to Nestan-Darejan, queen of Simon I – ibid., p. 16. From these facts it would appear that in his last years Wakhtang was an outlaw, out of favour with the King, and displaced by his sixteen-year-old nephew Irakli. His two sons were then infants, but from our text, at p. 495, it seems that in 1604–5 Irakli (and perhaps his brother Useyn) together with Wakhtang's sons, Taymuraz and Khozdrov, were all living on the Mukhranian appanage.

From the text at p. 496 it is clear that King Giorgi was suspicious of the pretensions of his kinsmen of the Mukhranian line. It was Tatishchev who discovered their eligibility. Brosset observes: 'One cannot admire enough the ability of a foreigner, not knowing the language of the country, who was able to find out exactly matters which were being carefully concealed from him.' But it would seem likely that the information was leaked by Eristav Nugsar (Prince Aristov). Taymuraz, the elder of the sons of Wakhtang (II) of Mukhrani, was born about 1573 and was therefore thirty-two at the time of Tatishchev's embassy. He was already married to a daughter of Eristav Nugsar – who, it may be borne in mind, was ambitious enough to seek for his eldest son the hand of King Giorgi's daughter, Khorashan. Again, Nugsar later became the father-in-law of Giorgi Saakadze, 'the great *mo'uravi*', the most dangerous and gifted adventurer in Georgian politics during the following two decades. Taymuraz of Mukhrani, indeed, found himself a member of the powerful northern faction which, under the leadership of Saakadze, became partisans of Shah Abbas, encompassed the downfall of Luarsab II and prepared the way for the ultimate succession to the throne of the Mukhranian Bagratids. (Here it should be observed that Luarsab twice affronted the pride of the rather parvenu leaders of this group, since he married off his sister Khorashan to Taymuraz I of Kakheti after she had been promised to Nugsar's son Bahadur; and he himself repudiated as his wife the sister of Saakadze under pressure from the higher nobility, particularly their wives. See *Chronique Géorgienne*, pp. 41 ff.)

Taymuraz of Mukhrani became administrator of Kartli for Shah Abbas in 1623; he died the following year and was succeeded by his younger brother Kay Khusrau (Khozdrov) who married a Gurieli princess and died in 1627. Taymuraz was the grandfather of Wakhtang V and ancestor of the brilliant line of Mukhranian Bagratids who ruled Kartli until 1724. Kay Khusrau was the father of the Catholicos Domenti II (1660–1676) (cf. Brosset, *HG*, Vol. 11/i, Genealogical Trees, p. 626).

To conclude, it would seem that 'King Yuri's uncle' was a brother of Simon I and was not Wakhtang of Mukhrani. The references to the second Wakhtang, Prince of Mukhrani, indicate that he was the father of the two princes, Taymuraz and Kay Khusrau, and it is unlikely that he was in fact living at the time of Tatishchev's mission. In any case it seems clear that King Giorgi's intuition that the Mukhranian princes were not to be trusted was valid.

COMMENTARY 69

Tsar Boris's daughter Xenia (ref. Chap. 14, p. 493, n. 1; p. 499, n. 1)

Boris Godunov's daughter, Xenia (Kseniya) was born in 1582. Contemporaries praised her intelligence, education and good looks; she was described as being of medium height, with pink cheeks and a white skin, wavy black hair and large black eyes. Her father's efforts to find her a husband of royal blood had proved unlucky. In 1598 the arrangements with the Swedish Prince Gustav fell through because he refused to embrace Orthodoxy or to discard his mistress. In a letter to Sir Robert Cecil from Archangel, dated 10 June, 1600, Sir Anthony Sherley had tentatively suggested that Queen Elizabeth might offer Tsar Boris 'any gentleman of spirit whom she will vouchsafe to call cousin' (cf. Ross, *Anthony Sherley*, p. 246, also p. 36). Another suitor, brother of King Christian of Denmark and brother-in-law of King James VI of Scotland, had died suddenly in Moscow in 1602, shortly before the wedding. The Tsar's insistence that the chosen bridegroom should embrace Orthodoxy narrowed the field. Marriages with members of royal houses of the Orthodox Church in the east were not without attraction for the Muscovite Tsars. Ivan III had married the exiled and impoverished Sofia Palaeologa; and Ivan IV had found it politic to take as his second wife Maria Temryukovna, daughter of the paramount prince of Kabarda, who had to be baptized for the occasion. By marriage into the Kartlian house the newly established Godunovs would inherit the blood, not only of the Bagratids, but also of the Byzantine Comnenes; and the connection with the imperial blood of Byzantium which had died out with the late Tsar Fedor Ivanovich was of significance for the prestige of the Muscovite rulers (cf. Commentary 39 above).

In this same summer of 1605, following the success of the False Dmitri, and the killing of her brother and mother, Xenia was forced to become for some months the mistress of the Pretender. Later she took the veil and was banished to a convent at Beloozero. She died in 1622 (cf. *RBS* under 'Kseniya'; also article by Allen in *OSP*, Vol. XII, 1965). In Müller's *Sammlung* (for the loan of which I am indebted to

La Ville de TARKU dans le Dagestan.

16. Tarku town, c. 1643. From Olearius/W., Vol. 1, pp. 1055/6.

Dr. Laurence Lockhart), Band 5, Stück 1 and 2, 'Versuch einer neureren Geschichte von Russland', Xenia is persistently called Arinia (=Irene) – a confusion with her Aunt Irina, widow of Tsar Fedor Ivanovich and sister of Boris Godunov.

COMMENTARY 70

Buturlin's catastrophe at Tarku (ref. Chap. 15, p. 512, n. 2)

This passage in Tatishchev's report helps to date the final catastrophe at Tarku which Russian historians give, rather indefinitely, as 'the Spring of 1605'. At the end of the first week of June, Aytek told the ambassadors that the Kumukhs had captured the fort on the Koysu (Sulak) and that Tarku was under artillery bombardment. Buturlin was besieged and cut off from the sea by a mixed horde of Kumukhs and Avars under the command of the Shevkal's son, Saltan-Mahmut, who had in the previous year been in touch with the Turks in Shemakha (see above, Chap. 11, p. 451, n. 1). For the siege he received cannon and some reinforcements in men from the Turkish Pasha in Derbent. Saltan-Mahmut proposed capitulation to Buturlin – whose position was further weakened by the mining of a bastion which collapsed and buried over a hundred musketeers. Terms were agreed: that the Russians should withdraw under arms, taking with them their sick and wounded; Saltan-Mahmut gave his own son as hostage for the proper carrying out of the agreement. But it was the day fixed for the celebration of the marriage of the Shevkal with a daughter of the Avar Khan. Hundreds of *tuluks* of *buʒa* (goatskin bags filled with Tartar beer) were distributed to the wild victors who were further excited by the preaching of their mullahs. The orgy proved fatal to the Russians. While their columns, with sick and wounded, were crossing the marshy land on both sides of the Osen river they were set upon by the fanatical and drunken hordes. Buturlin struck off the head of

Saltan-Mahmut's hostage son – who was, it was said, a substituted Tartar boy. But Buturlin and his own son, together with Pleshcheyev and his two sons, and many other boyars were slain; Saltan-Mahmut was also among the killed in this savage affair which resulted in the annihilation of some seven thousand Russian troops. Prince V. I. Bakhteyarov-Rostovski (*q.v. RSB*, under name), A. Blagoy and S. Mamatov were taken prisoners; the latter as a convert to Orthodoxy from Islam, was drenched with naphtha and burnt alive by his captors. For the Osen river and topography of Tarku see Commentary 51.

From our text it appears that the news of the disaster had not reached the commanders on the Terek when the ambassadors arrived on 10 June. But it did 'at that time' – when panic prevailed and a Turkish attack on Terek-town (Terki) was expected. It would therefore be reasonable to date Buturlin's disaster and death on the Osen towards the end of the second week of June. For a good account of these events, see Potto (pp. 10–13) citing I. Popko, *Terskoye voysko* (Vol. I, pp. 38–44) and *Prilozheniye* (not available to the present writer). For many picturesque details see Müller's *Sammlung* (Band V, pp. 176–9) who dates the battle 1604, instead of 1605. Karamzin, Vol. II, pp. 90–2, gives a good running account based on original sources; Solovyev, Vol. II, p. 712, is slight. For biographical note on Saltan-Mahmut, see *SSKG*, Vol. I, p. 58 (twice), n. 8.

COMMENTARY 71

Castelli and his drawings

The interests of the Papacy in the Black Sea lands had been manifest since the thirteenth century. In 1328, John of Florence had been appointed first Roman Catholic Archbishop of Tiflis and two years later, an Englishman, Peter Gerald, was named Bishop of Tzkhomi (Sukhum).[1] Anxious to engage the interest

[1] For a brief summary of these early contacts, see Allen, *HGP*, pp. 336–

of the west, the Georgian kings encouraged these missions, although they regarded Roman propaganda with reserve and conversions, sometimes, with hostility. During the middle of the seventeenth century, the Theatines were the most active of the teaching and preaching orders in Georgia. About 1630 Fr Christoforo Castelli was sent to Gori. In 1634, he was delegated to Guria and early in 1640 he moved to Mingrelia. Later he spent some years at the court of King Alexander III of Imereti and he was still living in Kutaisi in 1650 when the Russian embassy of Tolochanov and Yevlev was there. Castelli was an artist of real talent, an acute observer with a genial interest in architecture, agriculture, sports and all the details of the everyday life of the people. He was, too, a skilled portraitist and left many drawings of the princes and notables of the time and their ladies.

His four folio albums of drawings have survived in the Biblioteca Communale in Palermo (*Miscellanea di Oriente*, 92–95). Many of the drawings bear notes in Latin, Neapolitan and Georgian. Castelli left also a brief *Descriptio origines missionum Theatinorum in Regno Georgiae* (*Miscellanea di Oriente*, MS. 94). Castelli's drawings, with their wide range of interest for historians, sociologists and anthropologists, and their artistic merit have not been edited or published.[2]

338. For a detailed survey, Fr Michel Tamarati, *L'Eglise géorgienne*, Chaps. xiii–xvi. The Catholic missions were finally expelled by the Russian government in 1845.

[2] In the Museum and in the National Gallery of Tbilisi are 137 photographs of the drawings deposited by Tamarati, who published 19 of them in his *Eglise géorgienne*. Allen published 36 (most in line) in *HGP*. Mr Terence Gray gave a set of photographs (not complete) to the National Library, Dublin.

SUPPLEMENTARY DOCUMENTS
(FROM THE EMBASSY OF SOVIN
AND POLUKHANOV, 1596–9)

I. THE ADVENTURES OF THE GEORGIAN LUKOYANKO
(From Belokurov, *Snosheniya*, pp. 284–5)

To the Sovereign Tsar and great Prince Fedor Ivanovich of
all Russia, his servants Ivanets Vorotynski and his assistants
make obeisance. It is written in your Majesty's letter received
on the 28th of July of the current year ... that we are to send
off the Georgian ambassadors from Kazan to Astarakhan
together with Kuzma Sovin and under-dyak Andrey Polukhanov. Now, Dubrovin, a boyar's son from Murom who had
been attached to the Georgian ambassadors for their journey
home, has come to us, your servants, and told us that ambassador Khurshit wants to take one by the name of Lukoyanko,
who escaped from the Nogays, with him to Georgia. We had
him brought to us ... and on being questioned this Lukoyanko said that he was born in the Georgian land and that he
was taken prisoner by the Crimeans; and from the Crimeans
he was captured, Sire, by the Don Cossacks, Ivan Kishkin and
his comrades, who sold him at Azov. And, Sire, he says that he
went from Azov to Tsaritsyn when Ivan Buturlin was in
command; and from Tsaritsyn he was carried to Kazan by
Ivan Gubin. And, Sire, Lukoyanko wants to travel to Georgia
with the ambassador because he is a native of Georgia. He has
handed a petition to us, your servants; and, Sire, having glued
the petition underneath this dispatch, we are sending it to you.
Until we get your Majesty's command, we have entrusted
Lukoyanko to the boyar's son Derevnya Kaysarov.

To the sovereign Tsar and great Prince Fedor Ivanovich

of all Russia, his Majesty's servant, the Georgian expatriate Lukoyanko, son of Gregory, makes obeisance. My father, Sire, was a *strelets* captain in the Georgian land. Crimeans took me prisoner in the Georgian land, and I, your servant, spent seven years in captivity in Crimea, in the house of the Crimean Tartar Daud of the *ulus* of Sulesh murza. And in the Crimea I was captured by your Majesty's Don Cossacks under *ataman* Ivan Kishkin; and this Ivan Kishkin and his comrades sold me at Azov. I spent twelve years at Azov in the house of the Azov Tartar Memsha. I fled from Azov into Russia under your royal name, and I came to the Cossacks on the Don. From the Don I went to your Majesty's patrimony, the town of Tsaritsyn, when Foma Afanasyevich Buturlin[1] was your Majesty's commander there. At Tsaritsyn Foma Buturlin took from me thirty gold pieces, and a length of green *zenden* and a piece of purple morocco leather and a gold-embroidered *arakchin*.[2] Last year, in [7]103, I came to your Majesty's patrimony of Kazan with Ivan Gubin, when he was travelling from Terek-town to Moscow; and since then I have been living at Kazan. I have no orders from you, Sire. Merciful

[1] Foma Afanasyevich Buturlin was appointed senior commander at Tsaritsyn in 1593, after having spent a year as commander at Serpukhov. Transferred to the Tsar's court, he became one of the signatories of the petition to Boris Godunov asking him to accept the Crown. He was made an equerry in 1598 and died in 1602. Despite a life-time of soldiering he was an educated man and commissioned the translation of a Polish treatise on natural history (*RBS*). A member of the influential Buturlin family, he was kinsman of Ivan Mikhaylovich Buturlin who commanded in Daghestan in 1605; cf. Commentary 70.

[2] *Zenden*: a cotton fabric manufactured in Central Asia, named after the village of Zandana or Zendane in Bukhara, where such cloth was made as far back as the tenth century; by the sixteenth century *zenden* was manufactured in other villages in Bukhara as well. It was a fairly thick type of cloth, woven from coloured threads (and not dyed subsequently); it could either be plain or have a design. Its price in Russia at the end of the sixteenth century varied between 5 and 11 copecks the *arshin* (1 *arshin* = $2\frac{1}{3}$ ft.) (Fekhner, *TRG*, p. 75 and n. 1, p. 78). *Arakchin* = a skull-cap made of thin cloth.

Tsar, Sire, show your mercy, and have your royal command issued about me. Sovereign, Tsar, be merciful.

2. THE PROBLEM OF TRANSLATORS (From Belokurov, *Snosheniya*, pp. 298–300)

On the same day Khurshit and dyak Iaram who had been on an embassy to Moscow came to the ambassadors' camp with a message from the king and said to Kuzma and to Andrey:

'The king has commanded us to say to you: You have brought a letter from the great Sovereign, and letters from Patriarch Job and from the Sovereign's brother-in-law Boris Fedorovich – written in Russian. The king has not got anybody who can translate these letters; the man whom the king had before now to translate letters written in Russian has since died. The king wants to hear the contents of the letters soon. So you, Andrey, should forthwith ride with the interpreters to the king's court where the Bishop and the king's noblemen are waiting for you. You, Andrey, should read the letters which you brought with you and the interpreters should (orally) translate what is written in the letters into Turkish, and the king's clerks will write it down in Iberian.'

Kuzma and under-dyak Andrey replied: 'Our great Sovereign sent letters to King Alexander with his Majesty's ambassadors on several occasions before now, and they were written in Russian. And the king had these letters translated by the Greek monk Kiril, and none of the Sovereign's men ever translated letters for the king. The letters which have now been sent with us for king Alexander from our great Sovereign, and the holiest Patriarch Job and the Sovereign's brother-in-law Boris Fedorovich, are written in Russian as hitherto. We cannot translate the letters: such interpreters as we have speak Turkish; they cannot read and write in Russian or Turkish, and they are unable to translate the letters.'

Khurshit and his comrades said: 'The king has ordered us to say that you, Andrey and the interpreters should go to his court without fail and translate the letters.'

And Kuzma and Andrey replied: 'We cannot do such things as have not been done before now. Consider it yourselves: would it be possible to translate letters correctly by using three languages? It is not a proper job – only a muddle.'

And Khurshit and his comrades rode back to the king.

On the following day, Wednesday 15th of December, the bishop of Alaverdi Philip and the king's nobles, Prince Kanchinya and Prince Uman, together with the king's trusted nobleman Prince Aram and Khurshit who had been on an embassy to Moscow, came from the king to Kuzma and said to him and to Andrey: '. . . Our sovereign, King Alexander, has sent us with the letters which you brought from the Sovereign, the Patriarch and the Sovereign's brother-in-law Boris Fedorovich, so that you can translate them.'

Kuzma and under-dyak Andrey said . . . 'We cannot do things which have not been done in the past. Neither are we able to translate the letters: the interpreters we have speak Turkish and they cannot read or write in Russian or Turkish. The letters contain many wise words taken from Holy Writ, and the interpreters cannot say these words in Turkish because they do not exist in the Turkish language. A translation ought to be rendered correctly. Consider it yourselves: would it be possible for interpreters to translate correctly letters through three languages? If even one single word is not written correctly in the translation, the thing will be muddled and the whole matter will become null because of one word.'

Bishop Philip and the king's nobleman then said: 'We know that your great Sovereign, in his mercy towards King Alexander, commands that letters be written to him in Russian. And so long as the king had translators for these letters, he did not even mention the matter of translation to the Sovereign's previous ambassadors. But now that the king has no translator he has commanded us to tell you to translate the letters without fail. How can the king know the contents without having read the letters? And if you will not translate the letters, the king will be forced to look beyond his land for a man who can read and write Russian; and then all the affairs about which the Sovereign graciously writes will become known through your fault and not through the fault of King Alexander. For our sovereign King Alexander glorifies in all realms your great Sovereign's mercy and protection, but he keeps secret what is in writing. But since you do not want to translate the letters ... just read their contents to us, and let the interpreter render it in Turkish. All of us understand Turkish. And we shall notify our Sovereign of the contents of the letters.'

So Kuzma and under-dyak Andrey read the letters and had the contents ... conveyed in Turkish by the Sovereign's interpreters to Bishop Philip and to the king's noblemen ... And the bishop and the noblemen rode back to the king.

3. LOGISTICS ON THE TEREK AND THE STATE OF DAGHESTAN IN 1599 (From Belokurov, *Snosheniya*, pp. 291–2)

And we, your servants, have written to the commanders Petr Sheremetev and Ivan Nashchokin and to dyak Bogdan Ivanov at Astarakhan, to give them the news from the Koysu: On the 8th day of March Shevkal's son Surkay Shevkal came to the blockhouse on the Koysu and said that a small number of soldiers should not be sent from the Terek to meet the ambassadors, because the Kumyks have gathered together. In accordance with your Majesty's instructions given to us, your servants, over the signature of dyak Afanasi Vlasyev, we asked the commanders at Astarakhan to send us soldiers to the Terek: a captain of mounted *streltsy* and *sotniks* together with

500 mounted *streltsy* and *yurt* Tartars. As for the 100 Tartars who were sent from Astarakhan this winter under the drove headman Yarlagash, there were twenty-two young hired lads among them. Drove headman Yarlagash and his comrades petition you, Sire, and say that they were sent on your service from Astarakhan to the Terek; at Astarakhan they were given two rubles each of your bounty but no provisions for their service, although they travelled to the Terek on horseback in winter-time. We, your servants, are giving them for their needs out of your Majesty's treasury an eighth of a barrel of groats for every ten men a month. Of these one hundred nomad Tartars, twenty-two men fled from the Terek on the 2nd of April. And we, your servants, sent the names of the runaway Tartars to Petr Sheremetev, Ivan Nashchokin and dyak Bogdan Ivanov at Astarakhan; we asked them to send Tartars into your Majesty's service on the Terek so as to make up the number in accordance with your Majesty's instructions.

Thirty carts with horse-collars and shaft-bows for the train have also been sent this winter from Astarakhan to the Terek, but these carts are too few for the train, and there are no horses belonging to your Majesty on the Terek. And we, your servants wrote to Astarakhan about horses and carts, and asked that they should send us seventy carts with horse-collars and shaft-bows and one hundred horses for the train, when the horse captain, the *sotniks* and the *streltsy* come here – over and above what has already been sent.

We also wrote, Sire, about stores of grain and about boats and ship-stores, and asked them to send stores of grain to Terek-town and the blockhouse on the Koysu with the first convoy this spring, in accordance with your Majesty's order. In Terek-town no surplus of grain was left in the granaries of the Terek tax-payers after the time of St Sergius, while the stores of the soldiers, the *streltsy* and the Cossacks in the blockhouse on the Koysu were sunk in the autumn storms at sea.

Of your Majesty's boats which can be repaired there are on the Terek ten sea-going *strugi* and four rowing *strugi*; and of ship stores there are eight old canvas sails, twenty-three anchors with the flukes broken off, and eight old masts. We need boats, Sire, in order to fetch stores from Astarakhan by sea, and to send from the Terek to the Koysu with stores and troops, or up the Terek with troops for the blockhouse on the Sunzha, and to set up posts along the rivers and on the sea-shore to guard against attacks by Kumyks and men of Azov. And, Sire, as regards the boats and ship stores which are taken from soldiers and settlers on the Terek or from visitors who come from Astarakhan, and which are used to convey messages, these boats get damaged by storms during journeys; and there is nothing with which to repair them on the Terek; no staples or oakum or tar is to be had or to be bought on the Terek, and no stores for boat-repairing are sent from Astarakhan.

If no troops are sent to the Terek from Astarakhan in accordance with your Majesty's instructions, and if Prince Solokh and the Kabardan Cherkesses do not come to the Terek and do not accompany your Majesty's men to the gorges to meet the ambassadors, it will be impossible to escort your Majesty's and the Iberian ambassadors from the gorges with the help of such troops as are on the Terek, and there will be no troops to send against the Kumyks.

And we, your servants, sent to your Majesty on the 5th of January by the Terek guide Andryusha Sumnikov, who was travelling with a troop overland, a list of how many of your Majesty's men there are in Terek-town, in the blockhouse on the Koysu and in the blockhouse on the Sunzha.

We, your servants, have questioned Allaga, who had acted as guide to Prince Andrey Khvorostinin, about the Kumyks: In what numbers and where are there gatherings of Kumyk horsemen? And Allaga said: 'Shevkal's sons, Sultan Magmut and his brothers, who have 200 horsemen, are in Andreyevo village. The prince of Kuyen has 70 horsemen; Shevkal's son Nutsal has 200 horsemen in the village of Karagach; Sultaney of Tyumen has 100 horsemen; Shevkal's youngest son Surkhay has 50 horsemen at Tarkali; another of Shevkal's sons, Alkas, has 30 horsemen at Kapchaga; among the Kafyr-Kumyks, Shevkal's son Andey has 150 horsemen; at Shuran, Shevkal's *uʒden* Temir-khan has ten horsemen; Sarkay Shevkal has 50 horsemen at Tarku; at Kazanych Shevkal has 200 horsemen; beyond Tarku, Shevkal's son Akhmat-khan has 30 horsemen at the Hot Spring; the prince of Karabutak has 100 horsemen; at Kogden there is a nephew of Shevkal's with 200 horsemen; a nephew of Shevkal has the fief of Boynak, with twenty horsemen; the fief of Ukhli belongs to Shevkal's brother-in-law, who has 50 horsemen; Shevkal's *uʒden* Burunchi is in the fief of Arkusha, and he has 30 horsémen; Shevkal's *uʒden* Kazy is in the fief of Apshima with 20 horsemen; Krym-Shevkal's son Mekhdey is in the fief of Dergeli, and he has 100 horsemen; Krym-Shevkal's nephew Surkhay is in the fief of Yungutey, and he has 100 horsemen; Shevkal's nephew Saltan is in the fief of Ulushura with 30 horsemen; *uʒden* Alebek is in the fief of Khili, and he has 50 horsemen; Mirza, who has 50 horsemen, is in the fief of Kaldar; the fief of Erpeli belongs to Budachey of Erpeli and to his brothers, who have some 400 horsemen; Prince Alebek of the Kazy-Kumyks and his brethren have about 500 horsemen; Sultan Magmet, who has 50 horsemen, is in the fief of Kharakula; Kaitmaz is in the fief of Bortyu and he has 30 horsemen; there is the town of Tsakur lying between the Kumyk and the Georgian lands, and Prince Adikorklyu holds it with 200 horsemen; Prince Usmy is in the fief of Kalakura, and he has about 500 horsemen and about 700 foot; there is the fief of Utemish, with Prince Khalebek in it, who has about 300 horsemen; Zikhrar's son, Prince Kadit of Tabasaran is between the Kumyks and Derbent with 500 horsemen.' According to what Allaga says, the Kumyk and the mountaineers from various small states who are allied to Shevkal and his sons have some 5,000 horse in all. Should the Kumyks, and the mountaineers, and the Cherkesses all assemble, they will number about 15,000 horsemen, besides the foot. So, Sire, have your command issued about soldiers, about the Kumyk expeditions, about stores of grain, and about boats and ships' stores.

COMMENTARY ON THE SOURCES

I. ARCHIVAL SOURCES

It was Brosset, during the summer of 1844, who first systematically examined the documents relating to Georgian affairs preserved in the Main Archives of the Ministry of Foreign Affairs in Moscow. He found there a register which he states was arranged in 'perfect chronological order'. It covered thirty-two bundles of papers, sixteen bound journals of embassies and five hundred and thirteen scrolls or documents. He was able to read the journals of the twenty embassies exchanged between the years 1586 to 1620 and numerous other papers which he details in his report.

Brosset classified the documents as follows:

(i) The *nakaz* or instruction which indicated the route to be followed; the speeches to be made to the princes to whom the embassy was accredited; and the answers to be given to enquiries on the state of Russia and her relations with other powers. The attention to detail is impressive: the food to be provided for foreign ambassadors returning to their own country; the quality and prices of horses to be bought; lists of presents to be distributed to notables en route and at the court to be visited.

(ii) The *nakaz* was sometimes supplemented by a *pamyat* or aide-memoire.

(iii) The *otpiski* or particular letters exchanged on matters which had arisen during the course of the embassy.

(iv) The *stateyny spisok* or detailed journal of the journey and actions of the ambassador.[1]

Brosset published the results of his researches in 'Examen

[1] Brosset, *EC/BHP*, Vol. II, col. 144.

critique des annales géorgiennes, pour les temps modernes, au moyen des documents russes' in Vols. I, II and III of *Bulletin de la classe des sciences historiques, philologiques et politiques de l'Académie Impériale des Sciences de Saint-Pétersbourg*. Brosset's work was a summary only of the whole documentation for the period 1586–1620 but it remains the one complete survey of the documents surviving in 1844 and has not been superseded by later scholars. Brosset seems to have made use of some documents which had disappeared by the time Belokurov approached the same subject nearly half a century later; and he cites details from them. Again, Brosset, in his wide knowledge of the Georgian annals and of contemporary Persian, Ottoman, Armenian and European sources, was as an editor better equipped for his task than either Belokurov, who was primarily an archivist, or more recent Soviet historians. Indeed, it is a curious fact that Belokurov, while making use of some of Brosset's works, seems to have overlooked the 'Examen critique' buried away in the rare quarto volumes of the *Bulletin*.

The systematic publication of Russian diplomatic documents of the pre-Petrine period was begun in 1851 by the Second Department of the Imperial Chancellery. Towards the end of the nineteenth century the work was also taken up by learned societies such as the Eastern Section of the Imperial Russian Archaeological Society (which was responsible for the publication of the documents covering Russian relations with Persia edited by N. I. Veselovski)[1] and by the Imperial Society of Russian History and Antiquities of Moscow University. It was for the latter Society that Sergey A. Belokurov edited Vol. I of *Russian relations with the Caucasus (Snosheniya Rossii s Kavkazom)* which was published in 1889 and from which the accounts of the embassies of Zvenigorodski and Tatishchev and the extracts from Sovin have been translated.

[1] N. I. Veselovski, *TVOIA*, Vols. XX, XXI, XXII.

Although Belokurov produced some other important works,[1] it appears that he never brought out a second volume of his *Snosheniya*.

Despite the losses over three centuries due to fires and enemy invasions, and the hardly less serious damage by mice and damp – which seems to have continued even during the generation between Brosset and Belokurov – large quantities of documents from the Posolski Prikaz archives had survived and Belokurov's merit is that he began to edit them in full. Further, in contrast to Brosset, he did not confine himself to documents of Georgian interest but printed much material of interest on Kabarda to which he gives useful attention in his introduction. Until the publication by Kumykov and Kusheva in 1957 of two important volumes on Kabardino-Russian relations during the sixteenth to eighteenth centuries, Belokurov's work remained the only significant contribution on the subject for the sixteenth century.[2]

Prior to the turn of the sixteenth century documents relating to foreign affairs had been kept in the Royal Archives. The Archives of the Posolski Prikaz were established at the end of the sixteenth or at the beginning of the seventeenth century. In the time of Brosset and Belokurov these collections of ancient documents were still kept in the Main Archives of the Ministry of Foreign Affairs in Moscow. Nowadays they are stored in the Central State Archives of Old Records (*Tsentralny Gosudarstvenny Arkhiv Drevnikh Aktov = TsGADA*) in Moscow.[3]

The earliest surviving register of the Royal Archives, compiled between 1572 and 1575, includes the following references to the relations of Russia with Georgia: Chest

[1] *O Posolskom Prikaze* (Moskva, 1906); and *O Vivlioteke Moskovskikh gosudarey v xvi stoletii* (Moskva, 1899).

[2] *Kabardino-Russkiye otnosheniya* (= *KRO*), 2 vols (Moskva, 1957).

[3] S. O. Schmidt (ed.), *Opisi tsarskogo arkhiva xvi veka i arkhiva Posolskogo Prikaza 1614 goda* (Moskva, 1960) p. 6.

No. 23 – contents: ... Iberian quires; and Chest No. 226 – contents: ... Letters from Leon Prince of Georgia (Levan of Kakheti) and a letter to him.

By 1614, the *Posolski Prikaz* had accumulated a much larger Georgian Archive as follows:

(i) 'Bundle of letters from the Iberian King Alexander to the Tsar and great Prince Fedor Ivanovich of all Russia sent by Khurshit and Aram in [7]103';

(ii) 'Letters from divers Tartar and Georgian states put away in one box';

(iii) 'Two letters to the Tsar and great Prince Fedor Ivanovich of all Russia from the Georgian King Alexander sent in [7]103 by a Frenchman whose name is not indicated';

(iv) 'Letter to the Tsaritsa and Great Princess Irina Fedorovna from the Iberian King Alexander's Queen Tinatida [*G.* Tinatin] in 7[101]';

(v) Iberian books for the years [7]095 to [7]105;[1]

(vi) 'Georgian scrolls [*stolpy*]: two scrolls of the year [7]101 – arrival in Moscow and departure of the ambassadors Prince Iaram and his assistants; scroll of the year [7]109 – arrival in Moscow of the Georgian ambassadors Suleyman and Khurshit and their departure from Moscow, and the departure from Moscow of the Sovereign's ambassadors Vasili Pleshcheyev and dyak Timofey Kudrin; scroll of the same year – arrival of the Sovereign's ambassador Prince Andrey Zvenigorodski from the Georgian land; scroll of the year [7]110 – departure of the ambassadors Ivan Nashchokin and dyak Ivan Levontyev and the [*stateyny*] *spisok* of their embassy; scroll of the year [7]114 about Prince Pankrati [*G.* Bagrat] ...; two bundles of various Georgian documents of different years.'[2] By 1673 the original *stateyny*

---

[1] Iberian Book, No. 1, ff. 103–383 contains material on Zvenigorodski's embassy.

[2] Schmidt, *Opisi tsarskogo arkhiva*, pp. 20, 43, 87, 91, 94, 112, 135.

spisok of Zvenigorodski's embassy had 'rotted and fallen apart'.[1]

In the Main Archives of the Ministry of Foreign Affairs in Moscow the documents on Russia's relations with Georgia before the days of Peter the Great were divided into two sections: (1) 'Georgian kings' affairs, written in books, from 1586 to 1700,' and (2) 'Georgian kings' affairs of former years, written on scrolls, from 1586 to 1700.' Both sections were equipped with Registers, some of them compiled in the eighteenth century.[2]

When Belokurov was writing his *Russian relations with the Caucasus* he carried out an exhaustive search of the archives in the course of which he discovered documents placed in the wrong chronological sequence and others in wrong sections. He reached the conclusion that 'After our search, we are convinced that all the documents on the Muscovite State's relations with Caucasian peoples prior to 1613 which are preserved in the Main Archives of the Ministry of Foreign Affairs in Moscow have been included in this volume', with the exception of 'documents of an economic character relating to the equipping of embassies, the sums of money given to ambassadors, the provision of food stores, carts and escorts, etc.'[3] which he decided to omit.

Belokurov published the following documents on the three embassies with which we are concerned:

1. Embassy of Zvenigorodski and Antonov:
   (a) Georgian affairs for 23 April 1589–91 (with the original of Zvenigorodski's *stateyny spisok*);
   (b) Georgian affairs for 21 September 1590–May 1591;
   (c) Georgian *stateynye spiski*, Book No. 1, ff. 103–383

[1] Register (*Peripisnaya kniga*) of 1673.

[2] Polievktov, *Mezhdunarodnye snosheniya Gruzii s inozemnymi stranami,* Vol. 2, pp. 18–19 (Tbilisi, 1928).

[3] Belokurov, *Snosheniya* . . . , pp. cxvi and cxxviii.

(this book is a seventeenth-century copy of documents, in chronological order, for the period 1586–92).

2. Embassy of Sovin and Polukhanov:
   Georgian affairs: (a) 5 June–December 1596; (b) August 1597–98; (c) 8 June 1599.
3. Embassy of Tatishchev and Ivanov:
   (a) Georgian affairs for (i) 2 May–December 1604; (ii) 6 May 1604–12 Nov. 1605.
   (b) Georgian letters: 1605, No. 3.
   (c) Kabardan affairs: 1605, No. 2.

Russian official documents of the pre-Petrine period were classified by substance and format.

Classification by substance was into:

(i) Ambassadorial affairs (*Posolskiye dela*): these included instructions to Russian ambassadors and official correspondence concerning the stay of foreign ambassadors in Russia and the equipment and dispatch of Russian embassies abroad.

(ii) Letters and Treaties (*Gramoty i traktaty*), i.e. documents exchanged by the Tsar with foreign rulers concerning the relations between them.

(iii) *Stateynye spiski*, i.e. detailed reports submitted by ambassadors on their return home. The term (literally 'record of paragraphs') was applied to all official documents divided into paragraphs, each dealing with a specific item, such as ambassador's reports, papers submitted to the *boyarskaya duma* (council), etc.

The classification of documents by substance was not strict, with the result that documents properly belonging to one category were often included in another.[1]

The subdivision by format was, basically, into scrolls (*stolpy* or *stolbtsy*) and books (*knigi*). The former constituted

---

[1] Veselovski, *PDTS*, Introduction.

the files of original documents, glued to each other; at a later stage, the individual sheets were separated and sewn together. Periodically the original documents were copied into bound volumes. One volume often contained copies of documents relating to several embassies arranged in chronological order. The copies were sometimes less detailed than the originals. Clerks of the *Posolski prikaz* were not only industrious copyists but also compilers of registers (registers were compiled in 1614, 1626, 1632 and 1674). The state of the documents was often indicated in these registers. Many documents described in them as 'old and falling apart' or 'rotted' no longer existed in Belokurov's day.

Prior to the 1560s the normal manner in which ambassadors reported to the Tsar on the progress of their mission had been by letter from abroad. It was the exception for them to submit day-to-day detailed records (*stateynye spiski*) although the method itself had been in use at least since the beginning of the century (the earliest surviving *spisok* dates back to 1518; it was submitted by Vladimir Plemyannikov on his return from an embassy to Emperor Maximilian I).[1] The early *spiski* were confined to a description of the negotiations conducted abroad; gradually, however, the ambassadors also came to include accounts of the countries they visited and of their inhabitants.

Ya. Lurye and R. Muller indicate that the *stateyny spisok* of an embassy was drafted by the dyak or under-dyak accompanying the senior ambassador, but that responsibility for editing the final version lay with the latter.[2]

That the *stateynye spiski* of Russian ambassadors are important sources of information on the history and geography

---

[1] D. S. Likhachev (ed.) *Puteshestviya russkikh poslov* XVI–XVII *vv. – Stateynye spiski*, Moskva, 1954, pp. 326, 327.

[2] Ibid., pp. 347 ff.

of the countries they visited is not open to question. In assessing their accuracy, however, one must bear in mind the jaundiced remarks of Kotoshikhin, himself a clerk at the Posolski Prikaz: 'It might be that in carrying out his embassy, an ambassador has said things which were not in his instructions or has failed to say what he was instructed to say. Be that as it may, in his *stateyny spisok* he writes down his speeches not as they were made, but beautifully and wisely, extolling his skill in deception, with a view to being honoured by the Tsar and securing a rich bounty. Nor are the ambassadors ashamed to behave in this manner, since who can inform the Tsar against them in these matters?'[1] The inaccurate reports submitted by Nashchokin and Levontyev on the manner in which they had been treated in Kakheti[2] show that Kotoshikhin was not misjudging his fellow-countrymen. On the other hand, while his remarks might well apply to accounts of negotiations and audiences, there would seem to be no reason why ambassadors should report purposely inaccurate geographical information; in this respect one can agree with Belokurov that the *spiski* were impressively accurate and detailed.[3]

Russian diplomatic documents of the sixteenth and early seventeenth centuries are written in the 'officialese' (*prikaznoy yazyk*, literally 'language of Government departments') of the period. Like all officialese, it lacks literary grace: colloquial expressions abound side by side with archaisms and foreign words (mostly Turkish in the Caucasian documents); clauses and sentences are usually strung together with the help of conjunctions (mostly 'and'); to avoid all possibility of confusion, pronouns were seldom used – instead, the writer repeated the name of the person or object he had in mind.

---

[1] Kotoshikhin, p. 52.
[2] See Chap. 11, above.
[3] Belokurov, *O Posolskom Prikaze*, p. 72.

This has resulted in extreme repetitiveness which is carried a stage further in the substance of the documents. Thus, the reply to a letter begins by quoting the latter at length; an official message sent to a foreign sovereign begins by recapitulating the course of preceding negotiations; the Tsar's letter duplicates the oral message delivered by the ambassador. Accuracy was the aim of the dyaks of the Posolski Prikaz, and tedious repetitiveness was not regarded as too heavy a price to pay for it.

2. THE CAUCASIAN SECTIONS OF THE BOOK OF THE GREAT MAP

The extent to which Russian officials of the late sixteenth and early seventeenth century were acquainted with the geography of the Caucasian lands is reflected in the Book of the Great Map (*Kniga glagolemaya Bolshoy Chertezh*) compiled in 1626. In that year 'an old map of the whole of the Muscovite realm ... drawn a long time ago under former sovereigns ... was found in the Razryad'. Since the map was in a bad state of preservation and falling apart, with the names and markings becoming illegible, a copy of the old map was made to the same scale. Distances on the map were marked 'in versts and in miles and in travelling times – how far a body of horsemen can ride in one day'. The place-names on the map were listed in a book, 'the Book of the Great Map', under rivers, from the sources to the estuaries. The references to the topography of Caucasia are to be found in the sections covering the description of the rivers Don and Terek.

Numerous MSS. of the Book survive in a succession of revised recensions and it was printed several times during the eighteenth and nineteenth centuries in editions which are now bibliographical rarities. I am indebted to Mr. R. A. Skelton for drawing attention to Spasski's edition of 1840, a copy of which is in the British Museum. Serbina's edition, published in Moscow in 1950, has not been available but her articles published in *Istoricheskiye Zapiski*, Nos. 14 (1945) and 23 (1947) are of great value.[1] In these articles, however, Serbina does not discuss topographical identifications. Spasski made many identifications in the Caucasian sections but although he cites Güldenstädt he failed to pinpoint a number of place-names in the Kura valley and he had not the advantage of reference to Brosset's edition of Wakhusht which appeared two years after his own work, in 1842.

In papers published in *Imago Mundi*, the late Leo Bagrow and the late J. Keuning have made numerous comments on the Book and on the original missing map – to which the Book was a sort of primitive 'Baedeker'.[2]

Bagrow has observed that at different times, certainly during the sixteenth century, maps were made in Moscow for domestic use. There were military, frontier and route maps; they did not, however, cover the entire realm and the need for a general map was clear. Ivan IV made several efforts to invite foreigners to make a map: in 1577 negotiations were carried on in Gorlitz to engage the services of the well-known cartographer, B. Shultetus; and in 1586 the Englishman John Dee was approached. These efforts came to nought. 'Thereupon it was evidently decided to make the map by own (*sic*) efforts basing it on the river system. To judge from the data placed

---

[1] See G. I. Spasski, *Kniga glagolemaya Bolshoy Chertezh*, Imp. Ob. Ist. i Drev. Rossii, Moscow, 1840; K. I. Serbina 'Kniga Bolshogo Chertezha i eye redaktsii' in *IZ* No. 14 (1945), pp. 129–47; and 'Istochniki Knigi Bolshogo Chertezha' in *IZ* No. 23 (1947) pp. 290–324. Cf. also the author's *KBCh*, Moscow, 1950, pp. 229, not available to me but reviewed at length in *IM*, Vol. ix (1952) pp. 118–20.

[2] Leo Bagrow, 'The Book of the Great Map' in *IM*, V, 1948, pp. 81–2; J. Keuning, 'Hessel Gerritsz' in *IM*, VI, 1950, pp. 50–1; also K. Buczek, reviewing Bagrow's 'Anecdota Carthographica', Vol. 1, in *IM*, Vol. 11, 1937.

on the map it may be assumed that the map was made between the years 1597 and 1600'.[1]

In the year 1613, the Dutchman Hessel Gerritsz published a map of Russia dedicated to the new Tsar Mikhail Fedorovich Romanov. It bore the title 'Tabvla Russiae ex autographo, quod delineandum curavit Feodor filius tzaris Boris desumta'. In the left-hand top corner there is a plan of Moscow: 'Moscva ad Architypum Feodori Borissowitsi'. On the right there is a view of 'Archangelsckagoroda' surmounted by three gentlemen in Russian dress. Fedor the son of Boris Godunov was born in 1587 and was not more than eighteen at the time of his death in 1605. It would be difficult to allow that he participated seriously in the compilation of the map, but an intelligent boy in his teens may well have made a competent autograph copy of an original draft under the supervision of cartographers and drawing masters in the Kremlin. (In this connection it is only necessary to recall the precocious talents of contemporary youth – including the English Henry Prince of Wales.) The evidence satisfies Keuning who believes also that the persons responsible for the construction of the map disposed of Russian sources which were not available to European cartographers of the time.[2]

Keuning observes that 'we do not know whether Hessel Gerritsz had at his disposal the manuscript of the Tsarevich himself, or a copy of it; likewise we do not know how he obtained it. The original Great Map did not include the whole of Russia, but only the central and southern parts of it. The map seems to be founded entirely on Russian sources. Hessel Gerritsz must have completed this Russian map from other data . . . It is still unknown from whom H. Gerritsz derived his

[1] Bagrow, *IM*, Vol. v, p. 81.

[2] Keuning, *IM*, Vol. vi, p. 51; cf. also Serbina, *IZ*, Vol. 23, 1947, who favours the view that the map was made with the participation of the Tsarevich.

outline of the coasts of the Baltic Sea, Black Sea and Caspian Sea ... In spite of a whole series of errors the map of Hessel Gerritsz is distinct from all preceding maps of Russia by its authentic informations (*sic*) likewise by the greater exactitude regarding the general form and the many details; for a long time it remained the basis for many later maps of Russia'.[1]

The version of the Great Map attributed to Tsarevich Fedor Borisovich, published by Hessel Gerritsz in 1613, carries interesting details on Caucasia. The eastern half of Caucasia as far as the Terek occupies four-fifths of the width of the isthmus – a clear indication that the cartographers of the Kremlin, round the year 1600, were much better informed on the topography of Kabarda and Daghestan than they were on the Circassian lands to the west of the Terek as far as the Black Sea littoral. On the Gerritsz edition the Kuma river is clearly delineated but is named Tura, a form of Turkish origin which is also found as the name of a river in western Siberia. The Terek (Terca) and the Sunzha (Zunsa) are shewn with settlements of Baragun, Sunzha and Tumensko. To the south are the Aksu (Aksa) with its affluents and the Koysu (Koisa) with the towns of Koysu, Tarku (Tarca) and Buinak (Buimak). Shevkal's (Scalfhal) lands are indicated and, to the south the Kafir Kumukh (Cafurhumki Cirkassi) and the Gazi Kumukh. Archi (Arski), the stronghold of the Eristavs of the Aragvi near the source of the Terek is placed at the source of the Koysu. To the south of the main chain, the upper reaches of the Aragvi (Aragusa) and the Alazani (Lazan) rivers are indicated; and the towns of Gremi (Crim) and Zumtinsokia (? Shiomta-skaya). The Caspian is captioned 'Mare Caspium olim, nunc Mare de Bachu, Rhutheni vocant Gvalentscha More'. The Russians continued to call the Caspian *Khvalinskoye more*, 'the Khvalinian or Khwarazmian Sea', down to the

[1] Keuning, *IM*, Vol. VI, p. 51.

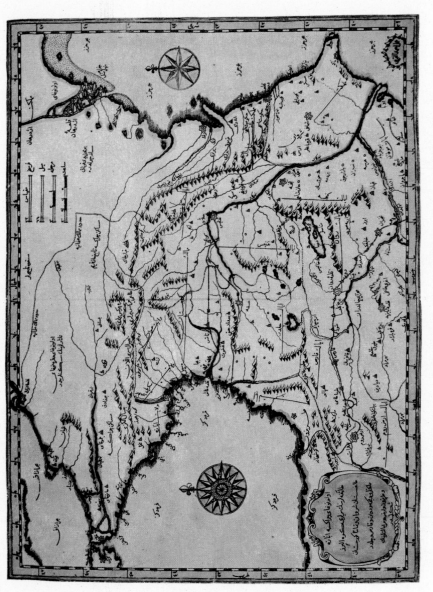

Map 6. The first Turkish map of Caucasia printed in Katib Chelebi's *Cihan Numa*, 1734.

end of the seventeenth century – as is evident from successive recensions of the Book of the Great Map.

The recensions of the Book, with various amendments and additions to the original text of 1626, have been analysed in detail by Spasski in his printed edition of 1840, and recently, by the Soviet scholar K. I. Serbina. The latter believes that the sections on the Don and the lower Volga, including the pages devoted to the Caucasus, were edited by Prince Grigori Sunchelevich Cherkasski, the paramount chieftain of the Pyatigorsk Cherkesses and, at the same time, a distinguished and efficient administrator in the hierarchy of the Muscovite state. He died about 1672; and the seventh recension of the Book was completed round 1680.[1]

Hessel Gerritsz's version of the Tsarevich Fedor's map, first published in 1613, may be fairly taken as a reflection of official Russian information on the Caucasus at the beginning of the seventeenth century, based without doubt on the reports of the embassies sent to Kakheti at the end of the sixteenth century. The seventh recension of the Book of the Great Map brings that knowledge up to date to the end of the third quarter of the seventeenth century, in the period preceding the massive intrusion of Peter the Great into the affairs of north-eastern Caucasia and the relatively modern and scientific explorations of officers and Academicians which followed during the course of the eighteenth century.

3. PRINCE WAKHUSHT'S 'GEOGRAPHICAL DESCRIPTION OF GEORGIA'

Prince Wakhusht Bagration was a natural son of King Wakhtang VI of Kartli (reigned 1711–14 and 1719–23). Composed during the third decade of the eighteenth century, his

---

[1] For Prince G. S. Cherkasski, see Commentary 12: The princely families of Kabarda.

work is the earliest detailed source for the study of the historical topography of Georgia and the central Caucasus. It is only available to western scholars in the rare edition of M.-F. Brosset, *Description géographique de la Géorgie*, Georgian text with interleaved French translation (St Petersburg, 1842), and in the equally rare Russian rendering by M. G. Janashvili in *ZKO*, kn. xxiv, vyp. 5 (Tiflis, 1904). In 1956 the Georgian scholar, L. I. Maruashvili, published an all too brief study: *Vakhusht Bagrationi: his predecessors and contemporaries.* Three years earlier he had presented the results of his analysis of Wakhusht in a paper read in Russian before the Section of the History of Geographical Knowledge of the Moscow Branch of the USSR Geographical Society, and printed in *Voprosy Istorii*, Vol. 31, 1953. A slightly abbreviated English translation is given below (pp. 574–86). The footnotes are mine [WEDA].

Wakhusht's geographical and cartographical works
(descriptive scheme)

A list of Wakhusht's works relating to geography can be set out as follows:

1. The Life of Georgia=History of Georgia (*Kartlis Tskhovreba*), his fundamental work, completed in 1745, includes a number of chapters devoted to the description of the geographical conditions of territories inhabited by the Kartvelian peoples and neighbouring tribes. These chapters taken together constitute 'The Geographical Description of Georgia' (*Geographiuli Aghdseri Sakartvelosa*) which is of fully independent significance as M. Brosset justly stressed.[1]

2. Early series of geographical maps of Georgia and adjoining lands, prepared in 1735 and supplemented in 1737–8.[2]

[1] Maruashvili notes that the original MS. of Wakhusht's *Kartlis Tskhovreba*, dated Moscow, 1745, is in the Central Archives of the Georgian SSR, Tbilisi.
[2] The first series of maps compiled by Prince Wakhusht are in the MSS.

3. Later series of geographical maps of the same territory dating to 1742–3.[1]

4. Georgian translation of a Russian edition of world geography, carried out in 1752, with the addition of 27 maps. The translation is free: some parts of the original text are summarized whilst, on the other hand, the descriptions of Turkey and Persia are supplemented with additional material by the translator.

Wakhusht's geographical work, 'The geographical description of Georgia', is a fairly bulky work in which the natural conditions and the population of a considerable part of the Caucasian isthmus are dealt with in detail; the area covered, in addition to the territory of the present Georgian SSR, includes parts of adjoining countries, Turkey, North Caucasus, Armenia and Azerbaijan.

The description is divided into an introduction, covering a general description of Georgia, and into several chapters with detailed descriptions of parts of the country – the kingdoms of Kartli, Kakheti and Imereti, together with subject and adjoining territories, as well as the non-Georgian part of the highlands of the Great Caucasus (Ovseti) and Samtskhe-Saatabago (the Pashalik of Akhaltsikhe which belonged to Turkey).

Inside these regional chapters the material is sub-divided either according to smaller administrative and ethnographic units (governorships and principalities) or else according to sharply defined natural areas such as the basins of mountain rivers. The material is set out in a strictly consecutive order, according to the topographical situation of a locality, taken up or down the principal river.

Section of the Georgian State Museum, Tbilisi. In September 1966, through the courtesy of Professor Ilya Abuladze, I was privileged to inspect these maps which were in beautiful condition. I was informed that it is intended to publish an Atlas of the two series.

[1] The originals of the second series of maps are in the Central Archives of the Georgian SSR, Tbilisi.

Thus, Wakhusht's geographical work from the point of view of its general character belongs to the type of topographical descriptions which predominated in Europe's geographical literature until the end of the eighteenth century.

Wakhusht's work is also related to the geographical works of European authors of the pre-Humboldt period by its encyclopaedic contents; the most varied material has been gathered in it in accordance with a definite system, customary at that time. This material consists of data about the configuration of the land, minerals, climate, hydrography, vegetation, fauna, ethnology and the economic activity of the population and its customs, language, beliefs, costumes and so on.

Whilst having much in common with European geographical works from the point of view of the method used, Wakhusht's work at the same time stands out among Caucasiological works by the originality of its factual material: not only is it not a compilation, but it does not even use any considerable quantity of data from other authors. As will be shown below, it is predominantly based on Wakhusht's own maps and on information gathered by him as a result of personal observation and questioning.

The fundamental merit of Wakhusht's 'Geographical Description of Georgia', compared to other eighteenth-century and earlier geographical works on the Caucasus, is the detailed and precise nature of the descriptive material assembled therein. To illustrate this premise it should be pointed out that Wakhusht describes 800 orographical units (mountain ranges, massifs, summits, valleys and plains), 440 rivers large and small, 22 lakes, and so on. It can be boldly stated that Wakhusht's work by the wealth of its contents and the detail and precision of descriptions is superior to all geographical accounts of the Caucasus compiled before the end of the eighteenth century (before the work of the Russian Academy expeditions headed by I. A. Güldenstädt and P. S. Pallas).

The fact that this description of a varied mountainous territory is founded on a sound conception of geographic zonality (though based on empirical, popular observations) must also be regarded as a major merit of Wakhusht's geographical work.

Wakhusht does not anywhere specially formulate his general views with regard to the laws and causes of the geographic division of phenomena: such a formulation would have been out of place in such a typical topographic description of a limited territory as his work was. However, his descriptions are based on a correct understanding of geographic laws and of the factors determining them.

Vertical zonality in Georgia's natural conditions is fully reflected in the Georgian scholar's work. Differentiating between the lowland and upland types of climate, flora, fauna and other components of the landscape, Wakhusht clearly delineates the areas of the two.

In the case of mountain valleys he always notes the limit of the lowland landscape in the given valley, which is characterized by warm climate, the existence of crops which thrive in warm weather (such as grapes, pomegranates, rice, cotton, various fruit trees) and a given structure of life of the population.

A similarly clear-cut delineation between the lowland and the upland zones is also made with regard to the fishes found in Georgia's rivers.

Quite detailed schemes of the geographical habitat of varieties of wild plants, crops and fresh-water fishes on the territory of Georgia can be compiled on the basis of the data of the 'Geographical Description of Georgia'. Academician I. A. Javakhishvili has done so in part (with regard to plants).

In so far as Wakhusht's cartographical works are concerned it should be noted that the originals of both sets of maps – the early and the late – referred to above in the list of works of the Georgian scholar, have reached us. These sets were compiled with an interval of four to five years between the dates of their production and they reflect two stages in the development of Wakhusht's cartographic notions. Each set consists of a general map of Georgia and the adjoining regions, and of several special maps of parts of Georgia and neighbouring areas.

The scale of the maps (the true scale is meant here; this differs considerably from the linear scale shown on the maps, as a result of imperfect cartography) is quite big taking the conditions of the time into consideration: the general maps are 1:1,500,000 (in the early series) and 1:2,800,000 (in the late series), whilst the scale of the maps of different parts of Georgia varies between 1:950,000 and 1:260,000 in the early series and 1:1,000,000 and 1:270,000 in the late series.

The maps give in detail the hydrography, inhabited localities, defensive and religious buildings, the political-administrative and the ethnographic subdivision of Georgia and adjacent provinces . . . In addition to these, the author also set himself other tasks which he has solved with a greater or lesser degree of success. The highlands are indicated by 'mole-hills'. There are signs standing for forests, snow fields, communications, inns, and so on. All the maps are coloured.

It should be noticed that the topographical material is not of equal value on all areas. Various parts of the Caucasian isthmus are given by Wakhusht with an unequal amount of detail or exactitude. The maps of the kingdoms of Kartli, Kakheti and Imereti where hardly a single inhabited locality or stream is omitted, are best of all. The remaining lands – Mingrelia, Guria, Abkhazia, Samtskhe-Saatabago, the Great Caucasus highlands, North Caucasus, Azerbaijan and Armenia, are less satisfactorily depicted.

In this latter part of Wakhusht's maps there are substantial omissions and errors which indicate the imperfection of the topographical material on which they were based. The fantastic presentation of the Kapetis-tsqali river is particularly apparent; in its lower course it is made to correspond with the Bzyb, and in its upper with the Ingur. Similarly crude mistakes are also encountered in the presentation of the hydrographical system of East Caucasus (Tusheti with adjoining areas), of the Javakheti lakes, and so on.

There are certain differences in the topographical contents of the maps of the two series, which bears witness to the fact that after compiling the first series of maps Wakhusht was in a position to acquire new topographical material.

One notices even more differences between the above-mentioned series of maps with regard to the cartographic basis. Maps of the early series are based on very crude astronomic measurement of the co-ordinates; they have a primitive (rectangular, devoid of mathematical grounds) cartographic grid, and as a result of this they considerably distort actual distances between geographical points (for instance, the total width of the Caucasian isthmus, measured along the Batum–Derbent line, is exaggerated nearly two times on the general map of the series under consideration).

These shortcomings of the early maps of the Georgian scholar were to a considerable degree rectified in the later series of his maps, where more exact measurements of latitude and longitude were used and where conical projection was applied. Exaggeration of distances on these late maps does not exceed 1.1–1.2.

Data about the origin of the topographical contents and the cartographical foundation of Wakhusht's maps are given in the next section.

From the point of view of their qualities and method Wakhusht's maps come between the numerous cartographical works of foreign travellers and cartographers of the sixteenth to eighteenth centuries (maps of Jenkinson, Olearius, Lamberti, de la Motraye, Lerch, Kaempfer and others) and Russian maps compiled in the nineteenth century.

Origins (sources of compilation) of Wakhusht's geographical and cartographical work.

The question of what Wakhusht's geographical work and maps were based on has always attracted the attention of scholars but it cannot, in spite of this, be regarded as finally solved. There exist a number of unclear points, particularly with regard to the origin of the topographical contents of the maps. These problems are still waiting for their investigator.

Wakhusht's geographical work is to a considerable extent based on his own cartographical work. This can be clearly seen through the juxtaposition of the descriptive text with the presentation of the corresponding areas on the maps. In a number of cases, the description, nearly *in toto*, is a paraphrase of the map, repeating the latter's qualities and errors.

A second important source for the Georgian scholar's geographical work is the factual material which he had himself gathered in the course of local observations (in Kartli, Imereti, as well as whilst crossing the Caucasus range in 1724) and through questioning people familiar with the locality... Among Wakhusht's observations one should note the data relating to the morphometric characteristics of the cañon of the Khrami river; the connection between the meandering sections of the Kura and the open nature of the territory traversed; the 'two-pointed' (i.e. bi-pyramidal) crystals in the neighbourhood of Samshvilde (magmatic quartz); the thickness and colouring of glacier ice in the Caucasian chain; the ice quarries of Saba-Tsminda and Khorkhebi; the possibility of foretelling windy weather in the Tbilisi area from the existence of clouds on the summit of the Kukheti (Sagurami) range; the peculiar symbiosis of the ibex and the mountain turkey; the positioning of mountain villages against mountain summits to avoid avalanche danger, and so on. The exactness of the majority of these and of other of Wakhusht's observations is being confirmed by modern research.

Finally, in compiling the 'Geographical Description of Georgia', Wakhusht also made use of literary sources (manuscript and printed), and, especially, of the Georgian chronicle *Kartlis Tskhovreba*; statistical census materials of various parts of Georgia, compiled on the orders of Georgian kings; the books of the Italian historian Baronius, which had been published in Russia, and possibly those of the Dutch scholar Varenius and the French text of J. Chardin's work.

Signs of the use of the literary sources listed above are clearly visible in the text of Wakhusht's work, but all these sources play a secondary role in it; they mainly supply the author with material for historical and toponymic asides. It is only exceptionally that literary data supplement the fundamental geographical kernel of the work under consideration.

The history of Wakhusht's maps is quite complicated and has not yet been fully elucidated. The origin of the topographical contents of the maps and of their cartographic foundations must be considered separately. We shall begin with the latter.

As has already been pointed out, Wakhusht's early maps, dated 1735, have a crude cartographical basis. The astronomical data for these maps were taken from ancient sources (Ulugh Beg, Ptolemy and others); this has been established by us through comparison of the materials from Delisle's portfolio described by M.-F. Brosset, with a surviving Georgian translation by Wakhtang VI of Ulugh Beg's work on astronomy.[1]

Wakhusht's later maps have a considerably improved

---

[1] The original of King Wakhtang's *Varskvlavt-mritskhveloba*, a translation from the Persian of Ulugh Beg's astronomical works is in the MSS. Section of the Georgian State Museum, Tbilisi.

cartographical basis, which, to all appearances, Wakhusht borrowed from the geographical department of the Russian Academy of Sciences through its director Delisle. This becomes clear through the juxtaposition of Wakhusht's general map with the corresponding sheet No. 11 of the Russian Atlas of 1745, based on Russian astronomical work of the beginning of the eighteenth century.

The question of the sources of the topographical material in Wakhusht's maps, of which it is the most remarkable trait because of its major qualities, has been less satisfactorily studied. The only clear thing is that the topographical contents of the Georgian scholar's maps result from comparison and compilation of different materials of different origin. Parts of the maps which depict the territory of the three Georgian kingdoms of Kartli, Kakheti and Imereti, and which stand out by their exactitude, are undoubtedly based on one type of topographical material, whilst the presentation of the remaining parts of the Caucasian isthmus is based on a different type.

The first and best part of Wakhusht's map is based on a close network of road surveys, carried out by the eye, along all river valleys of greater or lesser significance. The survey – as can be proved with the aid of documents in the case of the map of Imereti – was carried out on the orders of the Georgian kings, and the material of the surveys remained the property of the latter. It is probable, though not yet proved, that Wakhusht took a direct part in this survey.[1]

The presentation of the remaining territories is based on a

[1] For the background of Georgian cartography in the early eighteenth century see articles by W. E. D. Allen in *IM*, Vol. x, 1953, 'Two Georgian maps of the first half of the eighteenth century'; and Vol. xIII, 1956, 'The sources for G. Delisle's "Carte des Pays Voisins de la Mer Caspienne" of 1723'. The latter discusses the extent to which Wakhusht had drawn on material compiled by his kinsman and former tutor, Saba Sulkhan Orbeliani.

sparser network of itineraries; alongside materials derived from eastern cartographers and relating to Armenia and Azerbaijan, the Georgian scholar made use (especially in the later series) of Russian surveys of the North Caucasus and the Caspian shores carried out at the beginning of the eighteenth century. It is possible to determine the materials utilized in Wakhusht's cartographical works relating to the lands beyond the frontiers of the three Georgian kingdoms, by comparing Wakhusht's maps with the work of Russian, West-European and Moslem cartographers on the Caucasus.

Briefly summing up what has been said above with regard to the origin of Wakhusht's geographical and cartographical works, we find that they are the result of a synthesis of a number of materials of different origin and character. This statement is particularly true of the maps in compiling which Wakhusht made use of Russian surveys and of works of foreign cartographers, together with the fundamental topo-graphical material of Georgian origin.

Place of Wakhusht's geographical and cartographical works in the history of Caucasian studies and their present-day significance

In appraising the scientific significance of Wakhusht's works, and their role in the development of geographical knowledge of Caucasia, one must bear in mind the fact that there is a gap between the true position which these works occupy in Cauca-siological literature and cartography, and the position which they came to occupy formally in the history of the study of the Caucasian isthmus. As a result of some circumstances which proved unfavourable to Wakhusht's activity, the significance of his work, which is formally recognized, is lower than its merits.

The above statement particularly refers to the Georgian scholar's geographical composition, which for an entire century remained in MS. and which proved to be outdated by the time it came to be published, owing to the development of Caucasian geographical research in the latter half of the eighteenth and the first half of the nineteenth century. Wakhusht's geographical work, which had a number of merits from the point of view of the conditions of its era, was thus withheld from the general process of the evolution of geographical views of Caucasia, and did not play in this process the part it deserved.

The fate of Wakhusht's cartographical works proved to be better. His maps already became widely known in the author's lifetime; this is proved, for instance, by reports in a Leipzig paper about 'the excellent maps of the Caucasian mountains compiled by a Tiflis prince', published in 1737 and 1739. (See M.-F. Brosset, in *IRGO*, kn. 9, 1865, p6.) [But see Laurent Brosset, *Bibliographie analytique*, No. 229, from which it would appear that Maruashvili's page ref. is to the *tirage à part*.]

A number of printed and manuscript maps derive from the French (Delisle's) and the Russian (carried out by the Russian Staff) translations of Wakhusht's maps: French maps published in Paris in 1766 and 1783; the eleventh map of the 1745 Russian Atlas, the maps of I. A. Güldenstädt, S. D. Burnashev and others. The territory of Georgia and of adjacent provinces is depicted on the above-mentioned maps on the basis of Wakhusht's cartographical work; this fact is established by an analysis of the topographical contents and of certain other characteristics of the corresponding maps.

For nearly a century (from 1735 until the first decades of the nineteenth century) Wakhusht's cartographical work remained the principal source of detailed topographical material on Georgia, and directly or indirectly (through translations) it met practical and scientific requirements. Nearly all West European and Russian authors of Caucasian cartography of the middle and end of the eighteenth century based their maps on Wakhusht's work. The influence of Wakhusht's maps is also clearly visible in a number of works on geography of the end of the eighteenth and early nineteenth century – such as the works of I. A. Güldenstädt, O. Evetsky, Legkobytov and others.

It will not for this reason be an exaggeration to say that Wakhusht's cartographical activity indeed produced an entire epoch in the development of Caucasian cartography, thereby playing an important role in the general development of geographical conceptions about Caucasia.

The contemporary significance of Wakhusht's works for Georgia's historiography is very great. A picture of exceptional exactitude of the state of the country in the first half of the eighteenth century, which throws light on the most varied questions of the life of the population at that time, is engraved in them. In the justified words of Academician I. A. Javakhishvili, Wakhusht's works will never lose their great importance as sources of historical data about the Georgian people.

For geographers of the present day the significance of Wakhusht's works lies in the possibility of using the rich toponymic material contained in the Georgian scholar's composition and maps, for the purpose of improving regional descriptions, as well as in the existence of factual data contributing to elucidating the changes in Georgia's natural conditions during the past two or two and a half centuries.

With the help of the text of 'The Geographical Description of Georgia' it is possible to establish certain interesting facts relating to shrinkage of the area under forests (e.g. the destruction of the 'tugai' forests in the basin of the Kura) and of the habitat of certain mammals and birds (deer, chamois, pheasant and others) which has occurred under the influence of man since Wakhusht's work was written.

By his geographical description and maps of Georgia

Wakhusht has made a valuable contribution to the study of an interesting part of our boundless country [i.e. USSR].

Taking into account the significance of Wakhusht's works for our times, as described above, a re-publication of the Russian translation of the Georgian scholar's geographical work, accompanied by geographical commentaries, indices, dictionary of toponymy and reproduction of maps must be regarded as desirable. Such an edition would be a valuable addition to Soviet literature on the history of the country's geographical science.

GENEALOGICAL NOTES AND TABLES

I. THE RUSSIAN ROYAL HOUSES

(a) *The House of Rurik.* In Ivan IV Vasilyevich, called *Grozny*, the Dread, were united the strains of the Russo-Scandinavian Rurikovichi, of the Lithuanian Gedyminovichi, of the Byzantine Palaeologi, and (through the brilliant and erratic Glinskis) of the race of Chingiz Khan.

(b) *The House of Romanov.* Although he was married seven or eight times, Ivan's progeny were few and unhappy in their lot. By his first wife Anastasia Romanovna Zakharin-Koshkin, Ivan had two sons, Ivan Ivanovich (who was killed by his father in 1581) and Fedor I Ivanovich, Tsar, 1584–98. The name Romanov was assumed by the family of Anastasia's brother, Nikita Romanovich Zakharin-Koshkin, and, after the extinction of the Godunov line (see (e) below), Nikita's grandson, Mikhail Fedorovich, became the first Romanov Tsar in 1613.

(c) *The Kabardan Marriage.* For his second wife, Ivan IV took Maria Temryukovna, daughter of Temryuk (Kemirgoko), paramount prince of Great Kabarda. Maria died without issue, but the descendants of her brothers, russianised as the Princes Cherkassky, were prominent in Muscovite politics during the following three centuries. (See Commentary 12: The princely families of Kabarda.)

(d) *The Nagoy Marriage.* In 1581, near the end of his life, Ivan IV married Maria Fedorovna Nagoy, daughter of a boyar of Tartar descent. By her he had a son, Dmitri Ivanovich, known as Dmitri of Uglich, who died in 1591 in mysterious circumstances. In 1604, the appearance of a Pretender, 'self-named' (*samozvanets*) Dmitri, precipitated the fall of the Godunovs.

(e) *The House of Godunov*. Tsar Fedor Ivanovich married Irina, sister of Boris Godunov, the powerful favourite of Ivan IV. Feeble in health and weak in spirit, Tsar Fedor allowed his brother-in-law to rule under the title of Familiar Great Boyar and Viceroy of the Realms of Kazan and Astrakhan. Fedor and Irina had one daughter who died in infancy and, after the death of Fedor in 1598, Boris procured his own election as Tsar by vote of a popular assembly (*zemski sobor*). In April 1605, Tsar Boris died of a stroke – following the revolt of the false Dmitri (see (d) above). His son Fedor II Borisovich was killed two months later. His daughter, Xenia (Kseniya Borisovna) died a nun in 1622.

2. THE OTTOMAN SULTANS

1574–1595 Murat III, was the son of Selim II (called *Sarhosh* – the Drunkard), who was Russian (Ukrainian) on his mother's side. Murat's mother was Venetian, a kinswoman of Sebastiano Venier who commanded the Venetian galleys at Lepanto.

1595–1603 Mehmet III, son of Murat by Safiye Sultan.

1603–1617 Ahmet I, son of Mehmet by Handan Sultan. (For these two ladies, see the definitive article by Ettore Rossi in *Oriente Moderno*, Vol. 33 (1953), pp. 433–41.)

3. THE SAFAVID SHAHS

The Safavid dynasty was descended from the Sheikhs of Ardabil in Azerbaijan. Through the marriages of Sheikh Haydar of Ardabil and of Shah Ismail I (1502–24) with the ladies of the Turkoman dynasty of Ak-Koyunlu, the Safavids inherited the blood of the Trapezuntine Comnenes and of the Georgian Bagratids (ref. Allen, *PTP*, p. 76).

1578–1587 Muhammad Khudabanda was a son of Shah

Tahmasp II (1524–76) by a lady of the family of the Marashi Sayyids of Mazandaran (see Commentary 8, Vol. i, p. 257).

1587–1629 Abbas I, son of above, by a lady of the Marashi Sayyids of Mazandaran – a background which doubtless explains the Shah's love of that province. Amongst other ladies Abbas married Tinatin, daughter of Giorgi X of Kartli. (Brosset, *HG*, Vol. ii/i, Genealogical Trees, p. 627, citing Farsadan Giorgijanidze.)

4. THE GIRAY KHANS OF THE CRIMEA

The Girays were descended from Chingiz Khan, through Juchi, founder of the Golden Horde on the Volga. Mengli (Menkili) Giray, whose long reign in the Crimea lasted without interruption from 1467–1514, married his daughter Ayshe to the Ottoman Sultan Selim I (1512–20); and a daughter of Selim's married Mengli's son Sa'adet (Khan, 1524–32). In the event of the extinction of the Ottoman line, the Girays were regarded as their natural heirs. The Girays often intermarried with the princely families of Circassia and, under the *atalyk* (fosterage) system, their sons were frequently brought up among the Circassians. While the Girays avoided the many enervating effects on personality of the harim and, later, of the 'cage' system in Turkey, a conflict among turbulent brothers, supported often by the fostering clans among the Circassians, was a frequent phenomenon of dynastic succession in the Crimea.

1577–1588 Mehmet II, son of Devlet, a grandson of Mengli Giray, ruling intermittently with

1584–1588 Islam II
1588–1608 Ghazi II[1] } brothers of Mehmet II

---

[1] For Ghazi Giray ('Bora') see Chap. 9, p. 411, n. 3. For details of succession, see Mirza Bala, article 'Giray' in *IA*, cilt 4, cols. 783–8.

5. THE BAGRATIDS OF KARTLI

ALEXANDER I, 'The Great'[1] King of all Georgia, 1412–42 (common ancestor of the Bagratids of Kartli, Mukhrani and Kakheti)

GIORGI VIII, King of all Georgia, 1446–65; reigned as King of Kakheti 1470–6 (ancestor of Kakhian Bagratids)　　　　Dmitri, d. 1452

CONSTANTINE II, King of Kartli, 1478–1505

DAVID VIII, King of Kartli, 1505–26
　　(Giorgi IX, brother of above, 1526–34, became a monk)

Bagrat, Prince of Mukhrani in 1512 (see Table 6 – ancestors of the Mukhranian line)

LUARSAB I, King of Kartli, 1534–57

SIMON I, King, 1557–69 and 1578–1599 (m. Nestan Darejan, dau. of Levan of Kakheti)

DAVID IX (= Da'ud Khan) m. kinswoman of Alexander of Kakheti; King of Kartli, 1569–78

GIORGI X, 1599–1605[2] (m. 'Tomar' dau. of Giorgi Lipartiani)

BAGRAT VII King of Kartli, 1614–19

SIMON II, 1619–29

LUARSAB II, b. 1595, king 1605–14. Murdered near Shiraz, 1622

ROSTOM I (natural son of David IX) King of Kartli 1633–58, d. aged 91. Adopted as his heir, Wakhtang of Mukhrani (see Table 6)

[1] For dates and numeration, I have followed Gugushvili, 'The chronological-genealogical table of the Kings of Georgia' in *Georgica*, Vol. I, Nos. 2 and 3, based on I. Javakhishvili and S. Kakabadze. Some corrections of detail are necessary in Brosset's Genealogical Tables published in 1856, and in the text of my *HGP*, Chap. XI. For Giorgi IX, see Gugushvili, above, p. 133, n. 2.

[2] For the children of Giorgi X, see Additional Note, 5 (a).

5 (a). *Additional Note: The Children of Giorgi X*

1. *LUARSAB II*, born 1595. King of Kartli, 1605–1614. Later a prisoner in Persia, murdered near Shiraz, 1622.

2. *David*, died a hostage in Istanbul after 1606.

3. *Khorashan*, affianced to Bahadur, son of Nugsar, *eristavi* of the Aragvi (= 'Aristov Sonski'); married 1609, Taymuraz I, King of Kakheti.

4. *Tinatin*, married to Shah Abbas I, who repudiated her, and gave her to Pheikar Khan, governor of Kakheti in 1616.

5. *Elena*, destined for Tsarevich Fedor Borisovich Godunov.

6. THE BAGRATIDS OF MUKHRANI

BAGRAT, younger bro. of David VIII of Kartli, became Prince of Mukhrani, 1512; monk under name of Barnabas, 1539

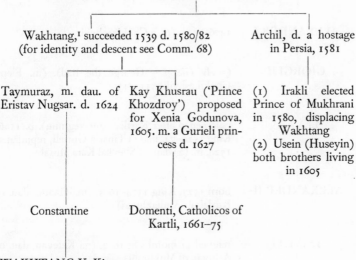

Wakhtang,[1] succeeded 1539 d. 1580/82 (for identity and descent see Comm. 68)

Archil, d. a hostage in Persia, 1581

Taymuraz, m. dau. of Eristav Nugsar. d. 1624

Kay Khusrau ('Prince Khozdroy') proposed for Xenia Godunova, 1605. m. a Gurieli princess d. 1627

(1) Irakli elected Prince of Mukhrani in 1580, displacing Wakhtang
(2) Usein (Huseyin) both brothers living in 1605

Constantine

Domenti, Catholicos of Kartli, 1661–75

WAKHTANG V, King of Kartli, 1658–75, founder of the Mukhranian line. (adopted by the last of the Kartlian line, see Table 5)

[1] Bagrat had a third son, Ashotan, died 1561. He was the father of Ketevan, who married David I, of Kakheti; she was martyred in Persia, 1624.

Bagrat also had a daughter, Dedis-Imedi, who married, c. 1545, Kay Khusrau II, Atabeg of Samtskhe – from whom descended the hereditary Pashas of Akhaltsikhe until 1828.

7. THE BAGRATIDS OF KAKHETI

GIORGI I   (= Giorgi VIII of United Georgian Kingdom – see Table 5), 1470–76

ALEXANDER I   1476–1511. (m. a Cholokashvili).

GIORGI II   (= *Av Giorgi* – George the Bad). (m. Elena Cholokashvili) 1511–13

LEVAN[1]   (succeeded after Kartlian interregnum). b. 1506. King 1520–74. m. (1) Tinatin Gurieli, repudiated 1529. m. (2) dau. of Shevkal Kara Musal

ALEXANDER II[2]   born 1527, King 1574–1605. (m. Tinatin, dau. of Bardzim Amilakhvari)

DAVID I   reigned 11 months in 1602. (m. Ketevan, dau. of Ashotan of Mukhrani)

     (CONSTANTINE, brother of David I, reigned six months during 1605)

TAYMURAZ I   ruled – with intervals – 1605–64. (m. (2) Khorashan, dau. of Giorgi X of Kartli)

[1] *Children of King Levan*: By Tinatin Gurieli, Levan had a second son, who may have been the elder and displaced by Alexander. He married a niece of Shah Tahmasp, became a Moslem and died 1580. A third son, Nicolaoz, was Catholicos *c.* 1580.

By Shevkal's daughter, Levan had four sons of whom one died in the father's lifetime and three were slain in battle with Alexander, *c.* 1574. Among several daughters, one – Nestan Darejan – married Simon I of Kartli. It was she who favoured Shevkal's house, and sustained the feud between Simon and her half-brother Alexander. She was the mother of Giorgi X of Kartli.

[2] *Children of King Alexander II*: Beside David I, Alexander had three other sons: (1) *Irakli*, became a Moslem and died in Istanbul, 1589. (2) *Giorgi*, killed with his father, 1605. He married (a) a daughter of 'Elisam Sultan' (= 'Krym Shevkal') cousin and foe of Andi Shevkal; and (b) a daughter of Kai Khusrau, Pasha of Genzha (see Commentary 47). By his first wife, Giorgi had a son, Yese (= Isa Khan) who commanded in Kakheti for Shah Abbas in 1615. (3) *Constantine* who murdered his father and brother Giorgi and ruled six months only in Kakheti in 1605.

Alexander also had a daughter Anna, who married Bagrat VII, King of Kartli (1614–19); and another unnamed who was wife of Hamza Mirza, elder brother of Shah Abbas. A third, Nestam Danejan, m. Dadian Manachar I (see p. 474, n. 2).

8. THE SHAMKHALS (SHEVKALS) OF TARKU

Information on the genealogy of the Shamkhals (Shevkals) of Tarku is incomplete. In 1868, *SSKG*, *vyp.* 1, *chast* iv, pp. 33–80, printed an article, 'Shamkhaly Tarkhovskiye', with a genealogical tree beginning only with Surkhai Khan (1643–82). In *OID*, Vol. 1, pp. 90–140, Kosven has elucidated the subject, using Russian archival sources. But he does not attempt to provide a genealogical tree and remarks on the confusion which arises from the pretensions of 'Shevkals' in Tarku, Enderi and Kumukh at the end of the sixteenth century. Kosven does not mention Kara-Musal who appears in the Georgian sources as the father-in-law of King Levan of Kakheti; nor does he identify 'the old Shevkal' stated by Don Juan, pp. 140, 153, to have been beheaded by Özdemiroghlu Osman Pasha, outside Derbent, in 1578. Kosven's Shevkals are as follows:

In Kazi-Kumukh
At end of fifteenth and beginning of sixteenth century. **ULKHAI I**

During first quarter of sixteenth century **ULKHAI II**
(son of Ulkhai I)

During second quarter of sixteenth century **BUGUDEI**
(killed in 1566–7 in Kabarda, Kosven, p. 128, n. 1)

In Kazi-Kumukh and Tarku
During third quarter of sixteenth century **CHUBAN (CHOBAN)**
(d. 1574, Kosven, p. 94, n. 5)
SURKHAI
(d. 1588 or 1589)
ANDI
(eldest son of Choban; ruling in Tarku in 1605; (Kosven, p. 94, n. 5

The following personalities of the Shevkal stock emerge from the contemporary sources:

(i) *Shevkal Kara Musal* (Brosset, *BHP/EC*, Vol. 2, Nos. 14/15, col. 214 and *HG*, *2me partie*, *1 livr.*, p. 634). A daughter became the second queen of Levan of Kakheti in 1529. He may be equated with Ulkhai II or Bugudei of Kosven's list.

(ii) *'The old Shevkal'* of *Don Juan* (pp. 140, 153). According to Don Juan, following Minadoi, he was decapitated on the orders of Osman Pasha. Asafi, the biographer of Osman, does not mention this incident but records the execution of Charagh, *bek* of Demir-kapu (=Derbent), in October 1578 (cf. Asafi MS., fol. 45 and miniature 45*v*.). This 'old Shevkal' cannot be equated with Choban (d. 1574) nor with Surkhai (d. 1588 or 1589). The story recorded by Don Juan and Minadoi was second-hand and must relate to the execution of Charagh.

(iii) *Krym Shevkal*: described as 'cousin germain' of the contemporary Andi Sultan Shevkal. As a serious pretender to the shevkalate he may have been the son of a brother of Choban Shevkal. As a protégé and ally of Alexander II of Kakheti, he was given the appanage of Elisu (*G.* Eliseni), hence the title 'Elisam Sultan'. His daughter married Alexander's son Giorgi.

(iv) *Progeny of Choban*: Besides the reigning Andi Sultan Shevkal, the following may be identified (for refs. see Commentary 8):

(a) daughter married to Shah Tahmasp, by whom she had a daughter *Perihan Khanum*, b. 1548, killed in Kazvin, 1579.

(b) son, *Shamkhal Saltan Charkas*, killed in Kazvin, with Perihan Khanum, 1579.

(c) son, *Imam Kuli Khan*, in Persian service, living after 1578.

(v) *Saltan Mahmut*: a son of Andi Saltan Shevkal by daughter of Saltan Ahmet, Utsmi of Karakaitakh (Kosven, p. 94 and n. 3).

BIBLIOGRAPHY AND ABBREVIATIONS

In the Bibliography an attempt has been made to include the titles of all books and articles to which reference has been made in the Texts, Commentaries and Footnotes. The editions used by the Translator and by the Editor have been cited – and in some cases a reference to the original edition has been added. In a few cases books and periodicals inaccessible to the Editor have been indicated for the benefit of readers who may have these works available.

Ackerman, Phyllis: 'A Russian document on Persian textiles' in Pope, *SPA*, Vol. III, Chap. 10, Section 52 (B).

AK=Arkhitektura Kakhetii, see Chubinashvili, G. N.

Akty: Akty sobranniye Kavkazskoyu Arkheograf123 cheskoyu Komissiyeyu, Arkhiv upravleniya Namestnika Kavkazkago, 12 vols., fol. (Tiflis, 1866–96).

Alderson, A. D.: *The structure of the Ottoman dynasty* (Oxford, 1956).

Allen, *HGP*=Allen, W. E. D.: *A history of the Georgian people* (London, 1932).

——, *PS*=Allen, W. E. D.: *The poet and the spae wife* (London/Dublin, 1960) (first issued as Vol. xv, part 3 of the Saga-Book of the Viking Society for Northern Research).

——, *PTP*=Allen, W. E. D.: *Problems of Turkish power in the sixteenth century* (London, 1963).

——, *Ukraine* = Allen, W. E. D.: *The Ukraine: A history* (Cambridge, 1940) (reprint, NY, 1963).

——, 'Two Georgian maps of the first half of the eighteenth century,' in *IM*, Vol. x (1953), pp. 99–122.

——, The sources for G. Delisle's 'Carte des pays voisins de la Mer Caspienne' of 1723 in *IM*, Vol. XIII (1956), pp. 137–50.

Allen, W. E. D.: 'Ex Ponto III: The Trialetian goblet' in *BK*, No. 32/33 (1959), pp. 29–35.

——, 'Ex Ponto IV: Dogs' heads and wolves' heads' in *BK*, No. 32/33 (1959), pp. 36–47.

——, 'Ex Ponto V; Heniochi – Aea – Hayasa' in *BK*, No. 34/35 (1960), pp. 79–92.

——, 'Trivia Historiae Ibericae: 1. Gerfalcons for the King' in *BK*, No. 36/37 (1961), pp. 104–10.

——, 'A note on the princely families of Kabarda' in *BK*, No. 41/42 (1962), pp. 140–7.

——, 'Trivia Historiae Ibericae: 2–4. Aristop Sonski; Sonskaya Zemlya; the Daryal Gorge' in *BK*, No. 45-6 (1964), pp. 164–77.

——, 'The Volga-Terek route in Russo-Caucasian Relations' in *BK*, No. 43/44 (1963), pp. 158–66.

——, 'The Georgian marriage projects of Boris Godunov' in *OSP*, Vol. III (1965), pp. 69–79.

Amiranashvili, Sh. Ya.: *Istoriya Gruzinskogo iskusstva*, 4to (1st ed. Tbilisi, 1950; 2nd (expanded) 1966).

Anderson, Andrew Runni: *Alexander's gate, Gog and Magog, and the inclosed nations* (Cambridge, Mass., 1932).

Arrian: *History of Alexander and Indica*, 2 vols. (Loeb ed., London, 1946).

Artamonov, M. I.: *Istoriya Khazar* (Leningrad, 1962).

Asafī: *Sheja'atname*: MS. TY 6043 of Istanbul University Library (995/1586)

Atalay, *DLT* = Atalay, Besim: *Divanü Lûgat-it-Türk* (Turkish Linguistic Soc., 1940–3).

Atlas Aziatskoy Rossii, large fol. atlas, published together with *Aziatskaya Rossiya*, 3 vols., 4to, by the Emigration Section of the General Directorate of Agriculture and Land Management (St Petersburg, 1904).

Atlas Rossiyskoy sostoyashchi iz devyatnadsati spetsialnykh kart predstavlyayushchikh Vserossiyskuyu Imperiyu s pogranich-

nymi zemlyami, large fol. (St Petersburg, 1745). The first ed. of the first Russian Academy Atlas.

Avalishvili (=Avalov), Zourab: 'T'eimuraz I and his poem "The Martyrdom of Queen K'et'evan" ' in *Georgica*, Nos. 4/5 (London, 1937), pp. 17–43.

Ayalon, David: 'The Circassians in the Mamluk Kingdom' in *JAOS*, Vol. 69 (1949), No. 3, pp. 135–47.

——, 'The Wafidiya in the Mamluk Kingdom' in *Islamic Culture*, Vol. xxv (Hyderabad, 1951), Part 1, pp. 89–104.

Baddeley, *RCC*=Baddeley, J. F.: *The Russian conquest of the Caucasus*, (London, 1908).

——, *RFC*=Baddeley J. F.: *The rugged flanks of Caucasus*, 2 vols., 4to (Oxford, 1940).

——, *RMC*=Baddeley J. F.: *Russia, Mongolia, China*, 2 vols., fol., with set of maps in folder at back of Vol. 1 (London, 1919).

Bagrow, Leo: 'The Book of the Great Map' in *IM*, Vol. v (1948), pp. 81–2.

——, 'Italians on the Caspian' in *IM*, Vol. xiii (1956), pp. 3–10.

Bakradze, Dmitri: 'Kavkaz v drevnikh pamyatnikakh Khristianstva' in *Akty*, Vol. v, pp. 993–1107.

Barbier de Meynard, C.: *Maçoudi, Les Prairies d'Or*, 8 vols. (Paris, 1883).

Beauplan, Sieur de: *Description de l'Ukraine* ... etc., with important contemporary map (Rouen, 1660).

Bédi Karthlisa: Revue de Kartvélologie=*BK* (Paris, Nos. 50–51 published to 1966).

Bell, James Stanislaus: *Journal of a residence in Circassia during the years 1837, 1838 and 1839*, 2 vols (London, 1840). (Louis Vivien's Paris edition of 1841 with its learned introduction and notes is in many ways to be preferred to the English original.)

Bell, John, of Antermony: *Travels from St Petersburg in Russia to diverse parts of Asia*, 2 vols. (Glasgow, 1763).

Belokurov, *Snosheniya*= Belokurov, S. A.: *Snosheniya Rossii s Kavkazom: Materialy, izvlechennye iz Moskovskago Glavnago Arkhiva Inostrannykh Del, vypusk 1, 1578–1613 gg.* cxxix pp. Introduction, 584 pp. Text – all published (Moskva, 1889). (This book, like other of B.'s works, was included in the series *Chteniya v Imperatorskom Obshchestve Istorii i Drevnostey Rossiyskikh pri Moskovskom Universitete.* It is now rare. The editor's copy bought in Tiflis in 1926 has a pencilled note indicating that only 410 copies were printed.)

——, *O Posolskom Prikaze* (Moskva, 1906).

(Sergey Alekseyevich Belokurov (1862–1918). Son of a dyak he studied in the Dukhovny Academy. From 1886 he was employed in the Archives Department of the Ministry of Foreign Affairs. His other works were

(i) *O Vivlioteka Moskovskikh Gosudarey v xvi stoletii*, 2 parts (Moskva, 1899) – where he ruled out the possibility of the 'secret' library of Ivan IV;

(ii) *Arseni Sukhanov*, 2 vols. (Moskva, 1891–3) – an account of the travels of a seventeenth-century Russian monk in the Middle East;

(iii) *Yuri Krizhanich v Rossii* (Moskva, 1902).

In his works B. appears as an honest explorer of archives aiming, for example, at the collection and arrangement of facts but not at working out conclusions and generalizations from them. Besides his own work, B. edited a large number of documents from the archives – the affairs of the Secret Office, records of the relations of Moscow with the Polish-Lithuanian state – many of which were printed in *Chteniya*. There is a list of B.'s works to 1907 in a small book published by him – 'S. A. B. – 1862–1907' (Moskva, 1907). See also articles on him by S. K. Bogoyavlenski in *Istoricheski Arkhiv* (1919) and by M. M. Bogoslovski in *Russki Istoricheski Zhurnal*, No. 8, (1922) pp. 229–40.)

Belon de Mans, Pierre: *Histoire de la nature des oyseaux* (Paris, 1555).

Berdzenishvili, N., Dzhavakhishvili, I., Dzhanashia, S.: *Istoriya Gruzii*: chast 1 (all published): *S drevneyshikh vremen do nachala xix veka*. (Tbilisi, 1946).

Berezin, I.: *Puteshestviye po Dagestanu i Zakavkazyu*, 3 parts bound in 1 vol., 2nd ed. (Kazan, 1850).

Bernoville, R.: *La Souanéthie libre*, 4to (Paris, 1875).

Bibliotheca Accipitraria (Hastings, 1891).

Biographie Universelle, ancienne et moderne (=*BU*): 1st ed., 52 vols, (Paris, 1811–38).

BK=*Bédi Karthlisa, q.v.*

Bogdanov, –.: *Zveri i ptitsy Povolzhya* (volume not available to editor but cited from Dresser's *Birds of Europe*).

Bolshaya Sovetskaya Entsiklopediya (=*BSE*): 1st ed., 65 vols. (Moskva, 1929–47).

Bond, Edward A. (ed.): *Russia at the close of the sixteenth century*, comprising 'Of the Russe Commonwealth' by Dr Giles Fletcher, and 'The Travels of Sir Jerome Horsey' (London, Hakluyt Society, 1856).

Botsvadze, T. J.: *Sakartvelos – Qabardos urtiertobis istoriidan: xvi–xvii ss* (From the history of Georgian-Kabardan relations: sixteenth–seventeenth centuries) (Tbilisi, 1963).

Bovill, E. W.: *The battle of Alcazar* (London, 1952).

——, *The golden trade of the Moors* (Oxford, 1958).

Brockhaus and Efron: *Entsiklopedicheski slovar* (St Petersburg, 1890–1906).

Bronevski, Semen: *Noveyshiya Geograficheskiya i Istoricheskiya Izvestiya o Kavkaze*, 2 vols – with important folding end map by A. Maksimovich (Moskva, 1823).

Brosset, Laurent: *Bibliographie Analytique des ouvrages de Monsieur Marie-Félicité Brosset, 1824–1879* (St Petersburg, 1887).

Brosset, Marie-Félicité: *Chronique Géorgienne* (Paris, 1830). Georgian text and French translation.

Brosset, *EC/BHP*= Brosset, Marie-Félicité: 'Examen critique des annales géorgiennes, pour les temps modernes, au moyen des documents russes' in *Bulletin de la classe des sciences historiques, philologiques et politiques de l'Académie Impériale des Sciences de St. Pétersbourg*, tomes 1–2, 4to (St Petersbourg, 1844–5).

Brosset, *HG*= Brosset, Marie-Félicité: *Histoire de la Géorgie depuis l'antiquité jusqu'au xix siècle*, 7 vols., 4to (St Pétersbourg, Académie des Sciences, 1849–58). The titles of the volumes are as follows:

(1) *Ie partie: Histoire ancienne jusqu'en 1469* (1849).

(2) *Additions et éclaircissements à l'histoire de la Géorgie* (1851).

(3) *IIe partie. I livraison: Histoire moderne* (1856).

(4) *IIe partie, IIe livraison: Histoire moderne* (1857).

(5) *Introduction et table des matières* (1858).

There are two volumes of Georgian texts – not generally found with the five volumes in French:

(6) *Ie partie, Histoire ancienne jusqu'en 1469 (Texte géorgien; publié par M. Brosset)* (1849).

(7) *IIe partie, Histoire moderne depuis 1469 jusqu'en 1800 de J. C. (Texte géorgien publié par M. Tchoubinof)* (1854).

(In 1923, N. Y. Marr undertook to re-edit Brosset's Georgian texts but the task was not completed. Only the following appeared in 4to – 220 pp. under Georgian and French titles: *Histoire de la Géorgie depuis l'antiquité jusq'au xix siècle, publiée en géorgien par M. Brosset: Ie partie jusqu'en 1469 de J. C., I livraison (en partie)*. (Académie des Sciences, Petrograd, 1923.) In two pages of introduction Marr makes some critical remarks on Brosset's treatment of orthographic problems. Marr's promised notes on the texts have never been printed.)

Brosset, *VA*= Brosset, Marie-Félicité: *Rapports sur un voyage archéologique dans la Géorgie et dans l'Arménie exécuté en 1847–1848 (Ielivraison avec Atlas, St Pétersbourg, 1849; IIe livraison, 1850)*.

Brosset, M.-F.: 'O zheleznykh vorotakh khranyashchikhsya v Gelatskom monastyre v Imeretii' in *Kavkaz* (1847), pp. 163–7.

Browne, Edward G.: *A year amongst the Persians* (Cambridge, 1926).

——, *A literary history of Persia*, 4 vols. (Cambridge, 1928).

BSOAS= *Bulletin of the School of Oriental and African Studies* (University of London).

BSE= *Bolshaya Sovetskaya Entsiklopediya, q.v.*

BTTK= *Belleten, Türk Tarih Kurumu* (*Bulletin of the Turkish History Society*) (Ankara, 1940).

BU = *Biographie Universelle, b.v.*

Bushuyev, S. K. (ed.): *Istoriya Severo-Osetinskoy ASSR* (Moskva, Academy of Sciences, 1959).

Butkov, P. G.: *Materialy dlya novoy istorii Kavkaza* (=*MNIK*), 3 vols. (St Petersburg, 1869).

Byron, Robert: *The Station: Athos – treasures and men* (London, reprint 1949, with introduction by Christopher Sykes).

Byzantion, Vols. I–XXIV (Bruxelles, 1924–64).

Canard, M.: 'La relation du voyage d'Ibn Fodlan chez les Bulgares de la Volga' pp. 145. (Extract from *Annales de l'Institut d'Etudes Orientales, Faculté des Lettres de l'Université d'Alger*, n.d. but after 1956.)

Caraci, G.: 'The Italian cartographers of the Benicasa and Freducci families and the so-called Borgiana Map of the Vatican Library' in *IM*, Vol. X (1953), pp. 23–50.

The Catholic Encyclopaedia, 16 vols. (New York, 1907–14).

The Caucasian Review, Nos. 1–10 – all published (Institute for the Study of USSR, Munich, 1955–60).

Caucasica, begründet von Adolf Dirr, herausgegeben von Gerhard Deeters, Nos. 1–11 – all published (Leipzig, 1924–34).

Cavaignac, E.: 'Alashia – Elise' in *JA*, Vol. CCX/vii (1959), pp. 297–301.

Cellarius, Christophorus: *Notitia orbis antiqui, sive geographia plenior* ... 2 vols. (Leipzig, 1731–2).

Chadwick and Mann: *The medical works of Hippocrates* (Oxford, 1950).

Chardin, Sir John: *Travels of Sir John Chardin into Persia and the East Indies, through the Black Sea and the country of Colchis*, fol. (London, 1686). See also Langlès, M. I.

Chichinadze, Z.: *sakartvelos vatchroba* ... *Indoetchi* (*Georgian trade with India*) (Tbilisi, 1905).

CHOID = *Chteniya v Obshchestve Istorii i Drevnostey* (published by Moscow University).

CHR = *Catholic Historical Review*.

Chubinashvili, G. N.: *Arkhitektura Kakhetii* (=*AK*), 4to, 1 vol. Text, 1 vol. Atlas of plates (Tbilisi, 1956–9).

Chubinov, David: *Russko-Gruzinski slovar* (St Petersburg, 1840).

——, *Kartlis Tskhovreba* (*The life of Georgia*), (St Petersburg, 1854). See also above, Brosset, *HG*, (7).

Chursin, G. F.: 'Narodnye obychai i verovaniya Kakhetii' in *ZKO*, knizhka xxv, vyp. 2 (1905).

——, 'Osetiny: Etnograficheski ocherk' (offprint from *Trudy Zakavkazskoy Nauchnoy Assotsiatsii*, Ser. *I*, vyp. *I*. (Tiflis, 1925), pp. 1–103.

Coon, C. S.: *The races of Europe* (New York, 1948).

Cordier, Henri: *Ser Marco Polo: Notes and addenda to Sir Henry Yule's edition* (London, 1920). See also Yule, Sir Henry.

Dal (= Dahl), Vladimir: *Tolkovy slovar zhivogo Velikorusskago yazyka*, 4 vols. (St Petersburg, 1903).

Danişmend, I. H.: *Izahli Osmanli Tarihi Kronologisi* (The chronology of Ottoman history elucidated) (=*IOTK*), 3 vols. (Istanbul, 1947–50): cilt 1, 1258–1512; cilt 2, 1513–73; cilt 3, 1574–1703.

Daniyalov, A. D. (ed.): *Narody Dagestana* (Moskva, 1955).

Déchy, Moriz von: *Kaukasus: Reisen und Forschungen im Kaukasischen Hochgebirge*, 3 Bände (Berlin, 1905–7).

De Lisle, Guillaume: *Atlas Nouveau, contenant toutes les parties du Monde . . .* fol. (Amsterdam, 1745).

Desheriev, Yu. D.: *Batsbiyski yazyk* (Moskva, 1953).

DNB = Dictionary of National Biography.

Dictionnaire de Théologie Catholique.

Don Juan of Persia (Ulugh Beg): (i) *Relaciones de Don Juan de Persia, dirigidas a la Magestad Catholica de Don Philippe III, Rey de las Españas . . . donde se tratan las cosas notables de Persia . . .* (Valladolid, 1604). (ii) English rendering by Guy Le Strange: *Don Juan of Persia: a Shi'ah Catholic, 1560–1604.* (London, 1926).

Dorn, Bernhard, *Beiträge zur Geschichte der Kaukasischen Ländern und Völker aus Morgenlandischen Quellen* (St Petersburg, 1840; reprint, Leipzig, 1967).

Dowsett, C. J. F.: *The history of the Caucasian Albanians by Movsēs Dasxurançi* (Oxford, 1961).

Dresser, Henry E.: *A history of the birds of Europe*, 4to (London, 9 vols, 1871–88; index vol. and supplement, 1889–96).

DRV – Drevnyaya Rossiyskaya Vivliofika: 1st series, vols. 1–10 (St Petersburg, 1773–5); 2nd series, vols. 1–20 (Moskva, 1788–91); *Prodolzheniye*, vols. 1–11 (St Petersburg, 1786–1801).

Dubois de Montpéreux, Frédéric: *Voyage autour du Caucase, chez les Tcherkesses . . . en Géorgie, etc.*, 6 vols. of text, 8vo, and 5 vols. of plates, fol. (Paris/Neuchatel, 1838–43).

Dunlop, D. M.: *The History of the Jewish Khazars* (Princeton, N.J., 1954).

Dyakonov, M.: *Vlast Moskovskikh Gosudarey* (St Petersburg, 1889).

Eck, Alexander: *Le Moyen Age Russe* (= *MAR*), préface de Henri Pirenne (Paris, 1933).

Efendiyev, O. A.: *Obraʒovaniye Aʒerbaydʒhanskogo gosudarstva Sefevidov v nachale xvi veka* (Baku, 1961).

EI, 1st ed.=*Encyclopaedia of Islam* (Leiden/London, 1913–1936).

EI, 2nd ed.=*Encyclopaedia of Islam*, new edition (Leiden/London, 1954–).

Evliya=*Evliya Efendi: Narrative of travels in Europe, Asia and Africa, in the seventeenth century*: translated from the Turkish by Ritter J. von Hammer-Purgstall, 2 vols. (London, Oriental Translations Fund, 1834–50).

Evliya Chelebi: Kniga puteshestviya: translation with commentary by A. D. Zheltyakov, vyp. 1, *Zemli Moldavii i Ukrainy* (Moskva, 1961).

(The various MSS of *EC* have not been collated; and the printed Turkish edition in 10 vols. – the first 8 of which were published under the censorship of the Hamidian régime – has many defects. While several sections of the great work have been translated and edited, there is no complete translation in any European language.)

EVT=*Early voyages and travels to Russia and Persia by Anthony Jenkinson and other Englishmen*... Edited by Edward Delmar Morgan and Charles Henry Coote for the Hakluyt Society (London, 1885).

Fekhner, *TRG*=Fekhner, M. V.: *Torgovlya russkogo gosudarstva so stranami vostoka v xvi veke* (Moskva, 1956).

Felitsyn, E. D.: Cartographer; his maps of Northern Caucasus printed in Potto, *q.v.*

Fletcher, Giles: see Bond, Edward A.

Freshfield, Douglas: *The exploration of the Caucasus*, 2 vols. (London/New York, 1896). (With numerous illustrations by Vittorio Sella.)

Gan (=von Hahn), K. F.: *Kaukasische Reise und Studien* (Leipzig, 1896).

——, 'Puteshestviye v Kakhetiyu i Daghestan (letom 1898

goda)' in *SMK*, tom xxxi, otdel 2 (1902), pp. 49–96.

——, 'Poyezdka k verkhovyam Bolshoy Liakhvy i Ksanki (letom 1903 g)' in *SMK*, tom xxxv (1905), pp. 248–69.

Gärber, J. G.: 'Opisaniye stran vdol zapadnogo berega Kaspiyskogo morya, 1728 g.' in M. O. Kosven, *q.v.*, pp.60–120.

Garstang, John and Gurney, O. R.: *The geography of the Hittite Empire* (London, 1959).

GCK= Geschichte der Chane der Krim, see Hammer–Purgstall.

Genko, A. N.: 'Iz kulturnogo proshlogo Ingushey' in *ZKV*, tom V (Leningrad, 1930), pp. 681–761.

Georgica: A Journal of Georgian and Caucasian Studies, published for the Georgian Historical Society, Nos. 1–5 (Hertford, 1935–7).

Gibb, Sir Hamilton: *The travels of Ibn Battuta*, vols. 1, 2 (Cambridge, Hakluyt Society, 1958, 1962).

Gmelin, Samuel Gottlieb: *Reise durch Russland* . . . 4 parts in 5 Bände (St Petersburg, 1770–84). Russian ed.: *Puteshestviye po Rossii* (St Petersburg, 1771–85).

Golubinski, E. E.: *Istoriya Russkoy tserkvi*, 2nd ed., 4 vols. (Moskva, 1901–17).

Gordlevski, V. A.: *Izbrannye sochineniya:* tom 1, *Istoricheskiye raboty* (Moskva, 1960).

GOPMK= Gosudarstvennaya Oruzheynaya Palata Moskovskogo Kremlya (Moskva, 1954).

Grabar, Igor: (i) *Istoriya Russkago iskusstva*, 5 vols. (Moskva, 1909). (ii) Revised and amplified ed. of the above, 13 vols. (Moskva, 1953–64).

Gray, Terence: 'Les Bagratides: la plus ancienne dynastie de la Chrétienté' in *La Science Historique*, xli ann., Nos. 22/23, p. 10.

Grousset, Réné: *Histoire des Croisades*, 3 vols. (Paris, 1934–6).

Gugushvili, Andro: 'The chronological-genealogical table of the Kings of Georgia' in *Georgica*, Vol. 1, Nos. 2/3 (London, 1936), pp. 109–52.

——, 'Ethnographical and historical division of Georgia', ibid., pp. 53–71.

Guliyev, G. A.: *Bibliografiya etnografii Azerbaydzhana*, chast 1 (Baku, 1962).

Güldenstädt, Dr Johan Anton: *Reisen durch Russland und im Caucasischen Gebürge*, edited by P. S. Pallas, 2 Bände, 4to (St Petersburg, 1787–91).

Gyul, K. K. (ed.): *Fizicheskaya geografiya Dagestanskoy ASSR* (Makhachkala, 1959).

Gvozdetski, N. A.: *Fizicheskaya geografiya Kavkaza*, vyp. 1 (Moskva, 1954).

Gvritishvili, D. F.: *Iz istorii sotsialnykh otnosheniy v pozdnefeodalnoy Gruzii* (Tbilisi, 1961).

Hakluyt, Richard: *The Principal navigations, voyages, traffiques and discoveries of the English nation* (=*PN*) ... 12 vols. (Glasgow, Hakluyt Society, 1903–5).

Hammer–Purgstall, J. Ritter, von: *Geschichte der Chane der Krim* (Wien, 1856).

——, *Histoire de l'Empire Ottoman* (=*HEO*), 18 vols. (Paris, 1835–43); with Atlas fol. by G. J. Hellert (Paris, 1844). See also under Evliya Efendi.

Hasan Beg Rumlu: *Ahsanu't Tawārikh*, ed. C. N. Seddon (Gaekwad Oriental Series, Baroda, 1931).

Hasluck, F. W.: *Athos and its monasteries* (London, 1924).

——, *Christianity and Islam under the Sultans*, ed. Margaret M. Hasluck, 2 vols. (Oxford, 1929).

HEO=*Histoire de l'Empire Ottoman*, see Hammer, Ritter J. von.

Herberstein, Sigismund von: *Notes upon Russia: being a translation of the earliest accounts of that country entitled 'Rerum Moscoviticarum Commentarii'* (=*NR*) by R. H. Major, 2 vols. (London, Hakluyt Society, 1851).

Herodotus of Halicarnassus: *The history*, translated by H. G.

Rawlinson, revised and annotated by A. W. Lawrence (London, 1935).

Heyd, W.: *Histoire du commerce du Levant au Moyen Age: ed. française refondue et considérablement augmentée par l'auteur*, 2 vols. (Réimpression, Leipzig, 1923).

Hills, D. C.: *My Travels in Turkey* (London, 1964).

HM=History of the Mongols: see Howorth, Sir H. M.

Holt, P. M.: 'The Beylicate in Ottoman Egypt' in *BSOAS*, Vol. xxiv, Part 2 (1961), pp. 214–48.

Hommaire de Hell, Xavier: *Les Steppes de la Mer Caspienne, Le Caucase,* ... 3 vols. with fol. Atlas (Paris/Strasbourg, 1843–5).

Horsey, Sir Jerome: see Bond, Edward A.

Howorth, Sir H. M.: *History of the Mongols from the 9th to the 19th century*, 5 vols.; Part I, Part II, Division 1, Part II, Division 2, Part III, and index volume (London, 1876–88, 1927).

HSD=A History of Sharvān and Darband: see Minorsky, Vladimir.

IA=Islam Ansiklopedisi (Istanbul, 1942–   ).

Ibn Battuta, see Gibb, Sir Hamilton.

IM=Imago Mundi: A Review of Early Cartography (Berlin/Stockholm/Leiden, 1935–   ).

Inalcik, Halil: *Osmanli-Rus rekabetinin menşei ve Don-Volga kanali tesebbüsü (1569)* (The beginning of the Ottoman-Russian rivalry and the attempted construction of the Don-Volga canal: 1569) (Ankara, Türk Tarih Kurumu, 1948 – offprint from the Society's Bulletin, No. 46).

Inan, Afet: *L'Anatolie, le pays de la race turque: recherches sur les caractères anthropologiques de la Turquie* (Geneva, 1941).

Interiano, Giorgio: *Della vita de' Zychi, altrimente Circassi* (Venezia, 1502).

Iosseliani, Platon: *Opisaniye Shiomgvimskoy pustyni v Gruzii* (Tiflis, 1845).

——, *Rod knyazey Cholakaevykh i Muchenik Sv. Bidzina Cholakaev* (Tiflis, 1866).

——, *Opisaniye goroda Dusheti* (Tiflis, n.d.).

IRAN: Journal of the British Institute of Persian Studies.

Islamic Culture (review published in Hyderabad).

Istoricheskiye Zapiski (=*IZ*) (Moskva, Academy of Sciences, 1937–).

Ist. Kab.=*Istoriya Kabardy:* see Smirnov, N. A.

Istoriya Moskvy: Tom 1: Period feodalizma, xii–xvii vv., 4to (Moskva, 1952). (There is a *Prilozheniye* to Tom 1 containing eleven plans of Moscow at different periods.)

IZ=*Istoricheskiye Zapiski*, see above.

Izhboldin (Ischboldin), B. S. 'Tsar F. B. Godunov' in *Novik* (New York, 1950).

Iz. Gos.=*Izvestiya Gosudarstvennoy Akademii Istorii Materialnoy Kultury* (Moskva, 1921–).

Iz. Kav.=*Izvestiya Kavkazskago otdela Imperatorskago Russkago Geograficheskago Obshchestva* (Tiflis, from 1872).

Iz. IMK=*Izvestiya Istorii Materialnoy Kultury.*

Iz. RAN=*Izvestiya Rossiyskoy Akademii Nauk.*

JA=*Journal Asiatique* (Paris)

Janashvili (=Dzhanashvili), M. G.: 'Izvestiya Gruzinskikh Letopisey o ... Didoeti', etc. in *SMK*, tom XXVI/i (1899), pp. 1–101.

JAOS=*Journal of the American Oriental Society.*

Javakhishvili, A. N., and Ryazanets (eds.): *Gruzinskaya SSSR: Ekonomiko-geograficheskaya kharakteristika* (Moskva, 1956).

Javakhishvili (=Djzhavakhov), I. A.: 'The Caucasian Race' in *Georgica*, Vol. 1, No. 2/3, pp. 92–108.

——, *Kartveli Eris Istoria* (History of the Georgian people) revised edition, 4 vols. (Tbilisi, 1941–50).

JRAS= Journal of the Royal Asiatic Society (London).

Jenkinson, Anthony: see *EVT*.

Joyce/*SHAI*=Joyce, P. W.: *Social history of ancient Ireland*, 2 vols. (Dublin, 1913).

Kabardino-Russkiye otnosheniya v xvi–xvii vv (=*KRO*) (2 vols., Moskva, 1957).

Kapterev, N. F.: *Kharakter otnosheniy Rossii k Pravoslavnomu Vostoku v xvi i xvii stoletiyakh* (2nd ed. Sergiyev Posad, 1914).

Karst, Joseph: *Les Ligures* (Strasbourg, 1930).

——, *Origines Mediterraneae* (Heidelberg, 1931).

——, *Mythologie Arméno-Caucasienne et Hétito-Asianique* (=*MA-C*) (Strasbourg/Zurich, 1948).

Kasayev, A. M.: *Osetinsko-Russki slovar* (Moscow, 1952).

Katip Çelebi: Hayati ve eserleri hakkinda incelemeler, Studies of the life and works of K.Ç. (Ankara, Türk Tarih Kurumu, 1957).

Kavkaz – newspaper (Tiflis, 1846–8), from which articles were reprinted in volume form as *Sbornik gazety 'Kavkaz'* (Tiflis, 1847).

Kav. Kal.=*Kavkazski Kalendar*, for the years 1854–1916 (Tipografiya Kantselyarii Namestnika, Tiflis).

Kav. Sbor=*Kavkazski Sbornik*, 32 vols. to 1912 (Tiflis).

Kazem-Beg, Mirza: *Derbend-Nameh or the history of Derbend translated from a select Turkish version and published with text and notes* ... 4to (St Petersburg, Imperial Academy of Sciences, 1851).

KBCh.=*Kniga glagolemaya Bolshoy Chertezh, q.v.*

Keuning, J.: 'Hessel Gerritsz' in *IM*, Vol. VI (1950), pp. 49–66.

Khakhanov (=Khakhanashvili) A. S.: 'Zakatalski okrug' in *MAK*, Vol. 7, pp. 28 ff.

Kilchevskaya, E. V. and Ivanov, A. S.: *Khudozhestvenniye promysly Dagestana*, 91 plates (Moskva, 1959).

Klaproth, Julius von: *Reise in den Kaukasus und nach Georgien, 1807–08*: 2 Bände (Halle, 1812–14).

Kniga glagolemaya Bolshoy Chertezh (= *KBCh*), ed. G. I. Spasski (Moskva, 1840).

'Kniga glagolemaya uryadnik: novoye ulozheniye i china sokolnichya puti' in *DRV*, chast III (1788), pp. 430 ff.

Kondakov, N. P.: *The Russian Icon*, translated by Ellis H. Minns, 4to (Oxford, 1927).

Kortepeter, Carl M.: 'Ottoman imperial policy and the economy of the Black Sea region in the sixteenth century' in *JAOS*, Vol. 86/2 (1966), pp. 86–113.

Kosven, M. O. (ed.): *Istoriya, geografiya i etnografiya Dagestana, xvii–xix vv: arkhivnye materialy* (Moskva, 1958).

——, *Ocherki istorii Dagestana* (= *OID*) (Moskva, 1957).

Kosubski, E. I.: *Istoriya goroda Derbenta*, 4to, plates (Temir-Khan-Shura, 1906).

——, *Bibliografiya Dagestana* (Temir-Khan-Shura, 1895).

——, *Pamyatnaya knizkha Dagestanskoy Oblasti* (Temir-Khan-Shura, 1895).

Kotoshikhin, G.: *O Rossii v tsarstvovaniye Alekseya Mikhailovicha* (4th ed., St Petersburg, 1906).

Kovalevski, A. P.: *Kniga Akhmeda Ibn-Fadlana i ego puteshestviya na Volgu v 921–922 gg.* (Kharkov, 1956).

Kovalevski, Maxim: *Sovremenny obychay i drevni zakon na Kavkaze*, 2 vols. (Moskva, 1886), summarized by Delmar Morgan in *JRAS*, Vol. 20 (1888).

Kreml Moskvy (Moskva, 1957).

KRO = Kabardino-Russkiye otnosheniya, q.v.

Kuftin, B. A.: *Arkheologicheskiye raskopki v Trialeti: i opyt periodizatsii pamyatnikov* (Tbilisi, 1941).

Kusheva, E. N.: *Narody severnago Kavkaza i ikh svyazi s Rossiey v xvi–xvii vv* (Moskva, 1963).

Kütükoghlu, Bekir: *Osmanli-Iran siyasi münâsebetleri, Vol I,*

1578–90 (Ottoman-Iranian political relations) (Istanbul, 1962).

Kuznetsov, B. A.: 'Alany i rannesrednevekovy Dagestan' in *Materialy po Arkheologii Dagestana,* tom 2 (Makhachkala, 1961).

Lang, D. M.: *Lives and legends of the Georgian Saints* (London, 1956).

——, *A modern history of Georgia* (London, 1962).

Langlès, M. I. (ed.): *Voyages du Chevalier Chardin en Perse et autres lieux de l'Orient,* 10 vols. with large fol. Atlas of 81 plates (Paris, 1811). This is the most complete edition of Chardin's travels. See above, Chardin, Sir John.

Larina, V. I.: *Ocherki istorii gorodov Severnoy Osetii* (Ordzhonikidze, 1960).

Larousse: *Encyclopedia of Mythology* (London, 1959).

Le Brun (Bruyn), Corneille: *Voyages par la Muscovie, en Perse, et aux Indes Orientales*: 2 vols. fol. with 320 maps and illustrations (Amsterdam, 1718).

Lefaivre, Albert: *Les Magyars pendant la domination Ottomane en Hongrie,* 2 vols. (Paris, 1902).

Le Strange, Guy: *The lands of the Eastern Caliphate* (Cambridge, 1930).

Likhachev, D. S. (ed.): *Puteshestviya russkikh poslov xvi–xvii vv – Stateynye spiski* (Moskva, 1954).

Lockhart, Laurence: *The fall of the Safavi dynasty and the Afghan occupation of Persia* (Cambridge, 1958).

Lurye, Ya. S. and Muller, R. B.: contributors to Likhachev's work, see above.

Luzbetak, Louis J.: *Marriage and the family in Caucasia* (Vienna-Mödling, 1951).

Lyayster, A. F. and Chursin, G. F.: *Geografiya Kavkaza: priroda i naseleniye* (Tiflis, 1924).

Lynch, H. F. B.: *Armenia: travels and studies,* 2 vols. with large folding map in end pocket (London, 1901).

Mango, Cyril: 'The Legend of Leo the Wise' in *Recueil des Travaux de l'Institut d'Etudes Byzantines*, No. 6 (Belgrad, 1960).

Mánkowski, Tadeusz: 'Some documents from Polish sources relating to carpet making in the time of Shah Abbas I' in *SPA*, Vol. III (1938), pp. 2431–6.

Manvelishvili, A.: *Histoire de Géorgie* (Paris, 1951).

MAK=Materialy po Arkheologii Kavkaza, ed. Countess Uvarov, Vols. 1–14, 4to (Moskva, 1888–1916).

*MAR=*Eck, *Le Moyen Age Russe, q.v.*

Maruashvili, L. I.: *Vakhushti Bagrationi: ego predshestvenniki i sovremenniki* (Moskva, 1956).

Maslov, E. P. (ed.): *Severny Kavkaz* (Moskva, 1957).

Masúdi (=Maçoudi), see Barbier de Meynard.

Merzbacher, Gottfried: *Aus den Hochregionen des Kaukasus*, 2 Bände with *Karte des Kaukasischen Hochgebirges in drei Blättern* bound separately (Leipzig, 1901).

Meskhia, Sh. A.: *Goroda i gorodskoy stroy feodalnoy Gruzii, xvii-xviii vv* (Tbilisi, 1959).

Minadoi, Gio Tomaso, *Historia delle guerra fra Turchi e Persiani* (Torino, 1588).

Minasian, C.: *The chronicle of Petros di Sarkis Gilanentz* (Lisbon, 1959).

Minns, Ellis, H.: *Scythians and Greeks*, 4to (Cambridge, 1913).

Minorsky, Vladimir: *Ḥudūd al-'Ālam: 'The regions of the world'* (Oxford, 1937).

——, *Tadhkirat al-Mulūk: A manual of Safavid administration: circa 1137/1725 (=TM)* (London, 1943).

Minorsky, Vladimir: 'Khaqani and Andronicus Comnenus' in *BSOAS*, Vol. XI/3 (1945), pp. 550–78.

——, *A history of Sharvān and Darband (=HSD)* (Cambridge, 1958).

Mongait, A. L.: *Archaeology in the USSR* (Moscow, 1959); also in Pelican ed. (Harmondsworth, 1961).

Morgan, Jacques de: *Mission Scientifique au Caucase*, 2 vols. (Paris, 1889).

MR= The Mongols and Russia: see Vernadsky, George.

Mtskheta: itogi arkheologicheskikh issledovaniy I: arkheologickeskiye pamyatniki Armaʒis-khevi po raskopkam 1937–1946 gg, large 4to, various contributors (Tbilisi, 1937–46).

Muir, Sir William: *The Mameluk or Slave Dynasty of Egypt: 1260–1517 A.D.* (London, 1896).

Müller, G. F.: *Sammlung Russischer Geschichte*, 9 Bände (St Petersburg, 1732–64).

Muskhelishvili, L.: 'The Caucasian counterpart of an old Egyptian racing chariot' in *Georgica*, Nos. 4/5 (1937), pp. 290–2.

Myers, A. R.: *England in the late Middle Ages* (Harmondsworth, Middlesex, 1953).

Namitok, Aytek: *Origines des Circassiens, Ière partie* (all published) (Paris, 1939).

Natroyev, A.: *Iverski monastyr na Afone* (Tiflis, 1909).

Neborovski, Lt.-Col.: *Kratki vʒglyad na severny i sredni Dagestan* (St Petersburg, 1847).

NED= New English Dictionary.

Nikitine, Basile: *Les Kurdes: Etude sociologique et historique* (Paris, 1956).

Nogmov, Shura Bekmurza: *Istoriya Adykheyskago naroda*, ed. A. Berzhe (Tiflis, 1860; published also in *Kav. Kal.*, 1861–2). For criticism of the author's *fantaisiste* derivations, see G. Dumézil, *Légendes sur les Nartes*, p. 8.

Novik – Journal (New York, 1950–).

Oberling, P.: 'Georgians and Circassians in Iran' in *Studia Caucasica*, I (1963), pp. 127–43.

Obolensky, Dmitri: 'Russia's Byzantine heritage' in *OSP*, I (Oxford, 1950), pp. 37–63.

OI/PF/xv–xvii vv.= Ocherki Istorii SSSR, Period Feodaliʒma, konets xv v. – nachalo xvii v. (Tom 5 of *Ocherki Istorii SSSR*, Moskva, Academy of Sciences, 1955).

OID= Ocherki istorii Dagestana: see Kosven, M. O. above.

Olearius/W.= Olearius (Oelschlaeger), Adam: *Voyages très curieux et très renommés faits en Moscovie et Perse . . . traduits de l'original par le Sr. de Wicquefort . . .* 2 vols., fol. (Amsterdam, 1727).

OSP= Oxford Slavonic Papers (Oxford, 1950–).

Pallas, *TSP*= Pallas, Peter Simon: *Travels through the southern provinces of the Russian Empire in the years 1793 and 1794 translated from the German,* 2 vols, 4to (London, 1812).

Pallas, Peter: *Zoographia Rosso-Asiatica,* 3 vols., 4to and Atlas, fol. (Petropoli, 1811–31).

Pamyatniki diplomaticheskikh snosheniy drevney Rossii s derzhavami inostrannymi, 10 vols. (St Petersburg, 1851–71).

Pares, Sir Bernard: *A history of Russia* (London, 1937).

Patkanov, K. P.: *Tsygane: neskolko slov o narechiyakh zakavkazskikh Tsygan: Bosha i Karachi* (St Petersburg, 1887).

PDTS= Pamyatniki . . . snosheniy Moskovskoy Rusi s Persiey: see Veselovski, N. I.

Perry, John: *The State of Russia under the present Czar* (London, 1716).

Petrushevski, I. I.: 'Vosstaniye remeslennikov i gorodskoy bednoty v Tebrize v 1571–1573 gg.' in *Sbornik Statey po Istorii Azerbaidzhana,* vyp. 1, pp. 220–4.

Planhol, Xavier de: 'Geographia Pontica, I–III' in *JA,* tome ccli (1963), pp. 293–310.

Platonov, *OIS*= Platonov, S. F.: *Ocherki po istorii smuty v Moskovskom gosudarstve, xvi–xvii vv,* 3rd ed. (St Petersburg, 1910).

Platonov, S. F.: *Boris Godunov* (Petrograd, 1921).

PN= The Principal navigations, etc.: see above, Hakluyt, Richard.

Polievktov, M. A.: *Mezhdunarodnye snosheniya Gruzii s inozemnymi stranami,* 2 vols. (Tbilisi, 1926–8).

——, *Evropeyskiye puteshestvenniki xiii–xviii vv. po Kavkazu* (Tbilisi, 1935).

——, *Novye dannye o Moskovskikh khudozhnikakh xvi–xvii vv. v Gruzii* (Tbilisi, 1941).

Pope, Arthur Upham: *A survey of Persian art* (= *SPA*), 6 vols., fol. (Oxford, 1938–9).

Po sledam: see Tolstov, S. P.

Potto, Maj.-Gen.: *Istoricheski ocherk Kavkazskikh voyn ot ikh nachala do prisoyedineniya Gruzii*, 4to (Tiflis, 1899).

Rabino de Borgomale, H. L.: *Mázandarán and Astarábád* (London, 1938).

Radde, Dr Gustav: *Die Chew'suren und ihr Land* (Cassel, 1878).

——, *Ornitologicheskaya fauna Kavkaza* (*Ornis Caucasica*) 4to with plates (Tiflis, 1885).

Radlov, V. V.: *Uigurische Sprachdenkmäler* (Leningrad, 1928).

RDMA= Russia at the dawn of the modern age, see Vernadsky, George.

RBS= Russki Biograficheski Slovar, *q.v.*

Reineggs/W.= Reineggs, J.: *General historical and topographical description of Mount Caucasus, etc.; translated from the works of Dr. Reineggs by Charles Wilkinson*, with a map and plates (London, 1807).

REW= Russisches Etymologisches Wörterbuch, see Vasmer, Max.

Ross, Sir E. Denison: *Sir Anthony Sherley and his Persian Adventure* (London, 1933).

Rostovtseff, Michael: *Iranians and Greeks in South Russia* (Oxford, 1922).

Runciman, Sir Steven: *A history of the Crusades*, 3 vols. (Cambridge, 1951–4).

Russki Biograficheski Slovar (= *RBS*), 25 vols. issued between 1897 and 1918 when publication ceased (St Petersburg, Imperial Russian Historical Society). (See also Alphabetical List of former Russian personalities to be included in *RBS* published as Tom 16, chasti i and ii of *Sbornik Impera-*

torskago Russkago Istoricheskago Obshchestva, St Petersburg, 1887.)

Salia, Dr K.: 'Les chefs de l'église géorgienne' in *BK*, No. 41/42 (1963), pp. 10–16.

——, 'La littérature géorgienne' in *BK*, No. 48/49 (1965), pp. 69–98.

Salmon, Lt.-Col.: *An account of the Ottoman conquest of Egypt* (London, 1921).

Sarre, F. and Martin, F. R.: *Die Ausstellung von Meisterwerken Muhammedanischer Kunst in München*, 1910, 3 vols. fol. (München, 1912).

Sbornik gazety Kavkaz (Tiflis, 1847).

Sbornik materialov dlya opisaniya mestnostey i plemen Kavkaza (=*SMK*), 44 vols. (Tiflis, 1881–1916); Vols. 45 and 46 (Makhachkala, 1926, 1929).

Sbornik Statey po Istorii Azerbaydzhana, vyp. 1 (Baku, 1949).

Sbornik svedeniy o Kavkazskikh Gortsakh (=*SSKG*), 10 vols. (Tiflis, 1868–81).

Sbornik svedeniy o Terskoy Oblasti (=*SSTO*), vol. 1 (Vladikavkaz, 1878).

SCCH = Studies in Christian Caucasian History, see Toumanoff, C.

Schmidt, S. O.: *Opisi tsarskogo arkhiva xvi veka i arkhiva Posolskogo Prikaza 1614 goda* (Moskva, 1960).

Serbina, K. I.: 'Kniga Bolshogo Chertezha i eye redaktsii' in *IZ*, 14 (1945), pp. 129–47.

Serbina, K. I.: 'Istochniki Knigi Bolshogo Chertezha' in *IZ*, 23 (1947), pp. 290–324.

Shakhmaliyeva, E. M. (ed.): *Puteshestvenniki ob Azerbaydzhane*, tom 1 (Baku, 1961).

Skene, William F.: *Celtic Scotland: A history of Ancient Alban*, 3 vols. (Edinburgh, 1876–80).

——, *The Highlanders of Scotland:* ed. Alexander MacBain (Stirling, 1902).

Slovar Tserkovno-Slavyanskago i Russkago yazyka,(=*STsSRY*) 4 vols. bound in 2, 2nd ed. (St Petersburg, 1867–8).

Smirnov, N. A.: *Istoriya Kabardy s drevneyshikh vremen do nashikh dney* (=*Ist. Kab.*) (Moskva, 1957).

——, *Rossiya i Turtsiya v xvi-xvii vv.* (=*RT*), 2 vols. (Moskva, 1946).

——, *Politika Rossii na Kavkaze* (=Smirnov, *Politika*) (Moskva, 1958).

SMK=*Sbornik materialov . . . Kavkaza*: see above.

Solovyev, S. M.: *Istoriya Rossii s drevneyshikh vremen*, 3rd ed., 6 vols and index vol. (St Petersburg, 1911). (Vol. 1 of the first edition appeared in 1851, and the author died in 1879 while writing the twenty-ninth 'book' which ends – like the great work of von Hammer on the Ottoman Empire – with the year 1774.)

SPA=*A survey of Persian art*, see Pope, A. U.

Spasski, A. M.: *Russkaya monetnaya sistema* (Moscow, 1957).

Sreznevski, I. I.: *Materialy dlya slovarya drevnerusskogo yazyka*, 3 vols. 4to reprint from original ed. of 1890–1912 (Moskva, 1958).

SSKG=*Sbornik svedeniy o Kavkazskikh Gortsakh* – see above.

SSTO=*Sbornik svedeniy o Terskoy Oblasti* – see above.

Steder, –: 'anonymous' author of *Tagebuch einer Reise . . . im J. 1781, q.v.*

Stevenson, R. H., transl.: *Amiran-Darejaniani* (Oxford, 1958).

Strabo: *Geography* – Loeb ed; Greek text with translation by H. L. Jones; 8 vols (London, 1917).

Studia Caucasica (The Hague, Vol. 1, 1963–   ).

Sulimirski, T.: 'The forgotten Sarmatians' in *Vanished civilizations* (London, 1963), pp. 279–98.

Sumner, B. H.: 'Russia and Europe' in *OSP*, Vol. II (Oxford, 1951), pp. 1–16.

Tagebuch=*Tagebuch einer Reise die im Jahr 1781 von der*

Gränzfestung Mosdok nach dem innern Caucasus unternommen worden (St Petersburg and Leipzig, 1797): see Steder, above.

Tamarati, Michel: *L'Eglise géorgienne des origines jusqu'à nos jours* (Roma, 1910).

Tarsaidze, A. G.: 'Boris Godunov i Gruziya' in *Novik*, No. 7.

Tatishvili, V. L.: *Gruziny v Moskve* (Tbilisi, 1959).

Tavernier, Jean Baptiste, Ecuyer Baron d'Aubonne: *Les six voyages en Turquie, en Perse et aux Indes*, 3 vols. (Paris, 1692, ed.).

Tbilisis Universitetis Moambe (Journal of Tbilisi University) Vol. III (Tbilisi, 1923).

Tikhomirov, M.: *The Towns of ancient Rus* (Moscow, 1959).

Togan, A. Zeki Velidi: *Bugünkü Türkili ve yakin Tarihi: cilt 1, Bati ve Kuzey Turkistan* (Modern Turkistan and its recent history: Part I, Western and Northern Turkistan $= TT$) (Istanbul, 1942–7). Only Part I has appeared.

——, *Türkili haritasi ve ona ait izahlar* (Map of Turkistan with relevant explanations – folding with 32 pp. of explanatory text).

——, *Ibn Fadlan's Reisebericht* (Leipzig, 1939).

Tolstov, S. P.: *Po sledam drevney Khorezmiyskoy tsivilizatsii* ($= Po\ sledam$) (Moskva, 1948).

Toumanoff, Prince Cyril: *Studies in Christian Caucasian history* ($= SCCH$) (Georgetown University, 1963).

——, 'Moscow the Third Rome: Genius and significance of a politico-religious idea' in the *Catholic Historical Review*, Vol. 40 (1955), pp. 411–47.

Travels of Venetians in Persia ($= TVP$), (London, Hakluyt Society, 1873).

Trever, N. K.: *Ocherki po istorii i kulture Kavkazskoy Albanii* (Moskva, 1959).

$TT= Türkili\ Tarihi$: see Togan, A. Z. V., above.

$TVOIAO= Trudy\ vostochnago\ otdeleniya\ Imperatorskago\ Russ$-

kago Arkheologicheskago Obshchestva (St Petersburg, Vol. 3 –
1858; Vol. 22 – 1898).

TVP= Travels of Venetians in Persia: q.v.

Valle, Pietro della: *Viaggi . . . divisi in tre parti: cioè la Turchia,
la Persia e l'India,* 4 vols. (Roma, 1662–3); French ed., 8 vols.
(Paris, 1745).

Vasiliev, A. A.: *The Goths in the Crimea* (Cambridge, Mass.,
1936).

Vasmer, Max: *Russisches Etymologisches Wörterbuch*
(=*REW*), 3 Bände (Heidelberg, 1953–5).

VDI= Vestnik Drevney Istorii: see below.

Vernadsky, George: *The Mongols and Russia* (=*MR*), Vol. 3
of *A history of Russia* (New Haven, Conn., 1953).

——, *Russia at the dawn of the modern age* (=*RDMA*)
Vol. 4 of *A history of Russia* (New Haven, Conn., 1959).

——, *The origins of Russia* (Oxford, 1959).

——, 'The Spali of Jordanes and the Spori of Procopius' in
Byzantion, Vol. XIII/i (1938), pp. 263–6.

——, 'The death of the Tsarevich Dmitry' in *OSP*, Vol. v
(1954), pp. 1–19.

Veselovski, N. I.: *Pamyatniki diplomaticheskikh i torgovykh
snosheniy Moskovskoy Rusi s Persiey* (=*PDTS*), tomes xx,
xxi, xxii of *TVOIAO* (1890–8).

Vestnik Drevney Istorii (=*VDI*), published by Institute of
History, USSR Academy of Sciences, quarterly (Moscow/
Leningrad, Vol. 15– , 1946–).

Victoria and Albert Museum: *Brief guide to Turkish woven
fabrics* (HMSO, 1950).

——, *Brief guide to Persian woven fabrics* (HMSO, 1950).

Viktorov, A. F.: *Dagestanskaya ASSR* (Makhachkala, 1958).

Wak./Brosset=*Description géographique de la Géorgie par le
Tsarévich Wakhoucht publiée d'après l'original autograph par
M. Brosset,* 4to, with six folding maps (St Petersburg, 1842).

Wak./Jan.= 'Tsarevich Vakhushti: Geografiya Gruzii; vvedeniye, perevod i primechaniya M. G. Dzhanashvili' (=Janashvili) in knizhka xxiv, vyp. 5 of *ZKO* (Tiflis, 1904). See also Maruashvili, L. I. above.

Wardrop, Marjory, transl.: *The man in the panther's skin*, by Shotha Rusthaveli, Oriental Translation Fund, New Series, Vol. xxi (London, 1912).

Wardrop, Sir Oliver, transl.: *Visramiani*, Oriental Translation Fund, New Series, Vol. xxiii (London, 1914).

Warkworth, Lord: *Notes from a diary in Asiatic Turkey* (London, 1898).

Witsen, Nicolaes: *Nord en Oost Tartarye* (Amsterdam, 1705).

Wood, C. A. and Fyfe, F. M. (translators and editors): *The art of falconry: being the 'De arte venandi cum avibus' of Frederick II of Hohenstaufen*, 4to (Boston/London, 1943).

Yessen, A. A. and Degen-Kovalevski, B. E.: 'Iz istorii metallurgii Kavkaza' in *Iz.IMK*, vyp. 120 (1935).

Yule, Sir Henry: *The book of Ser Marco Polo*, 3rd ed., 2 vols. (London, 1929). See also Cordier, Henri.

ZKO = *Zapiski Kavkazskago Otdeleniya Imperatorskago Russkago Geograficheskago Obshchestva* (Tiflis: tom iv (1875–7) – tom xxii (1913–14)).

ZKV = *Zapiski Kollegii Vostokovedov*, 5 vols. (Leningrad, 1925–30).

ZVO = *Zapiski Vostochnago Otdeleniya Imperatorskago Russkago Arkheologicheskago Obshchestva*, 25 vols. (St Petersburg, 1886–1920 – when it ceased publication).

Zevakin, F. S. and Panchko, N. A.: 'Ocherki po istorii Genuezskikh koloniy na zapadnom Kavkaze v xiii i xv vv' in *IZ*, Vol. ii (1939), pp. 73–129.

Zheltyakov, A. D.: see Evliya Chelebi.

NOTE ON MAPS CONSULTED

Caucasia – 1:210,000 (5 verst to the inch)
Issued by Geographical Section, General Staff. War Office
1941 (2nd ed.). In 52 sheets – complete.

Caucasia – 1:420,000 (10 verst to the inch)
'Map of the Caucasian region compiled at the Military-Topographical Section of the Caucasian Military Area, Tiflis, 1869.' 22 cloth-backed folders – complete. In Russian.

Wakhusht's maps – For particulars, including the varying scales of these maps, see Commentary on the Sources: 3, Prince Wakhusht's 'Geographical Description of Georgia'. The six maps reproduced by Brosset in his edition of Wakhusht are a basic source for the historical topography of Georgia.

Olearius's map of the course of the Volga is excellent. His general maps of Caucasia and of the south-east coastlands of the Caspian are superficial but his views of several cities and towns of the Volga and Caucasia are fine.

Guillaume Delisle – 'Carte des pays voisins de la Mer Caspienne' of 1723. Much of the original detail in this map can be traced to Saba Sulkhan Orbeliani (see Allen in *IM*, Vol. XIII (1956)).

Atlas Rossiiskoy of 1745; also *Atlas Russicus* – edition in Latin and French.

Joseph-Nicolas Delisle – 'Carte générale de la Géorgie et de l'Arménie' of 1766.

Many topographical details on later maps were drawn from the French and Russian translations of Wakhusht's maps; e.g. Güldenstädt's 'Neue Carte des Caucasus' (1787) and George Ellis's excellent 'General Map of the Countries Comprehended between the Black Sea and the Caspian' (1788).

The map published in Wilkinson's English edition of Reineggs's 'Description of Mount Caucasus' (1807) is a crude work but based on the author's personal observations and useful for the topography of Daghestan.

S. M. Bronevski, with his two volumes of 'Newest Information about the Caucasus', published A. Maksimovich's large folding map (1823) which is excellent for topographical detail. Bronevski was an official on the staff of Prince Tsitsianov in the first years of the nineteenth century.

E. D. Felitsyn, in Potto (q.v.) published two sheets (1899) which remain the best example of the historical topography of the Northern and Central Caucasus.

For the whole of the main chain of the Caucasus, including Daghestan, four great travellers at the turn of the nineteenth century produced superb cartographical material derived from personal observation: *Douglas Freshfield* (1896); *Gottfried Merzbacher* (1901); *Moriz von Déchy* (1905–7); *John F. Baddeley* (1940). (For details of their books, see Bibliography. Baddeley's travels in the Caucasus were between the years 1879 and 1902; the two volumes of his 'Rugged Flanks of Caucasus' were in the press when he died in February 1940 in his 86th year.)

INDEX

In Belokurov's text the same personal name or place name often appears in two or more variants; for the sake of clarity the spelling of such names has been standardized in the translation, the other variants having been relegated to the Index where they are given in brackets after the main entry. The following abbreviations have been used in the Index: *P*. Persian, *R*. Russian, *T*. Turkish, *G*. Georgian.